MURDEROUS SCIENCE

Elimination by Scientific Selection of
Jews, Gypsies, and Others in
Germany, 1933-1945

MURDEROUS SCIENCE

Elimination by Scientific Selection of
Jews, Gypsies, and Others in
Germany, 1933-1945

Benno Müller-Hill
Afterword by James D. Watson

Translated by George R. Fraser

COLD SPRING HARBOR LABORATORY PRESS

© 1998 Cold Spring Harbor Laboratory Press
All rights reserved
Printed in the United States of America

This English edition has been translated from the original German publication
Tödliche Wissenschaft © Copyright 1984 by Rowohlt Taschenbuch Verlag GmbH,
Reinbek bei Hamburg

English translation by G.R. Fraser © Oxford University Press 1988

Library of Congress Cataloging in Publication Data
Müller-Hill, Benno. 1933–
    [Tödliche Wissenschaft. English]
    Murderous science: elimination by scientific selection of Jews, gypsies, and others in Germany,
1933–1945/Benno Müller-Hill; afterword by James D. Watson: translated by George R. Fraser.
    p. cm.
    Includes bibliographical references and index.
    ISBN 0-87969-531-5 (pbk: alk. paper)
    1. World War, 1939–1945—Atrocities. 2. Science and state—Germany—History—20th century. 3.
Genocide—Germany—History—20th century. 4. Human experimentation in medicine—
Germany—History—20th century. I. Title.
    D804.G4M7713 1997
    940.54'05—dc21   97-40085
                                                                       CIP

Authorization to photocopy items for internal or personal use, or the internal or personal use of specific clients, is granted by Cold Spring Harbor Laboratory Press, provided that the appropriate fee is
paid directly to the Copyright Clearance Center (CCC). Write or call CCC at 222 Rosewood Drive,
Danvers, MA 01923 (508-750-8400) for information about fees and regulations. Prior to photocopy-
ing items for educational classroom use, contact CCC at the above address. Additional information on
CCC can be obtained at CCC Online at http://www.copyright.com/

All Cold Spring Harbor Laboratory Press publications may be ordered directly from Cold Spring Harbor Laboratory Press, 10 Skyline Drive, Plainview, New York 11803-2500. Phone: 1-800-843-4388 in
Continental U.S. and Canada. All other locations: (516) 349-1930. FAX: (516) 349-1946. E-mail:
cshpress@cshl.org. For a complete catalog of all Cold Spring Harbor Laboratory Press publications,
visit our World Wide Web Site http://www.cshl.org/

Contents

Afterword

Author's Preface to the English Edition

In this translation misprints and many errors in the German edition have been corrected. I am most grateful to the translator for his help in pointing them out. In a few instances, additional material has been incorporated into the text and, in collaboration with the translator, a number of explanatory notes have been added for the English-speaking reader.

Since the German edition first appeared in August 1984, my scientist friends have been concerned that some readers may interpret this book as a condemnation of science and as a denial of rationalism. This would be a complete misinterpretation of my intentions, which are to show that a world in which science flourishes but justice is absent is condemned to the same fate as Sodom. I might add that a world in which justice flourishes but science is absent would be condemned just as surely to a different, but equally horrible, fate. By justice I mean more than the mere existence of law schools and a legal system.

I want to take this opportunity of repairing an omission. I found it unbearable to dedicate the German edition to my wife, Rita. I did not even mention her in the acknowledgements. And yet she had listened patiently to me over the years, as I talked night after night about Fischer, von Verschuer, and Mengele, and about all this pain and death. I did not want to acknowledge in public that the piecing together of the story of so much bloodshed had to be carried out in the company of one who is so loving and beautiful. I say it here. Without her, I might not have had the strength to write this book.

B. M. H.
Cologne
June 1987

Acknowledgements

I thank the archivists of the Federal Archives in Koblenz, the Military Archives in Freiburg, the Political Archives of the Foreign Office in Bonn, the Central Archives of the German Democratic Republic in Potsdam and Merseburg, the National Archives in Washington and Suitland, Maryland, the Archives of the Yiddish Scientific Institute in New York, the Document Center in West Berlin, the Archives of the Centre of Contemporary Jewish Documentation in Paris, the Archives of the Max Planck Society in Berlin, the Archives of the University of Münster, and the Archives of the Institute of Contemporary History in Munich for their help. I thank the anthropologists, the psychiatrists, and their relatives, especially Professors Abel, W. Lenz, Loeffler and Rauch for their readiness to speak candidly to me. I thank my co-workers and colleagues who tolerated my absence and apparent lack of interest in science as friends, and later critically reviewed the manuscript of this book. Finally, the translator and I should like to express our appreciation of the unfailing patience and painstaking thoroughness with which the staff at the Oxford University Press afforded assistance during the preparation of the English edition.

Translator's Preface

Many thousands of books have been written about the aberration in world history represented by the 'New Order' which the Nazis imposed on Germany and on most of Europe. A substantial proportion of these books deal wholly or in part with that execrable aberration within an aberration, the Nazi policy of mass murder of 'inferior' peoples or groups. In a few cases, sterilization, or genetical death, took the place of actual murder.

Most of the books in this group are about the genocide of the Jews. Much less information is available about the effects of this policy, which included mass murder through starvation and exposure to the elements and to disease, as well as more active forms of killing such as gassing, shooting and hanging, on the Gypsies, mental patients, and many of the other peoples of Europe, especially Slavs.

Although it touches on these topics, this book does not aim to remedy these deficiencies in documentation. It is in no sense an enumeration of the statistics of mass murder. Its uniqueness lies in the examination of a parallel aberration in the history of science which involved some of the leading figures in the German academic establishment, especially in the fields of anthropology (including human genetics) and psychiatry. These individuals aided and abetted the racial policy of the Nazi state. They provided the intellectual and scientific basis for assumptions of racial and genetical inferiority (and, *ipso facto*, superiority) and they helped to build up the legal infrastructure of the mechanisms which were put into place to give expression to those ideas in the form of mass murder, genocide, and sterilization. This book attempts to trace the actions of many of these persons, which included actual participation in mass murder in the guise of scientific and medical experimentation, and to provide some understanding of the motivation of these individuals.

It is not only the book but the aberration which is unique. The study of this aberration should serve as an object lesson to all scientists in revealing the immense power for evil which they are able to wield through association with unscrupulous politicians and demagogues. It has been a privilege to bring this book to the attention of a wider public through this translation. I share the hope of the author that this slim volume will lead to more intensive investigation of this aberration of the recent past, including a detailed study of the copious literature of the period, concerned with supposed inferiority and superiority on racial or genetical grounds, both in textbooks and learned journals and in publications directed towards a wider public.

I also share the author's hope that such an enterprise will lessen the chance of a recurrence of a similar misuse and perversion of science and medicine in the future, especially as we enter the new era of molecular biology and its many potential applications.

Translator's Notes on Terminology

A note on German academic organization

A doctorate in medicine, which was gained by dissertation and oral examination, was a prerequisite for a career in academic medicine but was not necessary for the practice of medicine, for which a licence taken by examination was sufficient. Thus a doctorate in medicine was equivalent to the British MD, rather than the North American medical degree. Teaching and research staff in medicine often held a second doctorate, in a scientific subject, also obtained by dissertation and oral examination, which was equivalent to a PhD. The oral examination for a doctorate was known as a **Promotion**. To qualify for a university teaching appointment, **Dozentur**, required a further oral examination and dissertation, the **Habilitation**. Candidates who succeeded became **Dozent** if their teaching was in connection with a paid university position and **Privatdozent** if they taught only on an unpaid basis.

Either of these titles, **Dozent** or **Privatdozent**, could be held together with the university grade of **Assistent**, translated here as assistant. The grade of assistant was flexible with respect to both tenure and qualifications. Thus, some assistants might have two doctorates and have obtained their **Habilitation** while others might be working towards one or another of these qualifications.

The only other university rank was that of professor. The professor who was head of a university institute was usually an Ordinarius [**ordentlicher Professor**, o.Prof.]. Other professors were known as Extraordinarius [**ausserordentlicher Professor**, a.Prof.].

Depending on rank and degrees many composite modes of address were used, for example Professor Dr; Professor Dr med.; Dr Dr; Dr med. Dr phil.; and Dr habil. In this translation all such composite titles are rendered as Professor or Dr.

In addition to the universities, there were the research institutes of the KWG, Kaiser Wilhelm-Gesellschaft zur Förderung der Wissenschaften, Kaiser Wilhelm Society for the Advancement of Science. A Kaiser Wilhelm Institute, KWI, had a director and department heads who often also held a university professional title. The Kaiser Wilhelm-Gesellschaft was dissolved after the war but was reconstituted in West Germany as the Max-Planck-Gesellschaft, MPG, which has a very similar structure.

Research was supported by the Notgemeinschaft Deutscher Wissenschaft, NDW, Association for the Emergency Funding of German Science. This name was changed in 1936 to the Deutsche Forschungsgemeinschaft, DFG, German Association for Research. An equivalent independent agency of the Federal Ministry of Science in West Germany retains this name today. During the war, it was an agency of the Reich Ministry of Science within which a Reichsforschungsrat, Reich Research Council, was appointed to oversee research. The two terms, Deutsche Forschungsgemeinschaft and Reichsforschungsrat, were in fact used more or less interchangeably.

Glossary of terms and abbreviations used in the text (those which appear only once are explained in footnotes to the text)

Asozial   This word when used as a noun is translated as 'asocial individual'. It was a term applied to Gypsies and other individuals who were not part of 'normal society'. This quality of being outside society may lead, among other things, to constant friction with the police because of petty crime.

DFG   Deutsche Forschungsgemeinschaft. German Association for Scientific Research.

Document Center (West Berlin)   This Center was created after the war by the US Government. It contains personal files on almost all Germans who belonged to the Nazi Party, the SS, or to other National Socialist organizations. German citizens wishing to use the Center first have to ask a representative of the West German Government for approval. A final decision as to whether permission is given to see a particular document is then made by the American staff of the Center. This changed in 1989 when the Document Center became part of the German Archives.

Einsatzgruppe   Special action group organized under the aegis of the SD of the SS, after the invasion of the USSR on 22 June 1941, for the specific purpose of exterminating Jews, Gypsies, mental patients, and other 'undesirable elements', usually by shooting. Similar groups were active on a smaller scale in Poland in 1939-40.

Einsatzkommando   A detachment (commando) of an Einsatzgruppe.

Führer   Adolf Hitler, on assuming the functions of President and Chancellor [Der Kanzler] of the Reich, allowed the title of Reichspresident to fall into disuse and was always known as Der Führer, The Leader.

Gauleiter   Party political leader of a Gau - a large administrative region of the Reich.

Geheimrat   A high civic rank, Councillor, both before and during the Third Reich.

Generalgouvernement   Those parts of pre-war Poland which were not incorporated into the Reich but were under direct German rule. In 1939 this area consisted of the four districts of Warsaw, Lublin, Radom, and Cracow. Eastern Galicia (capital Lwów) was added in 1941 after being occupied during the war against the USSR, which had annexed the region in 1939.

Gestapo   Geheime Staatspolizei. Secret State Police. An agency of the RSHA of the SS.

IG-Farben   Interessengemeinschaft Farbenindustrie Aktiengesellschaft. [Union of Interests of the Dye Industry (Limited Liability Company)]. After the war, the monopoly exercised by this company over the chemical industry was ended during decartelization when it was broken up into a number of smaller, successor companies.

KWG   Kaiser Wilhelm-Gesellschaft zur Förderung der Wissenschaften. The Kaiser Wilhelm Society for the Advancement of the Sciences.

Land (Länder in the plural)   A state of the Reich. After the war a state of West Germany.

Liquidationsanstalt Translated here as extermination centre. Under the control of T4, a number of institutions were created or designated for killing adult patients during the euthanasia programme. In general, children were killed in other institutions (see Reichsausschuss) although there was some overlap.

Luftwaffe The Air Force.

MPG Max-Planck-Gesellschaft. The Max Planck Society. The postwar reconstituted form of the KWG in West Germany.

Nazi The full name of the Nazi Party was *Nationalsozialistische Deutsche Arbeiterpartei* (NSDAP). National Socialist German Workers' Party.

NDW Notgemeinschaft Deutscher Wissenschaft. Association for the Emergency Funding of German Science. Its name was changed to DFG in 1936.

Oberdienstleiter This is a title which indicates a high rank in the central hierarchy in Berlin of the Nazi Party.

Rassenhygienische und bevölkerungsbiologische Forschungsstelle Translated as 'Section for Research on Race-hygiene and Population Biology'. An agency of the Reich Department of Health (Ministry of the Interior) supported to a large extent by the Reich Ministry of Science through the DFG. Dr Ritter as head of this section worked on the identification and classification of Gypsies.

Rassenpolitisches Amt der NSDAP Translated as 'Race-policy Bureau of the Nazi Party'. Its function was to decide on theoretical questions about race and racial propaganda on behalf of the Nazi Party.

Reich Empire. The Nazi state was known as the Third Reich and, sometimes, as the Thousand-Year-Reich.

Reichsausschuss zur wissenschaftlichen Erfassung von erb- und anlagebedingten schweren Leiden The Reich Commission for the Scientific Registration of Hereditary and Constitutional Severe Disorders, abbreviated in the text as the 'Reich Commission for Registration of Severe

Disorders in Childhood'. Created in 1939, this Commission consisted of Professor Catel and Dr Wentzler, who were paediatricians, and Professor Heinze, a child-psychiatrist. It was directly responsible to the Führer's Chancellery. Beginning in August 1939, midwives were required to report all cases of handicapped and malformed liveborn infants. All physicians were required, in addition, to report children under the age of four years with the same specified range of defects. The Commission then decided after examination of the completed registration forms whether the infant should be killed, as part of the euthanasia programme. Later, the Commission also made decisions about the killing of older children. Dr Wentzler subsequently extended his role to signing requests by Gypsies for voluntary sterilization as an alternative to commitment to a concentration camp. His signature gave a semblance of legality to the procedure, and legality was an obsession.

Reichsführer-SS   Heinrich Himmler, the Leader of the SS. His full title was Der Chef der Polizei und Reichsführer der SS. The Chief of Police and Leader of the SS. As a result of this double role, each regional police organization contained some SS-officers.

Reichsleiter   Reich Leader. This is a title which indicates a very high rank in the central hierarchy in Berlin of the Nazi Party.

Reichsmarschall   A title specially created for Hermann Göring, the Chief of the Luftwaffe, on 19 July 1940, when he became the senior serving military officer.

Reichsminister   A minister of the Reich, or of Germany as a whole, as opposed to a minister in the government of one of the Länder.

Reichssippenamt   Reich Kinship Bureau. An agency of the Ministry of the Interior which decided on all questions of classification of Jews and part-Jews. In some cases, it asked for racial expert opinions or reports [Gutachten] from qualified investigators and institutes.

RM   Reichsmark. The currency of the Reich. One RM was made up of 100 pfennigs.

RSHA   Reichssicherheitshauptamt. Reich Security Head Office. An agency of the SS.

RuSHA   Rasse- und Siedlungshauptamt. Head Office for Race and Set-tlement. An agency of the SS. It included the Rassenamt, Race Bureau and Heiratsamt, Marriage Bureau. Among the functions of the Race Bureau were to decide on the 'Aryan qualities' of individuals belonging to con-quered nations and their potential for 'Germanization'. The Marriage Bureau conducted medical examinations of SS candidates and of their brides before marriage. In both cases, applicants were required to produce documentation of Aryan ancestry going back to 1800.

SA   Sturm-Abteilung. Storm troopers also known as the Brownshirts. Until 1934, this was a very important para-military organization of the Nazi Party. Himmler successfully conspired against its Chief of Staff, Ernst Röhm, who was summarily shot, together with many of his lieutenants, during the 'night of the long knives' of 30 June 1934. By this 'Röhm Putsch', Himmler destroyed the SA as a rival in his quest for power for the SS. The SA became little more than a military sports association under Röhm's successor, Viktor Lutze.

SD   Sicherheitsdienst. Security Service. An agency of the SS connected with the RSHA.

Stiftung Ahnenerbe   This was the Research Foundation of the SS. The name 'Foundation for the Heritage of our Forefathers' emphasizes its ini-tial interest in 1936 in Germanic archaeology and palaeontology. These interests soon expanded to encompass many other branches of science and of the humanities.

SS   Schutz-Staffel. Bodyguards of the Nazi Party, also known as the Blackshirts. Himmler led the SS from 1929 (when it had 280 members). The SS grew into a state within the state. Its divisions included the armed Waffen-SS, and the general Allgemeine-SS which provided the guards and staff of the concentration camps. An attempt was made to maintain the SS as an élite in terms of 'racial purity', but it consisted by no means only of German nationals. It contained 'Germanic' units (composed of Flemish, Danish, or Dutch) from 1942 onwards. Later there were even units of Poles and Ukrainians who possessed the requisite 'Aryan' physical qualities. In 1943, when the manpower shortage in the armed forces became acute, a Turkic-Moslem unit was formed under SS auspices.

T4   A code name for the office directing the euthanasia programme. It is derived from Tiergartenstrasse 4, the address of the villa in Berlin, once the home of a Jewish family, where the office was situated from April 1940. Created in 1939, the office was initially directly responsible to the Führer's Chancellery. The official title of the organization was the Public Foundation for Medical and Institutional Care (Gemeinnützige Stiftung für Heil- und Pflegeanstalten). From September 1941 onwards, it was also responsible to the Ministry of the Interior's Department of Public Health and Hygiene. In 1941, the office collaborated with Himmler to initiate a programme under the code name 14 f 13, to free the concentration camps of the burden of 'valueless lives' [Ballastexistenzen]. Such individuals were selected for killing by a board of physicians. Children were not, in general, killed in the death camps under the control of the T4 office. There were perhaps thirty 'paediatric departments' [Kinderfachanstalten] in other institutions which participated in the killing. When the staff of the psychiatric extermination centres moved to the East to become the personnel of the first extermination camp for the Jews, they remained on the payroll of the Gemeinnützige Stiftung.

Waffen-SS   See SS.

Wehrmacht   The Armed Forces. In 1938, Hitler created a High Command of the Wehrmacht which controlled the High Commands of the Army, Navy, and Air Force, and was directly responsible to him as Commander in Chief.

In the interest of consistency Polish place names are used for towns situated in pre-war Poland with the following exceptions, dictated by common usage in English-speaking countries: Auschwitz, Birkenau, Cracow, Monowitz, and Warsaw.

Identification, Proscription, and Extermination

Introduction

The history of the natural sciences has two themes, one, the formation of their foundations, and the other, an account of their effects on society. Everyone who follows the calling of a natural scientist experiences pleasure, when his work is done, in studying the unfolding of knowledge in his science; it is a story both beautiful and true. So it is that the history of genetics is, on the one hand, the story of how the nature of living things has been revealed and, on the other hand, the story of how genetics has changed the world in which we live. A look round a market place suffices to fill the spectator's eyes with the achievements of both old-fashioned and modern breeders—cherries, apples, pears, and grapes are evidence in themselves. The variety of animal breeds tells a similar story. But how has genetics affected Man himself? There is a special branch of genetics which concerns itself exclusively with human beings: human genetics. However, genetics also plays a fundamental role in many other branches of human biology; in anthropology, psychiatry, and psychology, for example. In these sciences it is easy to think that only what is new is true. But when I think today of the story of how genetics was once put to use in anthropology and psychiatry, I see a wasteland of desolation and destruction. The blood of human beings, spilt millions of times over, is completely and resolutely forgotten. The recent history of these genetically orientated human sciences in action is as full of chaos and crime as a nightmare. Yet many geneticists, anthropologists, and psychiatrists have slipped from this dream into the deep sleep of forgetfulness.

I, myself, am trying to wake from this sleep. A few years ago I gave a course of lectures on "Philosophers and living matter". In the last two lectures, I talked about biologists and physicians who, in the present century, and particularly in Germany between 1933 and 1945, substituted ideology for philosophy. At the time, I noticed that there were very few secondary

3

sources available for reference and I thought that the course was not very good. In 1980, the opportunity of having the course material published arose.[1] As I fashioned the text of a book from my lecture notes, it finally became clear to me just how little I knew about the role of anthropology and psychiatry under National Socialism. I began to read anthropological books and journals. When it was time to give my manuscript to the publisher, I hardly had an even half-way-acceptable chapter, but I knew then that I did not understand this problem and that I wanted to understand it. It so happened that I was free to devote the winter semester of 1980–1 entirely to research. Instead of following my original plan and returning to the laboratory bench to work with my own hands, I devoted the entire time to this problem. I read the writings of anthropologists and psychiatrists in books and journals, and I questioned some of the scientists who were still alive. I worked my way through the documents of various archives, and, when my time was up, I realized that I had completely underestimated the extent of the problem. I could not and did not wish to give up my own scientific work. The experimental work of my laboratory had absolute priority, for I really wanted to know how protein recognizes DNA, or whether a certain vaccine can be produced by a certain technique. Only a few hours or days, here and there, remained for further work on this historical problem, and in these circumstances even a decade would not have been long enough for me to write a comprehensive book. So I decided to publish the manuscript as an unfinished essay, leaving it to others to write the comprehensive book which is still lacking.

As I assembled the material for my essay, it seemed to me that the conversations with anthropologists and psychiatrists were particularly important. Most of the people I was able to talk to were assistants at the time of these events, and their professors are dead. Questioning people forty years after events which occurred when they were young scientists restricted the force of their evidence still further. Nevertheless it seemed to me that the anthropologists and psychiatrists whom I mentioned in my work, or whose chiefs I mentioned, had the right to tell *their* side of the story.

Most of those whom I asked to talk to me agreed; some did so straight away, others after hesitating at first. Only Professor Fleischhacker and Professor Lorenz did not answer my letters. I decided against using a tape recorder during the conversations since I thought it would probably inhibit the very people whom I wanted, above all, to talk frankly and openly. Instead, I wrote out the conversations while on my way home. What I wrote out could only ever be an extract, never the entire conversation. I reproduced what they said in direct speech, as well as I was able to remember, although when their sentences were long I subdivided them. When I began my work, it seemed precarious and even mistaken to base it on the assumption that these conversations could ever be published. Yet when the possibility of publishing them did arise, I placed my version of the conversation before every single person whom I had questioned. I asked them all to alter, to erase, or to amplify anything which I had quoted as being theirs and which they felt did not ring true. Those whose contributions are included in this book took the trouble to do this and, as a result, the manuscripts often had to be sent backwards and forwards several times. I made it clear to them all from the start that the material to be published should not be anything spoken in haste or based on a misunderstanding on my part, but should consist of remarks for which they were prepared to take responsibility.

When I started talking to these people, I knew them only from their publications or from files in archives. Sometimes, I expected to talk with a living agent of evil—after all, they had once been involved in the most evil events. But these old ladies and gentlemen in whose homes I sat and whose hospitality I accepted did not at all correspond to the images which I had formed of them. Did I have a preconceived notion of the evil in them, just as they, in their youth, had seen characteristics which should be stamped out in mental patients, the Gypsies, and the Jews? None of the people I talked to showed any desire to revive these measures, even though many of them continued to justify at least the first steps.

Not all of them were able or willing to correct their manuscripts. Professor Loeffler became very ill just before he received the manuscript; although he had promised me on the telephone that he would correct it, his heirs forbade publication. Professor Schmieder (a former assistant of Professor C. Schneider) also became very ill and could not fulfil his promise. Others did not wish to correct their manuscripts for publication. These included Professor Becker (formerly an assistant to Professor Fischer), Professor Butenandt (formerly Director of the KWI of Biochemistry and later President of the MPG), Professor Ehrhardt (formerly a co-worker of Dr Robert Ritter), Professor Gottschaldt (formerly a department head at the KWI of Anthropology), Dr Magnussen (formerly a scholarship-holder at the KWI of Anthropology under Professors Fischer and von Verschuer), Professor H. Schade (formerly an assistant to Professor von

Verschuer), Professor B. K. Schultz (formerly chief of the Race Bureau of the RuSHA), and Professor Wendt (formerly an assistant to Professor C. Schneider). They, or in some cases their lawyers, let me know that they did not intend to correct their manuscripts for the press and that they forbade their publication. Of course, I respected their wishes as I had told everyone to whom I had spoken that I would only publish these conversations with their consent. I understand and, at the same time, I do not understand the decision they made. None of them had incriminated themselves. Most of them had declared that they had not known anything of the mass murders of mental patients, Jews and Gypsies; that they had not known anything of the events which had linked their academic institutions with the murderers; that there were no traces of anti-Semitism in their field of work; that either they had not joined the Nazi Party at all, or that they had been forced to join; that their best friends were Jewish or half-Jewish; that, as pure scientists, they had never handled expert reports on racial origins; and that they had given little or no thought to the general context of these events. Perhaps the enormity of the claims of ignorance and innocence which fell so lightly from their lips frightened some of them when they saw them written down, whether they were accurate or not.

Whatever the truth may be, these conversations, whether published or not, have influenced my attitude. Before I spoke to these people, I expected to meet only archetypal representatives of the old regime, but I soon realized that all of them were fallible human beings who had protected parts of their minds from being deranged by National Socialism. On occasion, I was even unable to withhold my sympathy, especially for those like Professors Abel and Loeffler, who had become so deeply involved with the Nazi Party or the SS that they were not able to return to academic life. For what would I have done in their place? But in science there can be no appeasement. No man has the right to forgive in the name of the dead. And the memory of the dead should be revered. Reconciliation is only possible between living people who have equal rights.

A German Chronicle of the Identification, Proscription, and Extermination of Those Who Were Different

1900   The work of Mendel is rediscovered. Those who regard the mental traits of Man (intelligence and so on) as being primarily inherited, believe that their hypothesis is scientifically proved by Mendelian genetics. For them, the whole of human history becomes a part of the biological evolution Darwin had described in the animal kingdom. They see it as their duty to demand the prevention of procreation by 'other inferior races' and by 'inferior individuals' within their own 'race', in order to stave off the decline and ruin of European culture which they allege is near at hand.

1902   Dr Woltmann, a gentleman-scholar, founds the *Politisch-Anthropologischen Revue* [Political-anthropological review].

1904   Dr Ploetz, a gentleman-scholar, founds the *Archiv für Rassenkunde und Gesellschaftsbiologie* [Archives of race-theory and social biology].

1905   Dr Ploetz founds the 'Gesellschaft für Rassenhygiene' [Society of Race-hygiene].

1908   In the German colony of South-West Africa, all existing mixed marriages are annulled and such marriages are forbidden in the future. The Germans involved are deprived of their civil rights. Dr E. Fischer, a Dozent in anatomy at the University of Freiburg, begins to investigate the 'bastards' [persons of mixed blood, born mainly of unions between Dutch (Boer) men and Hottentot women] of Rehoboth in German South-West Africa [now Namibia].

1913   Dr E. Fischer's book *Die Rehobother Bastards und das Bastardisierungsproblem beim Menschen* [The Bastards of Rehoboth and the problem of miscegenation in Man] is published. In it he writes about the people of mixed blood in German South-West Africa: "We should provide them with the minimum amount of protection which they require, for survival as a race inferior to ourselves, and we should do this only as long as they are useful to us. After this, free competition should prevail and, in my opinion, this will lead to their decline and destruction."

11 November 1918   The war comes to an end. Germany has lost her colonies with their 'inferior' Negroes. About half of the patients in German mental hospitals have died from hunger and infectious disease.

1920   The jurist Professor Binding and the psychiatrist Professor Hoche publish a book, '*Die Freigabe der Vernichtung lebensunwerten Lebens*' [The sanctioning of the destruction of lives unworthy to be lived].

1924   Hitler reads the second edition of the textbook by E. Baur, E. Fischer, and F. Lenz, *Menschliche Erblichkeitslehre und Rassenhygiene* [The principles of human heredity and race-hygiene], while imprisoned in Landsberg, and subsequently incorporates racial ideas into his own book, *Mein Kampf* [My struggle].

1927   The KWG founds a KWI of Anthropology, Human Heredity, and Eugenics in Berlin-Dahlem and nominates Professor E. Fischer as its director.

27–28 September 1929   The International Congress of Eugenics takes place in Rome. Dr C. B. Davenport (Cold Spring Harbor, USA), President of the International Federation of Eugenic Organizations, sends Mussolini a memorandum, written by Professor Fischer (Berlin), on the importance of eugenics: "Maximum speed is necessary; the danger is enormous."

2 December 1929   Dr C. B. Davenport asks Professor Fischer to become chairman of the committee on racial crosses of the International Federation of Eugenic Organizations.

1930   The National Socialist Minister of the Interior of the government of the Land of Thuringia invites the race-investigator H. F. K. Günther to a chair of social anthropology at the University of Jena, against the wishes of the faculty. Professor Lenz comments: "We are happy about the appointment itself, despite our reservations about the way in which it was made."

January 1931   The general student committee of the University of Erlangen, dominated by the National Socialists, makes a request to the Ministry of Culture for the creation of a chair of race-investigation, race-science, race-hygiene, and genetics.

1931   In the third edition of his textbook (with E. Baur and E. Fischer) Professor Lenz writes: "We must of course deplore the one-sided 'anti-Semitism' of National Socialism. Unfortunately, it seems that the masses need such 'anti' feelings . . . we cannot doubt that National Socialism is honestly striving for a healthier race. The question of the quality of our hereditary endowment is a hundred times more important than the dispute over capitalism or socialism, and a thousand times more important than that over the black-white-red or black-red-gold banners." [The banner of the Weimar Republic, which replaced that of Imperial Germany, black-white-red.]

31 December 1931   Himmler orders that members of the SS must obtain permission to marry from the newly constituted Race Bureau of the SS. "Permission to marry will be granted or refused solely and exclusively on the basis of criteria of race and hereditary health." Professor Lenz calls this a "worthwhile exercise".

2 July 1932   A committee of the Prussian State Health Council advises and recommends that a law on sterilization be brought in under the title: "Eugenics in the service of public welfare." The law was to permit the 'voluntary' sterilization of the same groups of persons (with the exception of alcoholics) as were later specified in the law of 14 July 1933.

23 August 1932   Dr C. B. Davenport, speaking at the International Congress of Eugenics in New York, suggests Professor Fischer as his successor as president of the International Federation of Eugenic Organizations. Professor Fischer declines, because of other commitments, and Dr. Rüdin (Munich) is elected.

30 January 1933   Hitler becomes Chancellor of the Reich.

1 February 1933   Professor Fischer gives a lecture, entitled: "Racial crosses and intellectual achievement" in the Harnack House of the KWG in Berlin.

7 April 1933   The 'law for the restoration of the professional civil service' is proclaimed. In particular, it contains provisions for the dismissal of all Jewish and half-Jewish civil servants and state employees.

25 April 1933   The KWG receives a letter from the Ministry of the Interior containing directions that the law for the restoration of the professional civil service be applied to the society's employees. Two days later, the Secretary General instructs the directors to carry out these measures.

6 May 1933   The Reich Minister of Justice, Gürtner, speaks to his colleagues in state governments: "I should like to ask you all to consider whether you can envisage any legislative procedure whereby we can prevent marriages of mixed race."

14 July 1933   The 'law for the prevention of progeny with hereditary defects' is proclaimed. It allows for compulsory sterilization in cases of "congenital mental defects, schizophrenia, manic-depressive psychosis, hereditary epilepsy . . . and severe alcoholism".

29 July 1933   Professor Fischer, recently elected as Rector of the University of Berlin, in which capacity he is responsible for signing his Jewish colleagues' dismissal notices, says in his inaugural address: "The new leadership, having only just taken over the reins of power, is deliberately and forcefully intervening in the course of history and in the life of the nation, precisely where this intervention is most urgently, most decisively, and most immediately needed. To be sure, this need can only be perceived by those who are able to see and to think within a biological framework, but it is understood by these people to be a matter of the gravest and most weighty concern. This intervention can be characterized as a biological population policy, biological in this context signifying the safeguarding by the state of our hereditary endowment and our race, as opposed to the unharnessed processes of heredity, selection, and elimination."

5 June 1934   The possibilities for legislating on 'race-protection' are discussed at the 37th Meeting of the Criminal Law Commission. Professor

Dahm says: "Ideally, sexual relationships between Aryans and non-Aryans should be punished."

20 June 1934   The NDW, soon to be renamed the DFG, agrees to the creation of five posts for assistants to process the 'scientific material', available in connection with sterilization, for Professor Fischer, Professor Rüdin (Director of the KWI of Psychiatry in Munich), and Professor von Verschuer (a department head at the KWI of Anthropology under Professor Fischer).

25 June 1934   Professor Lenz says at a meeting of the Expert Advisory Council for Population and Race Policy: "As things are now, it is only a minority of our fellow citizens who are so endowed that their unrestricted procreation is good for the race."

1 October 1934–1 August 1935   The first course for SS doctors is given at the KWI of Anthropology under the direction of Professor Fischer.

11 March 1935   A meeting takes place of Workgroup II of the Expert Advisory Council for Population and Race Policy. Professors Fischer, Günther, and Lenz discuss with civil servants from the Ministry of the Interior the illegal sterilization of German coloured children. Professor Rüdin calls for the sterilization of psychopaths.

26 August–1 September 1935   The Jewish Berlin psychiatrist, Dr Kallmann, is allowed to speak for the last time at a meeting in Germany. At the International Congress of Population Problems, he claims: ". . . it is desirable to extend prevention of reproduction to relatives of schizophrenics who stand out because of minor anomalies, and, above all, to define each of them as being undesirable from the eugenic point of view at the beginning of their reproductive years."

15 September 1935   Proclamation at the Party rally in Nuremberg of the 'law for the protection of German blood and German honour'. "Article 1.1: Marriages between Jews and citizens of German or related blood are forbidden . . . Article 2: Extra-marital sexual intercourse between Jews and citizens of German or related blood is forbidden."

6 February 1936   Decree of the Ministry of the Interior that a system of records be set up to cover hereditary–biological data on all patients in mental hospitals and institutions.

15 July 1936   Professor Mollison, an anthropologist from the University of Munich, recommends to the Ministry of the Interior that the costs of expert reports on Aryan or Jewish origins should be recovered from the applicants. "It is not advisable to provide such a time-consuming investigation free for those who claim Aryan origins when they know they are not entitled to do so."

November 1936   Dr Ritter, a psychologist and psychiatrist, begins his work on Gypsies in the Section for Research on Race-hygiene and Population Biology in the Reich Department of Health in Berlin, funded by the DFG.

Spring 1937   A decision is made that all German coloured children are to be illegally sterilized. After the prerequisite expert reports are provided by Dr Abel, Dr Schade, and Professor Fischer, the sterilizations are carried out.

2 February 1937   In reply to a question from the Reich Minister of Science, Education, and National Culture about the number of Jews and half-Jews supported by the DFG, its president is able to report: "None at all."

20 May 1937   Von Verschuer, by this time a professor at the University of Frankfurt, mentions in a letter to Professor Fischer his report for Rosenberg, "Proposals for the registration of Jews and part-Jews".

14 October 1937   Professor von Verschuer protests to the Reich Minister of Justice Gürtner that his expert opinion incriminating the defendant in a 'race-dishonour trial', had not been accepted and that, as a result, the defendant had been set free.

24 March 1938   Professor Kleist, a psychiatrist, ends his report on the mental hospital in Herborn, where euthanasia by starvation was being practised, with these sentences: "As long as there is no law for the destruction of lives unworthy to be lived, those who are beyond cure have the right to humane treatment which assures their continued existence. The expenditure on these unfortunates should not fall below an acceptable minimum level."

3 May 1938   The DFG places a sum of 15 000 RM at the disposal of Dr Ritter, "for the continuation of your research work on asocial individuals and on the biology of bastards (Gypsies, Jews)".

19–20 August 1938   Meeting of the committee for public care and welfare law. Professors of medicine and law discuss with civil servants from the Ministry of the Interior the possibility of a 'law on asocial individuals' which would allow people so defined to be sterilized or committed to concentration camps. According to later drafts of this law, which was never passed, two physicians and a police officer were to decide on the sterilization and further disposal of these individuals to concentration camps.

30 January 1939   Hitler tells the Grossdeutsche Reichstag [German Federal Parliament]: "If the Jews in international financial circles, both in Europe and elsewhere, succeed once again in plunging the nations of the world into yet another war, then the result will not be that the world will succumb to Bolshevism, and the Jews will be victorious, but, on the contrary, that the Jewish race in Europe will be annihilated."

20 June 1939   Professor Fischer says in a lecture: "When a people wants, somehow or other, to preserve its own nature, it must reject alien racial elements, and when these have already insinuated themselves, it must suppress them and eliminate them. The Jew is such an alien and, therefore, when he wants to insinuate himself, he must be warded off. This is self-defence. In saying this, I do not characterize every Jew as inferior, as Negroes are, and I do not underestimate the greatest enemy with whom we have to fight. But I reject Jewry with every means in my power, and without reserve, in order to preserve the hereditary endowment of my people."

Summer 1939   A public announcement is printed: "The German Society of Race-hygiene is to organize the Fourth International Congress of Eugenics in Vienna on 26–28 August 1940. The President of the Congress will be Professor Rüdin."

31 August 1939   The sixth decree on implementation of the law on sterilization virtually puts an end to the sterilizations.

1 September 1939   With his assault on Poland Hitler begins the Second World War. He backdates his letter introducing 'euthanasia' to the same date: "Reichsleiter Bouhler and Dr Brandt are entrusted with the responsibility of extending the rights of specially designated physicians, such that patients who are judged incurable after the most thorough review of their condition which is possible can be granted mercy killing."

October 1939   Following these instructions, questionnaires for every patient are distributed to mental hospitals. They are completed, in their capacity as 'experts', by Professors Heyde, Mauz, Nitsche, Panse, Pohlisch, Reisch, C. Schneider, Villinger, and Zucker, all of whom are professors of psychiatry, and thirty-nine other doctors of medicine. Their payment is 5 pfennigs per questionnaire, when more than 3500 are processed per month, up to 10 pfennigs when there are less than 500. A cross signifies death. There are 283 000 questionnaires to be processed. These experts mark at least 75 000 with a cross.

5 January 1940   Professor Lenz sends a memorandum to Pancke, chief of the RuSHA, entitled: "Remarks on resettlement from the point of view of safeguarding the race."

9 January 1940   Hildebrandt, who is the chief of the SS and Police in Danzig and West Prussia (and, from 1943 onwards, head of the RuSHA), reports to Himmler on the shootings of German and Polish mental patients which he has carried out: "The other two units of storm troopers at my disposal were employed as follows during October, November and December. . . . For the elimination of about 4400 incurable patients from Polish mental hospitals. . . . For the elimination of about 2000 incurable patients from the Konradstein mental hospital. . . ."

January 1940   The killing of mental patients by means of gas (carbon monoxide) is tried out in the jail at Brandenburg. By September 1941, 70 723 mental patients will have been killed in Grafeneck, Brandenburg, Bernburg, Hartheim, Sonnenstein, and Hadamar, using carbon monoxide gas provided by IG-Farben.

20 January 1940   Dr Ritter writes in a progress report to the DFG: "Through our work we have been able to establish that more than ninety per cent of so-called native Gypsies are of mixed blood. . . . The Gypsy question can only be considered solved when the main body of asocial and good-for-nothing Gypsy individuals of mixed blood is collected together in large *labour camps* and kept working there, and when the further *breeding of this population of mixed blood* is stopped once and for all."

31 March 1940   One of Professor Fischer's assistants travels to the ghetto in Łódz´ to take photographs which are to be used for comparison with pictures in a book on Jewry in antiquity, which Fischer is planning.

June 1940   A paper by Professor Lorenz, "Disturbances of species-specific behaviour caused by domestication", appears. He writes: "There is a certain similarity between the measures which need to be taken when we draw a broad biological analogy between bodies and malignant tumours, on the one hand, and a nation and individuals within it who have become asocial because of their defective constitution, on the other hand . . . Any attempt at reconstruction using elements which have lost their proper nature and characteristics is doomed to failure. Fortunately, the elimination of such elements is easier for the public health physician and less dangerous for the supra-individual organism, than such an operation by a surgeon would be for the individual organism."

July 1940   Professor Lenz expresses his views on 'euthanasia' in writing: "Detailed discussion of so-called euthanasia . . . can easily lead to confusion about whether or not we are really dealing with a matter which affects the safeguarding of our hereditary endowment. I should like to prevent any such discussion. For, in fact, this matter is a purely humanitarian problem."

Between 1939 and 1941 Professor Lenz had proposed the following formulation for Article 2.1 of the proposed law on euthanasia "The life of a patient, who otherwise would need lifelong care, may be ended by medical measures of which he remains unaware."

July–August 1940   Dr Jaspersen of Bethel attempts to persuade the heads of departments of psychiatry in German universities to make a collective protest against euthanasia. These professors make no move. Professor Ewald remains an isolated protester.

23 March 1941   Himmler presents Hitler with a memorandum entitled: "Some thoughts about the treatment of foreign peoples in the eastern territories." "I hope to see the very concept of Jewry completely obliterated."

26–28 March 1941   A scientific meeting takes place to mark the inauguration of the Institute for the Investigation of the Jewish Question in Frankfurt am Main. Professor Fischer and Professor Günther are guests of honour. Dr Gross, head of the Race-policy Bureau of the Nazi Party says: "The definitive solution must comprise the removal of the Jews from Europe", and he demands sterilization of quarter-Jews: "The reproduction of the quarter-Jews left behind in European countries must be reduced to a minimum." Professor von Verschuer reports the meeting for his journal, *Der Erbarzt* [The Heredity-Physician].

28 March 1941 Brack, who has been placed in charge of the euthanasia programme, writes from the Reich Chancellery to the Reichsführer-SS, Himmler, that the problem of sterilizing large numbers of individuals by means of X-rays has been solved in principle.

22 June 1941 The German armies launch their attack against the USSR. The Einsatzgruppen begin their mass murders of Jews, Gypsies, and mental patients.

31 July 1941 Reichsmarschall Göring entrusts the 'total solution of the Jewish question in the German sphere of influence in Europe' to Heydrich, the chief of the Security Police and the SD.

3 August 1941 In Münster, Bishop (later Cardinal) Count von Galen preaches in public against the murder of mental patients. His sermon marks the high point of a protest movement supported by both churches and, in addition, by many individuals.

24 August 1941 Killings of mental patients by gas are stopped at the extermination centre in Bernburg. Other extermination centres follow this step for which no written order exists. Two centres (Hartheim and Sonnenstein) resume operations a few months later for concentration camp prisoners. A statistical report gives a figure of 70 723 for the number of mental patients killed using gas, up to September 1941. This figure does not include those mental patients from Pomerania, East Prussia, and West Prussia who were shot or killed by gas. Covert euthanasia by starvation, drugs, and failure to treat naturally occurring infectious disease is now introduced.

3 September 1941 Killing of Soviet prisoners of war with Zyklon B (hydrocyanic acid) is tried out for the first time in Auschwitz.

10 October 1941 Heydrich, entrusted with the final solution of the Jewish question, includes the Gypsies as also being subject to 'evacuation' [deportation to extermination camps] in a discussion about the solution of the Jewish question.

25 October 1941   Dr Wetzel, a race-expert in the Ministry of the Occupied Eastern Territories, writes in a draft of a letter to Himmler: "I should like to inform you that Oberdienstleiter Brack of the Führer's Chancellery has said that he is prepared to collaborate in the provision of the necessary accommodation and appliances for gassing people. . . . In the present situation, there are no objections to doing away with those Jews who are unfit for work with the aid of Brack's resources. . . ."

16 November 1941   Rosenberg, theoretician and Minister of the Occupied Eastern Territories, announces the final solution of the Jewish question at a press conference.

10 December 1941   Himmler orders that commissions, made up of those physicians who were formerly concerned with euthanasia, be set up to 'comb out' prisoners in concentration camps who are unfit for work, ill, or are 'psychopaths'. Some tens of thousands of prisoners, picked out in this way by Professor Heyde, Professor Nitsche, and other physicians, are killed by gas in the extermination centres, Sonnenstein and Hartheim.

11 December 1941   Germany declares war on the USA.

Winter 1941–2   Dr Ritter takes part in a conference which considers a plan to drown 30 000 German Gypsies by sending them out into the Mediterranean Sea on ships and then bombing the ships.

Winter 1941, Spring 1942, or Summer 1942   Professor Fischer, lecturing in Paris, says: ". . . the morals and actions of the Bolshevist Jews bear witness to such a monstrous mentality that we can only speak of inferiority and of beings of another species."

January 1942   The first gas chamber is built in Auschwitz, and the second in June 1942. From now on, the killings in Auschwitz take place by means of Zyklon B made by Degesch, a subsidiary of IG-Farben.

14 January 1942   Dr Mennecke, a physician involved in the euthanasia programme, writes in a letter: "The day before yesterday, a large contingent from our euthanasia programme has moved under the leadership of Brack to the Eastern battle-zone. . . . It consists of doctors, office personnel, and male and female nurses, from Hadamar and Sonnenstein, in all a group of 20–30 persons." They start up the operation of the extermination site of Chelmno where Polish Jews and Gypsies are killed using carbon monoxide.

20 January 1942 Details of how the final solution of the Jewish question is to be organized are discussed at the Wannsee Conference. Among those attending is Hofmann, the head of the RuSHA and the immediate superior of the anthropologist Professor B. K. Schultz.

4 February 1942 A meeting takes place at the Ministry of the Occupied Eastern Territories where the 'scrapping through labour' of the peoples of the East is discussed. Professors Fischer and B. K. Schultz are among those present.

14 March 1942 Dr Ritter mentions 'about 15 000 thoroughly studied Gypsy cases' in a progress report for the DFG on his research.

23 March 1942 The Minister of the Occupied Eastern Territories, Rosenberg, writes about the possible employment of staff for his projected Reich Centre for Research on the East: ". . . I have thought of Geheimrat Eugen Fischer, a person who represents biological research and is a leading member of the KWG."

27 April 1942 In his "Comments on the General Plan for the East", a plan formulated by the SS, Dr Wetzel mentions the anthropological investigation, supported by the DFG, and conducted by Professor Abel (a department head at the KWI of Anthropology), involving Soviet citizens in German prisoner-of-war camps: ". . . he [Abel] gave a stern warning that the Russians should not be underrated. . . . In these circumstances, Abel saw only two possible solutions: either the extermination of the Russian people or a Germanization of its Nordic elements."

1 November 1942 Professor Fischer retires. His successor as Director of the KWI of Anthropology, Human Heredity, and Eugenics is Professor von Verschuer.

8 December 1942 Professor Hallervorden, Department Head at the KWI of Brain Research, writes in a progress report on his research for the DFG: "In addition, during the course of this summer, I have been able to dissect 500 brains from feeble-minded individuals, and to prepare them for examination."

16 December 1942   Himmler issues an order that persons of mixed Gypsy blood be sent to Auschwitz.

December 1942   The research ward run by the Heidelberg psychiatrist Professor C. Schneider in Wiesloch comes into full operation. In this ward, idiots and epileptics are to be physiologically and psychologically investigated. After their euthanasia elsewhere, their brains are anatomically and histologically studied.

18 January 1943   Professor C. Schneider places his first requests for the killing of patients from his research ward in Wiesloch before the Reich Commission for the Registration of Severe Disorders in Childhood.

2 February 1943   The last German troops surrender in Stalingrad. Many Germans start to have doubts about final victory.

9 March 1943   Himmler specifies, in a decree, that only physicians trained in anthropology should carry out selection for killing, and supervise the killings themselves, in extermination camps.

17 March 1943   The head of the RuSHA, Hofmann, submits a proposal to Himmler for the final solution of the question of part-Jews prepared by his subordinate Professor B. K. Schultz: "It is proposed that: quarter-Jews should not be included in the same category as persons of German blood *without exception*, but that they should first undergo a racial classification. Every quarter-Jew in whom Jewish racial characteristics are clearly prominent, as judged from external appearances, should be treated in the same way as half-Jews [i.e. as Jews]".

23 March 1943   Dr Ritter reports to the DFG: "The registration of Gypsies and part-Gypsies has been completed roughly as planned in the Old Reich [pre-war Germany] and in the Ostmark [pre-war Austria] despite all the difficulties engendered by the war. . . . The number of cases clarified from the race-biological point of view is 21 498 at the present time." One of Dr Ritter's co-workers later told a court: "Dr Ritter himself gave me permission to travel to the Gypsy camp in Bialystok in 1943. . . . It was known in the institute that abominable conditions prevailed in the Gypsy camps of Bialystok and Auschwitz, leading to deaths on a large scale among the prisoners from under-nourishment and as a result of the poor conditions of hygiene."

23 March 1943   The SS-statistician, Dr Korherr, sends the report, for which Himmler had asked, on the final solution of the Jewish question to his secretary. The report states that, up to 1 January 1943, 2.4 million Jews had been "evacuated to the East", that is to say, "had received special treatment" [*i.e.* deportation to extermination camps].

28 March 1943   Professor Fischer begins an article in the *Deutsche Allgemeine Zeitung* with the sentence: "It is a rare and special good fortune for a theoretical science to flourish at a time when the prevailing ideology welcomes it, and its findings can immediately serve the policy of the state."

30 May 1943   Dr Mengele, a former assistant to Professor von Verschuer in Frankfurt, and a visiting scientist in Professor von Verschuer's KWI of Anthropology in Berlin-Dahlem, becomes a camp doctor in Auschwitz. His first act there is to send those Gypsies who are suspected of suffering from typhoid to the gas chambers.

7 June 1943   Professor Clauberg, a gynaecologist from Königsberg, writes to Himmler that the method which he has been developing in Auschwitz for large-scale sterilization of women is "as good as ready". "I can now see the answer to the question you put to me almost a year ago about how long it would take to sterilize 1000 women in this way. An appropriately trained doctor could most probably sterilize several hundred, although perhaps not 1000, in a day."

June 1943   The new crematoria of Auschwitz have a capacity of 4756 persons a day.

June 1943   Professor C. Schneider's research ward in Wiesloch is closed because of problems due to the war.

18 August 1943   The DFG approves Professor von Verschuer's application for a grant for study of 'specific proteins'. In his progress report of 20 March 1944, Professor von Verschuer writes: "My assistant, Dr Mengele, has joined this part of the research as a collaborator. He is employed as an SS-Captain and camp doctor in the concentration camp of Auschwitz. With the approval of the Reichsführer-SS, anthropological studies have been carried out on the very diverse racial groups in this camp, and blood samples have been sent to my laboratory for processing."

9 September 1943 Circular letter concerning receipts from expert reports. "In the financial year 1942, 2340.50 RM were received in the KWI of Anthropology." Thus, assuming an average fee of 50 RM, some 50 expert reports were drawn up, each of them determining whether the Jew concerned was to live or to die.

31 January 1944 Dr Ritter mentions "23 822 conclusively clarified Gypsy cases" in a report to the DFG.

9 March 1944 Professor Hallervorden writes to Professor Nitsche, the organizer of euthanasia at that time: "I have received 697 brains in all, including those which I took out myself in Brandenburg."

10 June 1944 Professor Fischer accepts the chairmanship of a workshop at an Anti-Jewish Congress convened in Cracow: "Dear Reichsminister! That you intend to create a scientific front line for the defence of European culture against the influence of Jewry, and to call together for that purpose scientists from all the nations fighting Jewry, seems to me a very good idea and absolutely necessary, if I may allow myself to express such opinions . . . I am delighted to accept your invitation to attend this congress . . ."

June 1944 Professor H. F. K. Günther declares his readiness to speak on "The encroachment of Jewry on the cultural life of the nation" at the Anti-Jewish Congress convened in Cracow. Rosenberg himself intends to speak on "Biological humanism". [This congress never took place due to the war situation.]

3 August 1944 Of the total of 20 943 Gypsies registered as prisoners in Auschwitz, the last 2897 are sent to the gas chambers. 3461 had been transferred to other camps, while all the others died in Auschwitz from starvation, infectious disease, or by gassing.

2 September 1944 Professor C. Schneider writes in a letter about the reverses which his research project has suffered: "The people in Eichberg . . . maintain that they knew nothing of our experiments being continued, even though one of our collaborators had been going there from time to time . . . so, I have to reckon with the fact that only half the idiots whom we have investigated here will be available to us for a full examination."

Summer and Autumn 1944   Dr Mengele has his Jewish slave-assistant Dr Nyiszli send large quantities of scientific material to the KWI of Anthropology. This material includes eyes from murdered Gypsies, internal organs from murdered children, the skeletons of two murdered Jews, and sera from twins infected with typhoid by Dr Mengele.

12 February 1945   Professor von Verschuer informs the general administration of the KWG that the contents of the KWI of Anthropology have been sent from Berlin to the West in a lorry. Before or after this move, all incriminating documents (correspondence with Dr Mengele, expert reports, memoranda) are destroyed.

8 May 1945   The war comes to an end. The survivors of the concentration camps are saved. Five to six million European Jews are dead. The number of European Gypsies who have been murdered is unknown. In German mental hospitals, the fifteen per cent of patients who have survived continue to suffer from hunger. The number of murdered psychopaths, asocial individuals, and homosexuals is unknown. The anthropologists and psychiatrists involved will say that they had not known anything about it. Some are sentenced by courts, others commit suicide. The rest go back to work rebuilding their science. The world goes on its way.

25 April 1953   Watson and Crick define the three-dimensional structure of DNA, the hereditary material first identified in 1944. Rapid, almost explosive, advances in the science of genetics begin. Soon, semisynthetic hereditary material engineered for specific purposes can be introduced into plant and animal tissues, even into the germ line, where it is inherited by the next generation. Has anything been learnt from the outbreak of barbarism in Germany or will it be repeated on a worldwide scale in a yet more dreadful form and to a yet more dreadful degree?

From the Ostracism of the Jews to the Sterilization of Mental Patients

"Man findet es als Erleichterung von einer bedrückenden Sorge, wenn man im Fall des deutschen Volkes sieht, dass der Rückfall in nahezu vorgeschichtliche Barbarei auch ohne Anlehnung an irgendeine fortschrittliche Idee vor sich gehen kann."
Sigmund Freud: *Der Mann Moses und die monotheistische Religion*, Amsterdam, 1939.

"An oppressive anxiety is lifted when we realize that, in the case of the German people, their relapse into almost prehistoric barbarism proceeded without incorporating a single progressive idea."
Sigmund Freud: *The man Moses and monotheistic religion.*

The ideology of the National Socialists can be put very simply. They claimed that there is a biological basis for the diversity of Mankind. What makes a Jew a Jew, a Gypsy a Gypsy, an asocial individual asocial, and the mentally abnormal mentally abnormal is in their blood, that is to say in their genes. All these individuals, and perhaps others, are inferior. There can be no question of equal rights for inferior and superior individuals, so, as it is possible that inferior individuals breed more quickly than the superior, the inferior must be isolated, sterilized, rejected, and removed, a euphemism for killed. If we do not do this, we make ourselves responsible for the ruin of our culture. The murder of others is the secret, mystic message. It is an ideology of destruction, of mystery, and of worship of the blood.

When we compare the ideological, scientific, and bureaucratic activities of psychiatrists and anthropologists (eugenicists, race-hygienists, ethnologists, behavioural scientists) we reach what is at first a surprising conclusion: they set themselves similar goals and adopted similar positions.

The anthropologists busied themselves with identifying and eliminating inferior non-Germans (Jews, Gypsies, Slavs, and Negroes), whilst the psychiatrists were busy identifying and eliminating inferior Germans (schizophrenics, epileptics, imbeciles, and psychopaths). However, we shall see that this distinction between their respective spheres of influence was never strictly observed. Psychiatrists and anthropologists competed over the vast numbers of asocial individuals to be eradicated. Even before the Nazis seized power, Professor Fischer (Director of the KWI of Anthropology, Human Heredity and Eugenics and Professor of Anthropology at the University of Berlin) was involved in a demarcation dispute with Professor Rüdin (Director of the KWI of Psychiatry) about criminal twins. The Gypsies fell into the hands of a psychiatrist, Dr Robert Ritter, despite the interest of the anthropologists.

Their involvement in the extermination of others, of those who were inferior, was a common bond between psychiatrists and anthropologists. This programme of extermination developed gradually. I would like to put forward the hypothesis that it was a stroke of genius on Hitler's part to provide others with the necessary environment, but not with detailed plans, for complete extermination. We see these cultured and learned men hesitating at times, but none the less making steady progress, step by step, along the path to the final solution. They did not all go the whole way. Those who stopped closed their eyes, or rather they blinded themselves to the truth. They knew nothing, just as many believed that Hitler knew nothing. These learned men wanted to know nothing, and so there came into being a remarkable community of self-blinded internal exiles coexisting with the annihilators, those who did go all the way to the final solution.

Those who had not noticed the reign of terror directed against Communists, Social Democrats, and Jews, such as the anthropologist and Rector of the University of Berlin, Professor Fischer ("I repeat: this is a peaceful, an orderly revolution, a revolution under civilized conditions and without bloodshed . . . You other nations just try to repeat this, our German, revolution!"),[2] also did not notice the blatant and odious anti-Semitism of the 'law on the restoration of the professional civil service' of 7 April 1933 which imposed the removal of Jews, half-Jews, political offenders, and others from public office. The zoologist Professor von Uexküll, a pioneer in the field of ecology, immediately discovered a biological basis for this law. In the new edition of his *Staatsbiologie* [Biology of the state], 1933, he wrote a fresh chapter on 'Parasitic diseases (the internal parasites)' in which he designates as 'parasites' those of 'alien race'. "No one will criticize the leader of the state when he puts a stop to the infiltration of the organs of the state by an alien race."[3] Tactful as he was, he did not specifically name the Jews, Christian as he was, he then went on to quote and interpret Jesus Christ: "Help your neighbour and your neighbour always turns out to be precisely that person who needs your help, to whatever class and whatever race he may belong." Von Uexküll continued: "As the editor of the literary estate of H. S. Chamberlain, I should like to emphasize that these statements correspond point for point with Chamberlain's teaching." Thus, this learned man believed that he was acting entirely properly.

The conduct of the general administration, the Senate and the directors of the KWG shows to how great an extent the type of thinking which the anthropologists applied to the 'segregation' [used in the sense of apartheid in South Africa] of the Jews—that is to say the vulgar anti-Semitism of the National Socialists—had become accepted by a significant proportion of the members of the scientific establishment. The KWG was no minor provincial university. In anthropology and in psychiatry, and in most other fields, it was at the forefront of scientific endeavour. On 25 April 1933, the general administration of the KWG received a letter from the Ministry of the Interior which instructed them to dismiss Jewish and half-Jewish department heads and assistants. This instruction did not apply to the directors of the institutes, who were exempted under regulations still in force at that time.[4a] On the same day, a telegram arrived from the president of the KWG, Professor Planck, in which he announced that he intended to return from holiday on the evening of 28 April.[4b] Professor Planck was spending his leave in Italy and, while there, he had been reassured by the general administration of the KWG that no serious problems were pending. The Secretary General of the KWG, Professor Glum, acted quickly. Two days after receiving the letter from the Ministry of the Interior and one day before the return of his president, the general administration circulated a letter signed by Professor Glum and marked "for immediate action" in which the demands of the Ministry of the Interior were passed on.[4c] The directors were required to name their Jewish or half-Jewish employees and to dismiss them. Professor Haber, whose scientific activities were effectively halted by the demands of the letter (he had to dismiss three of his four department heads and five of his thirteen assistants), reacted immediately. On 30 April, he submitted his resignation in writing to the Minister, Rust. On 2 May 1933, he returned the completed questionnaires to Professor Glum and enclosed a copy of his letter of resignation.[5] The other directors (including those who were themselves Jewish) reported their Jewish employees according to instructions.

There are no other reported protests against these anti-Jewish measures. On 5 May 1933, according to the record of a meeting of the directors of the Berlin institutes, Professor Planck gave a revealing explanation:[4d] "First of all, the President emphasized that the KWG had placed itself entirely at the disposal of the national Government. The KWG already maintained very close links with the Government; either he himself or Professor Glum had called on Frick, Rust, Gerullis, and Milch.* The attitude of the Government towards the KWG was very sympathetic. It was simply that, in accordance with Government wishes, a reorganization and a reduction in the size of the Senate† was envisaged. The importance of the KWG lay in the scientific work of its institutes; their scientific independence, and that of the KWG in general, must be preserved, but under the supervision of the Reich. They would develop more freely within a better defined framework. All matters which had previously been submitted to the directors would now be dealt with by the presidency; to ensure a consistent policy within the KWG, no director should act independently. In all these arrangements, he found himself in complete agreement with the ministers responsible". The following remarks, reflecting the opinions of the directors, appear in the record: "In the subsequent discussion, Professors Haber, Baur, and Eugen Fischer spoke first. They were united in recognizing that firm leadership was required, especially at the present time, and they expressed their complete confidence in the President. The measures taken by the general administration, which had refrained from taking precipitate action, were approved. . . ."[4d]

This report, signed by Professor Planck, is open to question, especially the part which concerns Professor Haber. There were, however, no dissenting voices to be heard in the 'old' or 'newly constituted' Senate, in the

* This is presumably Erhard Milch (1892–1972), who was partly Jewish. He owed his spectacular career in the Third Reich to the protection of Göring, who said of him: "Wer Jude ist, bestimme ich." [I decide who is a Jew]. Field-Marshal Milch (as he became on 19 July 1940) was sentenced in 1947 to life imprisonment for war crimes. He was released in 1955.

† The Senate was the decision-making body of the KWG. It was composed of the President; some, although not all, of the institute directors; and government officials, of whom those who were Jewish or not pro-Nazi were removed.

Scientific Council, or in the General Assembly of the KWG, all of which held meetings between 18 May and 23 May. Nor have I found a single letter of protest. Any anxiety which may have been felt over these developments was matched by enthusiasm for the newly vacated positions and, finally, enthusiasm won the day. "Do we not have sufficient talent in our own country?" The voices of the doubters died away. Only a few noticed that the KWG, and the universities in general, lost their scientific supremacy and became (as they remain to this day) provincial.

On 23 May 1933, the President of the KWG sent a telegram to Hitler from this General Assembly: "The members of the Kaiser Wilhelm Society for the Advancement of the Sciences, gathered at their 22nd General Assembly, have the honour of sending their respectful greetings to the Chancellor of the Reich. They solemnly vow that German science is ready to make every possible effort to collaborate in the reconstruction of the new national state, which, in turn, has declared itself to be our protector and our patron. Planck." And Hitler sent the following telegram in response: "I thank you most sincerely for the oath of loyalty which you have taken and which you have communicated to me. May the KWG continue to apply the advances of science, as it has done in the past, for the good of the Reich. Chancellor of the Reich, Adolf Hitler."[6]

On 16 May 1933, Professor Planck visited Hitler to introduce himself, and during that visit tried to demonstrate the absurdity of dismissing Jews 'of value', using the case of Professor Haber as an example. The dismissal of Jews 'of less value' had already been accepted. Professor Planck has described this visit as follows: "After Hitler seized power, it was my duty, as President of the KWG, to pay my respects to the Führer. I thought I should use this opportunity to put in a good word for my Jewish colleague, Fritz Haber. I said that the last war [First World War] would have been lost from the outset had it not been for his techniques for producing ammonia by fixing nitrogen from the air. Hitler answered in these words: "I have nothing against Jews as such. But the Jews are all Communists, and the Communists are my enemies. It is against them that I fight." I commented that, even so, there do exist different types of Jews, some of value to humanity and some of no value, and that, among the former, there were long-established families who had absorbed the best of German culture. I said that we should make a distinction between them. He replied, "That is not correct. A Jew is a Jew; all the Jews stick together like burrs. Where there is one Jew, all kinds of other Jews gather. The Jews themselves should have established those distinctions. They did not do so and therefore I must proceed against all of them equally." I then remarked that we were inflicting damage on ourselves by forcing Jews whose talents we needed to emigrate and that their talents would now be used for the benefit of foreigners. This he did not accept at all and held forth at great length about quite general matters, ending up by saying: "It is said that I suffer on occasion from weak nerves. That is a slander. I have nerves of steel." With that, he slapped his knee with great force, spoke more and more rapidly and began to shake with such uncontrollable rage that there was nothing I could do but keep silent and take my leave as soon as I decently could."[7]

The directors of the KWG went about the task of dismissing their Jewish and half-Jewish assistants, secretaries and other co-workers. Some even showed 'foresight'.[4e] Thus Professor Kuhn had dismissed one of his two Jewish assistants even before he received Professor Glum's letter. In a letter to the Ministry of the Interior dated 4 October 1933,[4f] Professor Glum named in all 54 'non-Aryan' and 1007 'Aryan' employees of the KWG. Most of the 'non-Aryans' had been dismissed by their directors with the Jewish directors participating in this process. Professor Haber,* the only director who did not take part in this shabby and disgusting performance, died soon afterwards, on 29 January 1934, whilst travelling through Switzerland. As a last gesture of self-assertion, the KWG arranged a memorial service for him on 29 January 1935. The professors were told by the Ministry of Science, Education, and National Culture not to attend. Nevertheless, the memorial service took place. Those who did attend lamented the loss of a great scholar and German citizen and forgot, or rather repressed, the fact that the loss of Professor Haber was a consequence of the programme of dismissals which the eminent participants themselves had carried out.

During this period, a few 'difficult cases' and the Jewish directors were spared dismissal. However, the pressure finally became so strong that even they had to yield. It is not known which directors condoned false declarations made by their employees by remaining silent during the initial phase. Professor Meyerhof, under threat himself as a Jew, tried to keep Jewish employees in his institute, but he could not count on the support or the tolerance of his co-director, Professor Kuhn. On 27 April 1936, Professor

* Professor Haber had left Germany, hoping to find work in England, at Cambridge. He was on his way to Italy, to escape the rigours of the English winter, when he died.

Kuhn wrote to Professor Glum: "An enquiry from the State Police prompts me to ask you to check the questionnaires carefully. I informed Professor Meyerhof at the appropriate time that I did not intend to try to control his choice of collaborators. But I did so only on condition that he sent the questionnaires, completed according to instructions, to the general administration in Berlin. It now seems that three people of non-Aryan extraction are being employed by Professor Meyerhof in this institute (Mr Lehmann, Miss Hirsch, and another lady whose name I do not know). This situation has given rise to speculation about the KWG in general and the Heidelberg institute in particular. I should like to propose that you send precise guidelines to Professor Meyerhof on how he should select his collaborators once you have seen the questionnaires. In order to make the position of the KWG absolutely clear and to put an end to speculation, you should consider sending these guidelines not only to Professor Meyerhof but, in the form of a circular letter, to all institutes, even though the others may not be harbouring any similar cases."[48] In 1938, Professor Meyerhof was dismissed himself, as were most of the 'difficult cases'. Professor Planck resigned as President of the KWG. Professor Glum, the Secretary General, was dismissed at the same time. It became impossible to retain him, his 'purely Aryan' administration notwithstanding, for he had forgotten, in his zeal, that he too was not indispensable. The fact that his wife was partly Jewish (see p. 171) precluded his further employment.

A decision was made at a meeting of the Senate on 11 November 1943 that quarter-Jews could be members of the KWG, as long as they were suitable in all other respects for 'assimilation'. In the end, of all the Jews in the KWG, only Professor Warburg was left and he has told his own story: "The KWI of Cell Physiology was built, equipped and, in part, supported by funds from the Rockefeller Foundation. I was its director from the outset, So I kept my position until 1941, even though I am half-Jewish. In 1941, I was dismissed by the KWG. Phillipp B. Bouhler, then Chief of the Führer's Chancellery, learnt of this dismissal and ordered his chief of staff, Viktor Brack, to look into my case. A few weeks later, Viktor Brack succeeded in having my dismissal revoked and, in so doing, he probably saved my life. He also saved, for science, a world-famous institute which was working exclusively for peaceful ends. "I did this," Brack told me on 21 June 1941, "not for you, not even for Germany, but for the world." When we consider that Brack's action came at a time when racial hatred and war psychosis were reaching their peak in Germany, we can only marvel at his courage in allowing the tolerance and the peaceful aims which characterize science to take precedence over the basic principles of National Socialism.*"[8]

On 14 July 1933, the day after the treaty with the Vatican, the 'law for the prevention of progeny with hereditary defects'[9] was passed. This law allowed for compulsory sterilization in cases of "congenital mental defect, schizophrenia, manic-depressive psychosis, hereditary epilepsy, hereditary chorea, hereditary blindness, hereditary deafness, severe physical deformity, and severe alcoholism". A draft version of a similar statute had been prepared by experts in 1932, during the Weimar Republic (the draft version did not mention severe alcoholism). At that time Professor Fischer had shouted at a young National Socialist, Dr Conti, during a committee meeting: "Your party has not been in existence nearly as long as our eugenic movement!"[10] Professor Goldschmidt, one of those who compiled the draft statute, would later recall: "The Nazis took over the whole draft and then used the most inhuman and execrable methods to put the humane measures, which we had conscientiously and responsibly drafted, into everyday practice."[11] Professor Goldschmidt was director of the KWI of Biology until, being a Jew, he was forced to retire on 1 January 1936. He, like the other directors, had dismissed his Jewish employees.[12]

But even this law was not wide enough in its scope for some psychiatrists. Dr Kallmann advised compulsory sterilization of healthy, heterozygous, carriers of the abnormal gene for schizophrenia, for which he postulated recessive inheritance.† The lifetime incidence of schizophrenia of about 1 per cent would imply that no less than 18 per cent of the population are heterozygous carriers of the gene. Dr Kallmann thought that these carriers, although outwardly healthy, could be identified by the presence of minor anomalies. This enormous project would have involved the testing of all close relatives of cases of schizophrenia (who might be expected to include a substantial proportion of the 18 per cent of carriers in the population) and the subsequent sterilization of a half or

---

* Professor Warburg gave evidence on Brack's behalf when the latter was tried as a war criminal in Nuremberg in 1947. The charges included supplying equipment for gassing people. Brack was sentenced to death and hanged in 1948. Warburg affirmed after the war that the Nobel prize committee had proposed his name for a second Nobel prize after his dismissal.

† In the case of recessive inheritance, individuals are affected by a disease only if they have two abnormal genes at the same chromosomal locus, one inherited from the father and one from the mother.

more, selected through these minor anomalies. The patent absurdity of this proposal led Professor Lenz to oppose it at the meeting where Kallmann gave his lecture.[13]

A single psychiatrist, Professor Ewald,[14] and the Catholic Church protested against the law. The Minister of the Interior invited the bishops to a meeting;[15] they had no objection to sterilization as a punishment, but this was not enough for the Minister. The bishops and the clergy continued to object, often from the pulpit, but with no effect.

Government medical officers and the directors of secure mental hospitals were obliged by the law to submit requests for sterilization. Many university psychiatrists realized very quickly that these requests would drive patients out of their clinics and towards their competitors in internal medicine, so they announced that henceforward their clinics would be 'open'. The psychiatrists continued to send diagnoses of their patients to the government medical officers, but they left it to them to fill in the applications. A decision on the application was made by majority vote of a 'tribunal of hereditary health' consisting of a government medical officer, an 'independent' physician, and a judge. In other words, the physicians made the decision. Frequently the person concerned discovered what was happening only when the tribunal was actually in session. At a meeting of the 'expert advisory council', Dr Linden, from the Ministry of the Interior, said, without his opinion being questioned: "Government medical officers must exercise a certain caution in their summons to persons suffering from hereditary diseases and avoid causing undue alarm. Perhaps we should even recommend that in certain cases the patients, or alcoholics, should not be informed of the reason for the summons, but should be told only when the tribunal is in session."[16] The person concerned had no right to inspect the documents. His right to a legal adviser (who was not allowed to see the documents either) could be turned down without the possibility of an appeal. It was a costly parody of a legal process which had the effect of reducing the individual to an impersonal object without any rights at all.

Science did not do badly out of all this. By 1934, the Ministry of the Interior had already created (through the NDW) five new posts for assistants to Professors Fischer, Rüdin and von Verschuer to deal with the task of evaluating the data.[17] The scientists had ambitious plans. Professor Lenz said at a meeting at the Ministry of the Interior: "Our goal must be to establish a certificate of hereditary biology for every citizen [non-Jewish, non-Gypsy Germans] and every inhabitant [Jews and Gypsies]." He continued: "Those who do not suffer from hereditary disease within the meaning of the law are not necessarily hereditarily healthy and fit to breed." And later: "As things are now, it is only a minority of our fellow citizens who are so endowed that their unrestricted procreation is good for the race." Later still: "Safeguarding the hereditary endowment and safeguarding the race are basically the same thing. The biological foundations of the race are the biological foundations of the hereditary endowment and vice versa."[18]

The ultimate aim of many anthropologists was to make all sexual acts subject to authorization. This dream never became a reality, but the 'health in marriage' law of 18 October 1935 was a step in that direction. Under this law any person who "suffers from a mental disturbance which makes their marriage undesirable from the point of view of the community", was forbidden to marry. Thus substantial numbers of sterilized schizophrenics and individuals suffering from depression were not allowed to marry. However, there was not enough time before the war began to cast the net of hereditary–biological supervision over all Germans and there were too few personnel available to seek out all undesirable 'psychopaths'. Only for the SS was the authorization of a marriage dependent on an intensive investigation, which included a vaginal examination of the bride. It was not until the end of 1942, shortly before the defeat at Stalingrad, that Himmler put an end to this 'playing doctor'.[19]

A meeting of 'Workgroup II of the Expert Advisory Council for Population and Race Policy'[20] was convened on 11 March 1935. The topic for discussion was the sterilization of coloured children, overlooked when the law for the prevention of hereditary defects was drafted. Among others, Professors Günther and Lenz (both from Berlin), Rüdin (Munich), and Doctors Gütt and Linden from the Ministry of the Interior took part in this discussion. Three possible approaches were considered: widening of the scope of the law, 'export', i.e. deportation, and compulsory sterilization without changing the law. In 1937, a decision was handed down from the Chancellery of the Reich, but was never put on record: compulsory sterilization without any basis in law. An expert opinion had to be obtained on each child. The experts included Dr Abel and Professor Fischer (both from Berlin), and Dr Görner and Dr Schade, both assistants of Professor von Verschuer (Frankfurt).[21] The children were brought for examination to Professor von Verschuer's university institute in Frankfurt. The 'material' was also scientifically evaluated.[22] The Gestapo then took 385 coloured children* to university clinics, where they were surgically sterilized.[21]

During the second part of this 11 March meeting, Professor Rüdin presented his ideas on "widening of the spectrum of diseases necessitating sterilization". Professor Rüdin, Director of the KWI of Psychiatry, called for the compulsory sterilization of, amongst others, 'valueless individuals [Ballastexistenzen]', "all who were socially inferior psychopaths on account of moral confusion or severe ethical defects" and "the great mass of serious and incorrigible constitutional criminals".[20]

Because asocial individuals were being taken into custody, as well as sterilized, the legal profession began to take an interest in them too. For example, in April 1938 at the 'constituent meeting of the legal committee for public care and welfare law' Professor Emge, of the Academy of German Law, said that: "the law for the prevention of progeny with hereditary defects, which provides for the detention of persons with hereditary defects until they are sterilized, by no means removes the need for a law covering their custodial care, for they often contribute to the spread of epidemics; for example, their uninhibited behaviour could lead to epidemics of sexually transmitted disease."[23a] Four months later, Dr Ehaus from the Ministry of the Interior explained to a meeting of the same committee what was meant by 'custodial care', namely "state concentration camps, where they may pursue productive work which is useful to the general public."[23b] At the same meeting, Dr Linden referred to this problem again: "Requests that we settle the matter of the sterilization of asocial and antisocial individuals by a special law are reaching us from every quarter. For this reason, I am making this request here."[23b] Asocial individuals presented no problem to a practising physician, Professor Villinger, a child psychiatrist and director of the Bethel mental institution: "Concerning widening the scope of the law for the prevention of progeny with hereditary defects, I may say that, in general, we have trouble with asocial and antisocial individuals brought to us with a view to an application for sterilization, only when we can find no indication of a defect in intelligence. But there are rather few such people, although they do exist."[23b] The discussion then turned to the possibility that committal to a concentration camp should be decided by a tribunal, made up, like

---

* These coloured children were born as a result of the occupation of the Rhineland, from the end of the First World War until 1930, by the victorious French army, which included colonial units.

tribunals of hereditary health, of two physicians and a judge. I shall return to this proposal later.

The scope of the law for the prevention of progeny with hereditary defects was never widened. The number of individuals involved was large enough already. The judge of a 'tribunal of hereditary health' arrived at a figure of 200 000 sterilizations annually in the Reich. He made this estimate by extrapolating from the figures available from Hamburg for 1934.[24] The publication of this figure in a German legal journal stimulated the Ministry of Justice to embark upon research of its own. The result of this investigation, a figure of 62 463 sterilizations for 1934, was published in the German press as a correction of the previous article.[25] The figures for 1935 (71 760 sterilizations) and 1936 (64 646 sterilizations) were later obtained but remained unpublished at Hitler's request.[26] The same survey revealed that in these three years, a total of 367 women and 70 men had died as a result of these operations. While the figures for sterilizations are probably substantially correct, I suspect that the figures for deaths are too low, since it was not in the interests of the clinics concerned to make accurate reports of such deaths to the ministry.

The law gave rise to much dispute. Should those who drank too much as a result of brain injuries received during the First World War be sterilized, or should exceptions be made for them? The Ministry of the Interior turned to Professor Rüdin for an answer. He advised that no exceptions be made: "Any allowances we make today for the war-wounded will tomorrow be extended to party veterans who have been injured in street fights and the day after to industrial injuries."[27] In the summer of 1937, the Chief Physician of the Reich, Dr Wagner, sent an angry memorandum[28] to the Reich Chancellery about the irresponsible manner in which verdicts concerning sterilizations were made known. He complained that it was resulting in an alarming loss of the population's confidence in government medical officers. The reactions of the state secretary of the Reich Chancellery,[29a,b] of the Ministry of the Interior,[30] and of Himmler: "clear instructions to discuss matters with the person to be sterilized, in as humane a manner as possible, once the decision is reached,"[31] show that there was no inclination or intention to reduce the rate of sterilizations. In an unpublished circular,[32] sent out in 1936, the Minister of the Interior had previously ordered the introduction of a system of records of hereditary–biological data on all patients in psychiatric clinics. In 1938, the circular was sent to various offices and departments. The provincial ministries were unhappy about the scheme because of its cost.[33a] However, academics were more enthusiastic. Professor Pohlisch made detailed proposals about how this documentation should be organized—a preparation for the registration of those to be killed.[33b]

No substantial changes in sterilization procedures were made until the beginning of the war, so that we may estimate that 350–400 000 individuals were sterilized between 1934· and 1939. The programme with its 'tribunals of hereditary health' effectively ended with the 'sixth decree implementing the law' which prohibited almost all sterilizations after 31 August 1939. At the same time, investigations to determine suitability for marriage, required under the same law, were discontinued. The doctors and judges were needed not only for the war but for the killing of those who would previously have been sterilized. Hitler's letter authorizing such killing was backdated to 1 September 1939.

The Reich Minister of Justice had already approached his colleagues in the ministries of the Länder on 6 May 1933, before the law on sterilization was even passed, about another matter. "I should to ask like you all to consider whether you can envisage any legislative procedure whereby we can prevent marriages of mixed race."[34] The legal experts of the Criminal Law Commission discussed 'race-protection' at their 37th Meeting on 5 June 1934.[35] The following university professors also took part: Kohlrausch, Klee, and von Gleispach (Berlin); Dahm (Kiel); Metzger (Munich); and Nagler (Breslau). The professors and the judges were in agreement. Professor Klee: "The alien race, the Jewish race, is inferior given the need to preserve the purity of our race." Professor Metzger: "Unfortunately the fundamental criminal act does not lend itself to prosecution on any legally defined basis . . ." Professor Dahm: "Ideally, sexual relationships between Aryans and non-Aryans should be punished . . ." So this circular discussion went on and on. The wishes of professors and judges alike were granted with the passing on 15 September 1935 of the 'law for the protection of German blood and German honour':* Article 1.1: Marriages between Jews and citizens of German or related blood are forbidden . . . Article 2: Extramarital sexual intercourse between Jews and citizens of German or related blood is forbidden . . . Article 5.1: Those who contravene the regulations of Article 1 will be sentenced to penal servitude . . . Article 5.2: Any man

---

* This was one of the anti-Semitic Nuremberg Laws, so called because they were drafted, rapidly and on Hitler's personal initiative, whilst the annual party rally was taking place in that city. Another of these laws defined German citizenship.

who contravenes the regulations of Article 2 will be sentenced to a prison term or to penal servitude. The anthropologists were duly grateful. Professor Fischer, for example, addressed the Faculty of Theology of the University of Berlin. "Professor Fischer ended by thanking the Führer for giving geneticists the opportunity, by means of the Nuremberg laws, of making the results of their researches useful to the general public."[36]

The director of the KWI of Anthropology spoke straight from the heart. However, his department chief, Professor Lenz, had previously found anti-Semitism vulgar; how did he now react? In 1927, he had written in the third edition of *The principles of human heredity and race hygiene* "Prominent Jewish revolutionaries include not only Marx and Lassalle, but also, in more recent times, Eisner, Luxemburg, Leviné, Toller, Landauer, Trotsky, Szamuely and others besides. Kahn* who values the Jewish revolutionary as a liberator of humanity, sees in these individuals "a specifically Jewish conception of the world and of historical activity". Many Jewhaters are of the opinion that the character of the Jews is essentially subversive and negative. I do not think that this is correct. The fact that most of the leaders of revolutionary movements are Jews can be simply explained by the very qualities that Kahn had perceived, which, of themselves, are not in any way directed towards upheaval. Even when the Jew destroys, he intends as a rule to reconstruct. The marked sense of family of the Jews is anything but subversive and the same applies to their strong sense of community, their readiness to help each other and their feeling for humanity as a whole. The Jewish intellect, alongside the German, is the principal driving force of modern western culture!†"[37a] Enlightened by the recent persecution of the Jews, Lenz rewrote this section for the fourth edition of his book in 1936: "Prominent Jewish revolutionaries include not only Marx and Lassalle but also, in more recent times, Eisner, Rosa Luxemburg, Leviné, Toller, Landauer, Trotsky, Szamuely and others besides. Kahn, who values the Jewish revolutionary as a liberator of humanity sees in these individuals "a specifically Jewish conception of the world and of

---

* Lenz refers to Kahn. F. *Die Juden als Rasse und Kulturvolk* [The Jews as a race and a people of culture] (3rd edn). Berlin, 1922.

† Lenz here adds in a footnote: "This point of view provoked indignation among anti-Jewish readers of the first edition, as evidenced by their published criticisms. Nevertheless, I continue to believe that this view is correct. I often feel regret that so much youthful energy and enthusiasm is wasted in the anti-Jewish movement, to the accompaniment of so much useless clamour. If only all that youthful energy could be directed towards goals which are of real use to our race." This footnote was deleted in the 1936 edition.

historical activity". The Jewish race has been depicted by Schickedanz* as a race of parasites. There is no doubt that the Jews can constitute a grave handicap for their host nation, and it is no accident that as long as there have been Jews there have been hostile feelings towards them, persecutions, and expulsions. A living creature develops better without parasites. On the other hand, a parasite develops better in a host which is only slightly weakened. If the parasite destroys its host, it ensures its own destruction. Therefore, Jewry does not go as far as to destroy its host nation. If it were to do so, it would deprive itself of the basis of its own existence. But it cannot thrive among very strong nations. So, a certain amount of subversion of the host nation is in its interests."[37b]

The Nuremberg laws afforded the anthropologists many opportunities to give expert opinions. These expert opinions were required by the 'Reich Kinship Bureau', an agency of the Ministry of the Interior, from authorized institutes and investigators. A debate occurred in 1936 about who should bear the expenses for this work, which clearly reflects the attitudes of the academics. Professor Fischer writes: "On the other hand, I think it is unfair that our fellow countrymen, who happen to have the means, should enjoy the benefit of being able to obtain an expert opinion certifying them to be Aryan, while our poor fellow countrymen are denied this opportunity."[38] Professor Mollison, an anthropologist from Munich, writes: "It is not advisable to provide such a time-consuming investigation free for those who wrongly claim Aryan origins when they know they are not entitled to do so."[39]

The writing of expert reports all too often developed into charlatanism. The data, often consisting only of a photograph of a putative father, were almost never of such a nature that a statement could be made with any degree of certainty. If these anthropologists falsified the data on humane grounds, they became party to fraud, even though it might be a morally justifiable fraud. If, on the other hand, they did their work scrupulously they became accessories to murder, at least after 1941, when the verdict 'Jewish' became equivalent to a sentence of deportation to Theresienstadt or Auschwitz. Of those whom I questioned later, most said that

---

* Schickedanz, A. *Sozialparasitismus im Völkerleben* [Social parasitism in the lives of nations]. Leipzig, 1927. Schickedanz, a journalist and ideologue, was an early collaborator of Rosenberg, later the Minister of the Occupied Eastern Territories, who nominated Schickedanz overlord of the Caucasus, a post he never took up. He committed suicide at the end of the war like many other Nazi dignitaries.

someone else had provided the expert opinions. In the rare cases they admitted to, they said that it had always been done on a strictly scientific basis, which cannot be checked now because the academics concerned destroyed the evidence and the expert opinions were kept secret even from the individuals concerned. So I had to depend on a few examples that were preserved by chance. In 1937, Professor von Verschuer who was then director of the 'Institute of Hereditary Biology and Race-hygiene' of the University of Frankfurt and also the University's Rector, gave evidence in a 'race-dishonour case' [brought under the Nuremberg Laws] with his assistant Dr Mengele, who had obtained his doctorate in Professor Mollison's department in Munich. The accused proclaimed his innocence since he had always believed himself to be a Christian. Even in childhood, he had been teased that his Jewish legal father was not his real father and that his mother had had a lover who was not Jewish. A court believed the defendant and set him free. Professor von Verschuer and his assistant Dr Mengele, however, had come to the conclusion that the defendant was indeed the son of his Jewish legal father. Professor von Verschuer complained bitterly to the Reich Minister of Justice that the expert opinions that he and Dr Mengele had submitted had been disregarded.[40]

At the same time, Professor von Verschuer wrote a 'report' making "proposals for the registration of Jews and part-Jews". In a letter to Professor Fischer (Berlin), the Director of the KWI of Anthropology, Human Heredity and Eugenics, he set out the main points of his idea: "It seems to me that a promising method would be to widen the scope of military recruitment examinations so that, in the case of Jews and persons of mixed blood (as defined by the law on citizenship), it would be combined with an anthropological survey."[41a] At this time, if not before, Professor von Verschuer earned himself the hostility and contempt of Dr Gross, the chief of the Race-policy Bureau of the Nazi Party, for it was quite obvious that the arrangements proposed by Professor von Verschuer were absurd. An anthropological investigation of German Jews would only have shown that 'doubtful' Jews could not be positively identified in this way. It would only have served to increase the number of suspects. Being realistic, the Nazi Party was satisfied with evidence of ancestry since 1800, the assumption being that conversions to Christianity had been very rare before that time, while conversions to Judaism had never taken place. The Jews were actually registered in the general census of 17 May 1939. Everybody had to report, in addition to the usual data, any Jewish grandparent. These answers were to be returned in sealed envelopes; confidentiality was assured. The results were published and the individual data were used to plan deportations. Professor von Verschuer commented on the published data that he was pleased to see that the number of Jews had substantially decreased since 1933.[42a]

The fact that Professor von Verschuer destroyed his 'report' shows that he did not regard his proposal as representing an attempt on his part to provide some sort of covert assistance to the Jews. (Perhaps it should be added here that, after the war, almost all Germans 'discovered' that the acts of persecution, in which they had been involved, had in fact been cleverly designed subterfuges to help the persecuted.) When he was preparing his 'report', he wrote to Professor Fischer to try to persuade him to participate in a meeting organized by Dr Grau, the chief of the 'Research Section for Jewish Questions' of the 'Reich Institute for the History of the New Germany', Rosenberg's creation. "International Jewry", wrote Professor von Verschuer, "already knows full well where we stand and so taking part will not really change anything. Still, it is important that our racial policies should be based on objective scientific criteria which have gained wide acceptance."[41b] Professor Fischer attended the meeting.

Professor von Verschuer's contribution was published later in the series *Researches on the Jewish Question*, which was financed by Rosenberg.[42b] After the pogrom of November 1938* Professor Fischer had his turn when, on 20 June 1939, he made a speech to the coal barons of the Ruhr. "When a people wants, somehow or other, to preserve its own nature, it must reject alien racial elements, and when these have already insinuated themselves, it must suppress them and eliminate them. The Jew is such an alien and, therefore, when he wants to insinuate himself, he must be warded off. This is self-defence. In saying this, I do not characterize every Jew as inferior, as Negroes are, and I do not underestimate the greatest enemy we have to fight. But I reject Jewry with every means in my power, and without reserve, in order to preserve the hereditary endowment of my people."[43] It is certainly no accident that Professor Fischer began and ended this speech by singing the praises of that most German

---

* On 7 November 1938, Herschel Grynszpan, a 17-year-old Polish Jew whose family had been deported from Germany to Poland, shot and fatally wounded Ernst vom Rath, a third secretary at the German Embassy in Paris. This assassination was followed by the anti-Jewish pogrom of 9–10 November in Germany, known as the Kristallnacht, the night of broken glass.

of all heroes, Hagen.* Thus he closed the door on his return to the peaceful scientific community.

Activities which involved the giving of such expert opinions increased until the beginning of the war, when hundreds of unprocessed applications began to pile up in the institutes which dealt with these matters because the staff who had been handling them had been conscripted. This did not prevent another of the squabbles typical of the academic world. In 1940 Professor Lenz (Berlin) wrote to the district court in Cologne saying that he could not give an expert opinion in a particular case without serological tests.[44] The Ministry of Justice became involved and referred the matter to his colleagues. Professors Claussen (Cologne), Fischer (Berlin), Gieseler (Tübingen), Mollison (Munich), and Reche (Leipzig) replied that they did not share Professor Lenz's views at all and that *they* had no difficulty in making reliable assessments on the basis of photographs alone.

The KWI of Anthropology had another public duty. It provided intensive short courses for government medical officers and one-year courses for SS-doctors, in anthropology and genetics. Dr Geyer, Dr Poppendick from the RuSHA, Dr Schade, Dr Renno (who later became the director of an extermination centre), and others took part in the first course for SS-doctors, which ran from October 1934 to August 1935.[45] Professor Fischer was responsible for their scientific instruction while the RuSHA, an agency of the SS, took charge of their ideological training.[46]

It is not possible to document here the entire spectrum of investigations envisaged, or actually carried out, in collaboration with the anthropologists, but I should like to quote from a research application made by a professor of psychology from Berlin, Rieffert, which can be regarded as typical: "I have devoted more than ten years of work to developing methods for investigating the race-psychology of the Jews. Our institute will carry out its race-psychological investigations in collaboration with the Institute of Race-science headed by my colleague Günther and with the Institute of Anthropology headed by my colleague Fischer. We also intend to organize expeditions to the interior of Germany, especially to the districts where people of long-established German stock and pure race live. The first objective will be to make a psychological study of these communities and, in addition, to make observations and enquiries about the way

* Hagen is a major character in the Nibelungenlied, a medieval German heroic poem. He ferries the Burgundian host over the Danube into Hunland and then destroys the boat so that there can be no return.

of life of Jews living there. In this way, we will study the 'tactics' employed by Jews at various times to adapt to the particular characteristics of each community, as well as the ways in which these German communities defend themselves against Jewry in their day-to-day affairs."[47]

Let us return now to the psychiatrists. In the 1920s, the provincial psychiatric hospitals had become custodial institutions in which the patients waited, without treatment, either for death or for discharge. In the 1930s, innovations were introduced as various types of shock treatment (electricity, insulin, leptazol*) became available. This new era is well represented by the textbook written by Professor Carl Schneider.[48] From the 1920s onwards, the introduction of unpaid forced labour ('work-therapy') made these institutions important from an economic point of view too. The Wiesloch mental hospital, for instance, with approximately 1200 inmates, made 222 505.40 and 223 965.06 RM in clear profits in 1936 and 1937 (Schneider[48], p. 414). The psychiatric institutions were very much like the concentration camps. Once in, there was no way out for the inmate. He carried out forced labour. "Work gives health." He had no rights. If he remained uncooperative, a course of up to twenty treatments with leptazol, insulin or electricity would be prescribed as therapy, of course, and not as punishment (Schneider[48], p. 283). If the patient believed that this painful shock therapy was a punishment, the psychiatrist saw it as a further sign of insanity, which could only be cured by more electricity. Courses of sixty shock treatments were not uncommon. Broken bones and even deaths caused by the shocks were regarded as unavoidable accidents which were a normal consequence of the therapy.

---

* A neuroleptic drug (pentylenetetrazol) which causes seizures similar to those induced by electroconvulsive shock treatment.

From the Killing of Mental Patients to the Killing of Jews and Gypsies

In addition to the model institutions, like Wiesloch, there were others where killing mental patients through hunger and illness was a deliberate policy. Professor Kleist ended his report of 24 March 1938 on the Herborn mental hospital with these sentences: "As long as there is no law 'for the destruction of lives unworthy to be lived', those who are beyond cure have the right to humane treatment which assures their continued existence. The expenditure on these unfortunates should not be allowed to fall below a certain minimum level."[49] Some time later, the professors of psychiatry de Crinis, Mauz, Kihn, Pohlisch, and C. Schneider; the anthropologist Professor Lenz; the mental hospital directors Dr Faltlhauser, Dr Heinze, and Dr Pfannmüller together with a few SS-doctors and medical civil servants put the finishing touches to a draft of a law for 'euthanasia'. The 'expressed opinions' of these academics on the law have been preserved, but they are undated. It could be that they wrote them before the beginning of the war, during the time of the euthanasia programme, or after its cessation.[50a] They all agreed that a law which permitted the killing of psychiatric patients was necessary. If these academics conferred in 1939, then the 'euthanasia programme' was organized according to their proposals; if they met later, then they formulated a law in retrospective as well as in future justification of the 'euthanasia programme'. I leave it to the reader to decide which of these possible datings has the more frightful implications. To quote from these 'expressed opinions',[50b] C. Schneider proposed the title: "law for the granting of medical assistance to die . . .", Kihn: "law for the granting of last aid . . .", and Faltlhauser: "law for the granting of special or specially assessed help".

42

According to these men, the decisive article, Article 2, should be worded as follows: Pohlisch: "A human life which, because of a seriously abnormal constitution, or because of an incurable chronic mental illness, needs continuous care . . ."; C. Schneider: "The concept of degeneration does not apply to incurables who are doing socially worthwhile and, in particular, economically important work in the institution"; Heinze: "Individuals who need constant nursing care on account of an abnormal constitution or of incurable chronic mental illness or who for other reasons do not pass the test of life . . ."; and Lenz: "The life of a patient, who otherwise would need lifelong care, may be ended by medical measures of which he remains unaware . . ."

Of Article 4, the experts said: Kihn: "In Article 4.4 we should replace "two years' observation in a mental hospital" by "at least two years' observation by a medical specialist" "; Mauz: ". . . does not wish, as a matter of principle, to allow any exceptions for schizophrenia; he much prefers extending the minimum stay to five years"; Lenz ". . . is fundamentally uneasy about exceptions. They are not advisable for adults and for those with severe malformations special regulations are necessary. No apprehension about treatment in institutions should be allowed to spread among the public"; and de Crinis: ". . . in general, the discharge of patients from these hospitals should only be allowed with the consent of the representative of the Reich." Lenz wishes to replace the words "or by detaining patients in institutions" by "care or continuing care of the patient". Of the terms for carrying out the law, in Article 3.4, Lenz says: ". . . changes due to age alone, especially senile dementia, are not covered by the definitions of Article 2." Of course these statements were strictly confidential. For the public world of science, Professor Lenz said in July 1940, when the euthanasia programme was in full swing: ". . . detailed discussion of so-called euthanasia . . . can easily lead to confusion about whether or not we are really dealing with a matter which affects the safeguarding of our hereditary endowment. I should like to prevent any such discussion. For, in fact, this matter is a purely humanitarian problem"[51] So saying, he disclaimed all responsibility—for humanitarian questions are no concern of science.

Shortly after the beginning of the war, in a one-sentence letter backdated to 1 September 1939, Hitler launched the programme of murder. "Reichsleiter Bouhler and Dr Brandt are entrusted with the responsibility of extending the rights of specially designated physicians, such that patients who are judged incurable after the most thorough review of their condition which is possible, can be granted mercy killing."[52] While the 'once-and-for-all' euthanasia programme was intended to empty the majority of provincial mental hospitals and homes rapidly and for ever (National Socialist departments and offices were already fighting over the valuable buildings), a parallel, long-term programme was designed to prevent new mental patients, who could not be discharged, coming forward for admission. To this end, a 'Reich Commission for the Registration of Severe Disorders in Childhood', which consisted of paediatricians, was created. Professors Catel and Heinze were among its members. During the years that followed, this commission established criteria for euthanasia of children and made decisions about individual cases. In the beginning (1939–1940) the Commission had restricted itself to defining various categories of handicapped newborn babies and infants under the age of four and to making decisions about individual cases within this age group. But in later years, it also made recommendations and decisions about the killing of adolescents.

The mental patients of Pomerania and West Prussia, like those from Poland, were shot without recourse to expert opinions. Thus, the chief of the SS and Police of Danzig and West Prussia wrote to Himmler on 9 January 1940,[53] "The other two units of storm troopers at my disposal were employed as follows during October, November and December . . . For the elimination of about 4400 incurable patients from Polish mental hospitals. . . . For the elimination of about 2000 incurable patients from the Konradstein mental hospital . . ."

In the Reich itself procedures were more formal. A one-page questionnaire was completed in the clinic in which the patients were housed and was then 'processed' by two authorities. One positive decision meant death. Two lists of assessors have been preserved.[54] In addition to 39 doctors of medicine they included Professors Heyde, Mauz, Nitsche, Panse, Pohlisch, Reisch, Carl Schneider, Villinger, and Zucker. Their payment was 5 pfennigs per questionnaire when more than 3500 were processed per month, up to 10 pfennigs when there were less than 500. Each decision, which meant life or death for a human being, cost about as much as one cigarette. The patients who had been selected to be killed by this procedure were transferred to an 'observation institution' and from there they were soon taken to one of the extermination centres. There they were murdered, naked, with carbon monoxide, supplied by IG-Farben, now BASF.

The Jewish patients were first killed in the same extermination centres as the non-Jewish ones. With the end of 'euthanasia' by gas in August 1941 and the simultaneous inception of the mass murder of the Jews in Poland and the Soviet Union, the remaining Jewish patients were deported to the East to be included in the Final Solution in order to avoid their possible survival in hospitals.[226] These procedures, which began in the greatest secrecy, soon became known to almost everyone in the German population. Public prosecutors and judges protested because, as the President of the Superior Provincial Court of Frankfurt said, " 'their' defendants disappeared in the 'extermination centres' ".[55b] The presiding party court judge, Buch, forwarded to Himmler a letter of protest from a very perplexed lady who had long been a member of the party. Relatives, mental hospital administrators, and the Catholic and Protestant clergy of all ranks addressed questions and protests to the departments of justice.[56] Among all the letters, I have not found one from a psychiatrist, although one psychiatrist, Professor Ewald, is known to have walked out in protest when other professors were meeting to hear the facts about the euthanasia programme. Who were these others? Professor Ewald has maintained silence.

After the sterilization law was passed anthropologists and psychiatrists faced a progressive loss of esteem. It was bad enough that their patients had lost confidence in them, but what was worse was that the new generation of students was avoiding their subjects. Since the introduction of sterilization, specializing in psychiatry no longer appealed to students. The patients were 'inferior' beings, to be sterilized and now even killed. To make matters worse, psychology was becoming more respectable and psychologists were poised to take away the few remaining patients. The army was full of psychologists looking for clients. Alarmed by this prospect, Professor Wuth, the chief physician of the Army, wrote to the psychiatrist Professor Bumke: "I warned him [Professor de Crinis] of the danger of psychologists and psychotherapists taking over psychopathy and 'neurosis'. And with mental patients being taken care of by euthanasia, who will wish to study psychiatry when it becomes so small a field?"[57] Moreover, for the psychiatrists of provincial mental hospitals losing their patients meant losing their wards and often the loss of the entire hospital; and with that went their position and their power. It is, therefore, entirely understandable that the pioneers of 'euthanasia' were also pioneers in efforts for reform, so that they could pursue a 'modern' form of psychiatry with the patients who were left. The 'new arrivals' were discharged as quickly as possible thanks to shock therapy. The psychiatrists recommended 'forced-labour-therapy' for patients who had by some accident survived the euthanasia programme or, if they were unable to work, a covert form of euthanasia which did not use gas. A memorandum from the chief expert witness of the euthanasia programme, Professor Nitsche; Professor C. Schneider; Professor Heinze, the representative of the Reich Commission for the Registration of Severe Disorders in Childhood; Professor de Crinis; and the Director of the KWI of Psychiatry, Professor Rüdin, illustrates the point.[58] They said of euthanasia: "Even the euthanasia measures will meet with general understanding and approval, as it becomes established and more generally known that, in each and every case of mental disease, all possible measures were taken either to cure the patients or to improve their state sufficiently to enable them to return to work which is economically worthwhile, either in their original professions or in some other occupation." In order to put these reforms into effect, the Reich Commission bought 95 appliances for electroconvulsive therapy from Siemens and placed them at the disposal of mental hospitals.[59] This mixture of new ideas, electricity, forced labour and covert euthanasia formed a package with which almost all German psychiatrists could fully identify.

Those colleagues who were not well disposed towards the efforts of the protagonists of euthanasia tried to find a more wholesome environment in the armed forces. But even in the armed forces there were advisers such as Professors Heyde and C. Schneider who advocated sending 'psychopaths' to concentration camps, that is to say all those 'abnormal' enough to rebel against the large-scale killing which was taking place. These psychiatrists recalled the contribution which 'psychopaths' had made to the collapse, in 1917–18, of the Kaiser's Reich. Their scientific opponents, such as Professors von Baeyer, Kleist, Kurt Schneider, and others found concentration camp 'treatment' repugnant, and yet did not want to expose themselves to the suspicion that they would tolerate this 'psychopathic behaviour' again. For example, Professor Kurt Schneider said, at a working conference held at the Academy of Military Medicine, "We are uniformly of the opinion that no general concessions can be made for psychopaths under paragraphs 1 and 2* of Article 51."[60] There was to be no repetition of the quaking war neurotics of the First World War, whose rifles fell from their hands

---

* These paragraphs cover those who are no longer held responsible for their actions because they are mentally disturbed.

in their fright. Those who trembled with fear were caught just behind the frontline and sent back; if they could not accustom themselves to the conditions of the front-line they risked a court martial. Thus, only a few 'neurotics' or 'psychopaths' returned home for psychiatric treatment. This consisted of a method for which the only suitable term is 'torture by electricity'. This 'treatment' by painful galvanic current had been used during the First World War, when Professor Wagner-Jauregg had been one of the psychiatrists practising it.[61] The methods were 'improved', especially by Dr Panse, as the Second World War continued. This 'improved' treatment filled soldiers with such terror that they would risk anything rather than be exposed to it again. Professor Kleist wrote, in an August 1944 report, that up to the present time the soldiers had actually asked for the treatment. That had only changed because "an increasing number of hysterical patients of poor character and malevolent personality" were now coming for treatment. "One galvanizing apparatus had even been deliberately damaged." The report continues: "Until now such unpleasant occurrences have been only sporadic."[62a] In December 1944, Professor Mauz made a similar report.

After the war, Professor Bumke was critical of this treatment by electricity. He answered in the negative when asked by the interrogating officers of the Counter Intelligence Corps if the problem of neurotics had been successfully solved in the German army, and continued, "In one respect it was handled well in that it was prevented from playing a great practical numerical role. This was due to the policy of retaining neurotics at the front in whatever limited capacity duty was possible. But what I disapproved of was the Kaufmann type of electric treatment with which people were freed from their symptoms and good symptomatic results were achieved without making good soldiers or more stable human beings out of them. Furthermore, I considered the whole way in which the treatment was given as non-medical and unsoldierly. I never could get myself to even look at it because I did not like the whole idea."[62b] During his interrogation, another army doctor called this treatment "pure unadulterated sadism".

A full analysis of the activities of army psychiatrists would require thorough study of their expert opinions. This is not possible, and thus we must be content with an analysis of their reports. A few traces of compassion can be detected among the psychiatrists, although they remained helpless. For example, Professor Kurt Schneider concluded his talk in

Berlin to a working group of psychiatrists of the medical corps of the army of the Eastern Front with the sentence, "In many cases we should like to say to the courts martial, please do not ask us for our opinions at all."[60] I have excluded from my analysis one group of psychiatrists in the armed forces, those of the Luftwaffe. Psychotherapy rather than electricity was provided for any of the tiny élite group of pilots who had 'flown away'. There was of course a good reason. It is not possible to put such outstanding technicians back into their machines by the use of electricity.

When the war began, the deportations of Jews and Gypsies to ghettos or concentration camps in occupied Poland started. Soon after the pogrom of November 1938 the ultimate aim of that programme was clearly set out in the 24 November 1938 edition of *Das Schwarze Korps*, the newspaper of the SS. "So, we are now going to have a total solution to the Jewish question. The programme is clear. It reads: total separation, total segregation! What does this mean? It does not only mean the total exclusion of the Jews from the German economic system . . . It means much more! No German can be expected to live under the same roof as Jews. The Jews must be chased out of our houses and our residential districts and made to live in rows or blocks of houses where they can keep to themselves and come into contact with Germans as little as possible. They must be clearly identified . . . And when we compel the rich Jews to provide for the 'poor' of their race, which will certainly be necessary, they will all sink together into a pit of criminality. As this happens, we will be faced with the harsh necessity of eradicating the Jewish underworld, just as we root out criminals from our own orderly state: with fire and sword. The result will be the certain and absolute end of Jewry in Germany: its complete annihilation!"

In November 1940, Hitler shared with his confidants his decision, already taken in July, to attack the USSR. On 23 March 1941, Himmler presented Hitler with a memorandum, which he had written in November 1940, and which was entitled: "Some thoughts about the treatment of foreign peoples in the eastern territories."[63] It contained the sentence: "I hope to see the very concept of Jewry completely obliterated." Hitler's reaction to the memorandum was favourable, but he expressed a wish that it should remain 'top-secret'.

A few days later, on 26–28 March 1941, Rosenberg held a conference to mark the inauguration of his 'Frankfurt Institute for the Investigation of the Jewish Question'. There was discussion in front of a large audience, on the "total solution of the Jewish question". The rectors of many universities were present and Professors Günther and Fischer were guests of honour. The proceedings were published.[64] In addition, Professor von Verschuer wrote a report for his journal *Der Erbarzt*.[65] Rosenberg proclaimed the coming of a "cleansing biological revolution". "The Jewish question will only be resolved in Europe when the last Jew leaves the European continent." Professor P.-H. Seraphim, Dr Gross, and Rosenberg said that the "genocide [Volkstod] of the Jews" was the ultimate aim of the "total solution". But how was this goal to be achieved? Two possibilities were discussed: the pauperization of the European Jews through forced labour in huge camps in Poland, or in a colony. Professor Seraphim also spoke about the disadvantages of such a solution: "The social pauperization and regrouping of the Jews might well be achieved, but not the physical disappearance of Jewry, for the death of a people [Volkstod] is never a swift death . . ." A few months later, voluntary emigration of Jews was totally prohibited. Those who had heard or read the lectures could come to only one logical conclusion: the 'necessary and total solution' was to be achieved more quickly by violent killing.

The fate of the quarter-Jews was also discussed during the conference. Dr Gross demanded that "reproduction of the quarter-Jews remaining in European countries be reduced to a minimum". This sentence was interpreted behind the scenes as heralding the compulsory sterilization of quarter-Jews.[66a] Presumably, Dr Gross knew that at the very same time Brack was writing to Himmler with complete, if unfounded, optimism that experiments with sterilization by X-ray had been successful. "One way of carrying out the sterilization would be, for example, to have the person concerned step up to a counter where questions have to be answered or forms filled in; this would keep the person occupied for two or three minutes. The official, who would be sitting behind the counter, could use the apparatus during this time by turning on a switch which would activate both tubes simultaneously, since irradiation from both sides is necessary."[67] The Reich Chancellery was irritated[66a] by the candid remarks made by Dr Gross, which were not authorized, but this disagreement was soon settled after a discussion between the parties concerned.[66b]

The German armies launched their attack on the USSR on 22 June 1941. The murder detachments of the Einsatzgruppen began their work in the USSR within three months, shooting Jews, Gypsies, and mental patients.* A report of the activities of one such group says: "Einsatzkommando 6 shot 800 out of the total of 1160 inmates of the mental hospital at Dnepropetrovsk, up to 12 November 1941."[68] Professor Fischer travelled to Paris with the aim of convincing the French intelligentsia that Bolshevism and Jewry were identical and that the final solution was a scientific necessity. According to the published text of his lecture,[69] Professor Fischer said: ". . . the morals and actions of the Bolshevist Jews bear witness to such a monstrous mentality that we can only speak of inferiority and of beings of another species". This anthropologist had recognized that the Jews were animals to be eradicated. On 31 July 1941, Göring signed a letter, probably formulated by Himmler and Heydrich, entrusting the total solution of the Jewish question to Heydrich.

The similarities between Göring's letter and the one, written by Hitler, which unleashed the campaign of murder against mental patients, should not be overlooked. Hitler's letter was written shortly after the beginning of the war against Poland and the Western Powers; Göring's was written shortly after the beginning of the war against the Soviet Union. Hitler's letter consisted of one sentence; Göring's of three sentences, since this new problem was greater by one or two orders of magnitude. As a matter of urgency, Heydrich set up Einsatzgruppen within the SS to shoot the Jewish civilian population behind the front lines. However, it was not possible to kill eleven million European Jews in this way. Modern technology in the form of gas would be needed. Heydrich could call upon the experience of those who had been trained to kill mental patients with carbon monoxide since, at about this time, the euthanasia programme was stopped (see p. 45). It is not known who made the decision to put an end to the programme but it seems logical to assume that Heydrich was involved in order to free these trained staff to work on the extermination of the Jews. So it came about that a young psychiatrist, Dr Eberl, wearing a white coat scurried around one of the first extermination camps and supervised the process.[70]

On 25 October 1941, Dr Wetzel, the expert on racial matters in Rosenberg's Ministry of the Occupied Eastern Territories, drafted a letter to Himmler.[71] "With reference to my letter of 18 October 1941, I should like

---

* Four such Einsatzgruppen had been active on a smaller scale in Poland in 1939–40. Acting under direct orders from Hitler and Himmler, their primary objective had been to destroy the fabric of the Polish ruling class by shooting prominent citizens, but they had also shot Jews where they found them.

to inform you that Oberdienstleiter Brack of the Führer's Chancellery has said that he is prepared to collaborate in the provision of the necessary accomodation and appliances for gassing people. For the time being, the appliances in question are not available in sufficient numbers so they must first be assembled. Since, in Brack's opinion, the assembly of these appliances would cause far greater difficulties in the Reich than in the places where they are to be used, he believes that the most expedient course would be to send his people to Riga, in particular his chemist, Dr Kallmeyer, who will arrange everything. Oberdienstleiter Brack has indicated that the process in question is not without its dangers, so that special protective measures are necessary . . . In the present situation, there are no objections to doing away with those Jews who are unfit for work with the aid of Brack's resources . . ."

On 16 November 1941, Goebbels wrote in the newspaper *Das Reich* "that the Führer's prophecy of 30 January 1939, concerning the extermination of the Jewish race in Europe, was now coming true". Two days later Rosenberg informed representatives of the German press of the enormous resettlement operations which were planned and of the final solution of the Jewish question.[72] He unveiled the plans for mass murder and at the same time declared them to be secret: "These eastern regions are called upon to solve a problem which faces the nations of Europe, the Jewish question. There are still about six million Jews living in Russia, and the problem can only be resolved by a biological elimination of the entire Jewish population of Europe. The Jewish question will only be resolved for Germany when the last Jew has left German soil, and for Europe when no Jew remains on the European continent this side of the Urals. That is the task to which destiny has called us. As you can imagine, only those are called to carry out these measures who can understand this question as an historical responsibility, who do not act from motives of personal hate, but who have, on the contrary, totally clear-headed political and historical insight. November 9 [Kristallnacht] was a day of decision and destiny for us. On that day Jewry showed us that it stood for the annihilation of Germany. We can only thank the Führer and the strength of character of the German people that they did not succeed. We must prevent a sentimental future generation from accepting the Jews back into Europe again. That is why it is necessary to drive them to the other side of the Urals or to eliminate them in some other way. Gentlemen, we cannot permit ourselves to say these things in public today. It is self-evident that we should neither speak nor write about the setting of political goals. In the delicate situation in which Germany finds itself, it would be extremely harmful if the public got to know about these things. The Führer indicated in his speech on 9 November what can be said and the press should act within these guidelines . . ." They wrote their articles within the guidelines. For example, Professor von Verschuer wrote: "The policies of National Socialism have finally put an end to the last threat to the race—that which comes from the Jews."[73] The initiated understood. But anyone could later say that he had not understood, in spite of what he had read or even written.

Dr Mennecke, a psychiatrist who worked in the Eichberg mental hospital, wrote from Berlin to his wife: "My dear little wifey . . . I have just had an explanation from Dr H. [Hefelmann] of these brand new arrangements, which Miss Schwab had previously hinted at over the telephone. The day before yesterday, a large contingent from our euthanasia programme has moved under the leadership of Brack to the Eastern battlezone. It consists of doctors, office personnel, and male and female nurses, from Hadamar and Sonnenstein, in all a group of 20–30 persons. This is all top secret. Only those who, for the most pressing of reasons, cannot be spared from our euthanasia programme are not coming along."[74] So it was that doctors and other medical personnel in white coats supervised the process of exterminating Jews in the camps at Chelmno and Treblinka.[70]

The scale of the exterminations can be estimated from an official 'note' written on 5 June 1942, by a civil servant from the RSHA, detailing "technical modifications of special vehicles put into service".[75] "Since December 1941, using three vehicles, 97 000 persons have been 'processed', without any defects occurring in these vehicles. The explosion which is known to have occurred in Chelmno should be considered as an isolated case, caused by a technical failure. Special instructions have been sent to the depots involved, in order to prevent such accidents in the future. These instructions require safety levels to be increased by a substantial margin. Our experience to date has indicated that the following technical modifications would be appropriate . . ." Thirty vehicles were delivered and put into service on 23 June 1942; they were of improved construction. According to the estimates made by the RSHA, the eleven million European Jews could just have been exterminated in six years, using 30 gassing-vans. In fact, prior to 1 January 1943, some 2.4 million Jews were 'evacuated to the East', a euphemism for killed, according to a 'statistical report' prepared for Himmler by Dr Korherr on the 'final solution of the European Jewish question'.[76]

On 20 January 1942, various high-ranking representatives of the ministries and departments involved in the practical problems of transporting European Jews to extermination sites were summoned to a conference at a villa on the Wannsee [a lake near Berlin]. The 'Wannsee conference' was convened to acquaint the participants with the precise nature of these problems and to make plans to solve them. Of the fourteen participants whose names are known, seven had doctorates.[77] The Wehrmacht, which had already agreed to the extermination of Russian prisoners by starvation, was not represented.* In the spring of 1942 the Wehrmacht was to change its policy from one of 'extermination by hunger' to one of 'extermination by work' (Reichsminister Thierack's phrase). At 'the Wannsee conference', and at subsequent ones, discussions were held to define those categories of persons who were to be killed immediately, those to be sterilized, those to be 'scrapped through labour' [durch Arbeit zu verschrotten] and those to be 'Germanized'. At the same time, complicated, but necessary, administrative measures had also to be discussed.

Rosenberg lacked power, despite being Minister of the Occupied Eastern Territories. He wanted to monopolize research on the East and to found a 'Reich Centre for Research on the East'. In a 'note for the record for the Führer' dated 23 March 1942,[78] he wrote: "I have of course not entered into any negotiations concerning employment of personnel, as I do not yet have the Führer's consent, but I have thought of Geheimrat Eugen Fischer, an individual who represents biological research and is a leading member of the KWG." By that time, Professor Fischer had already taken part in a conference at the Ministry of the Occupied Eastern Territories where 'resettlement in Siberia' and 'scrapping through labour' were discussed,[79] as possible solutions to the problem of disposing of the racially undesirable millions of the East, by experts from the Ministry, and from the SS, among them Professor B. K. Schultz of the RuSHA. Professor Fischer expressed doubts about the concept of 'scrapping through labour'†, if this

---

* Approximately 3 million Russian prisoners of war were murdered or allowed to die through lack of care in German captivity (see Dallin, A. *German Rule in Russia 1941–1945. A Study of Occupation Policies*, 2nd edition, pp. 409–27. London, 1981).

† It might be thought that Professor Fischer did not understand the full horror of the expression 'scrapping through labour', in that the working conditions were secret and were of such an unimaginable nature. I should, therefore, like to quote a short extract from a book which was newly published at the time: "In 1941, Jews from the Jewish district of Warsaw were employed to work for the water company. However, this caused a lot of problems. About fifty per cent were unfit for work, and a further proportion were ill. The efficiency of the remaining Jews was so limited that the cost of their upkeep was higher than the profit which their work brought in. Later on, Russian prisoners of war were put to work instead of the Jews." Fischer, L., and Gollert, F. *Warschau unter deutscher Herrschaft* [Warsaw under German rule] p. 201. Cracow, 1942.

labour was to be paid and if education was to be allowed, since, in his opinion, "improvements in living standards could easily lead to an increase in the birth rate".

However, the SS moved more quickly than the planners at the Ministry, producing the first version of their own 'General Plan for the East' on 15 July 1941. Commenting on this plan, Dr Wetzel mentioned Professor Abel, a department head in Fischer's institute, as having carried out "thorough anthropological investigations on Russians during the course of the winter on behalf of the High Command of the Wehrmacht".[80] These investigations were financed by the DFG.[81] Professor Abel, troubled by the organized mass murder of Soviet prisoners-of-war which he had seen in the camps with his own eyes, gave a lecture to some 160 experts.[82] Dr Wetzel reported on it as follows: "Professor Abel demonstrated the special threat the Russians pose to the future of our people because of their substantial component of Nordic blood; he gave a stern warning that the Russians should not be underrated . . . In these circumstances, Abel saw only two possible solutions: either the extermination of the Russian people or the Germanization of its Nordic elements. Abel's proposal that we consider the possibility of exterminating the Russian people is out of the question on political and economic grounds, quite apart from the fact that it is hardly feasible."[80]

By this time, Professor Fischer and Professor Lenz had also given their expert opinions on the question of resettlement. Dr Wetzel writes: "In the south of the Ukraine and in the Crimea, a steppe climate predominates, and this is to be distinguished from the climate of the areas considered for settlement in the 'General Plan for the East'. Professor Lenz took the view that climatic conditions in these areas made them unsuitable for settlement by people of Nordic stock. Professor Fischer had expressed the opinion, in December 1941, that settlement of Germans in these areas could only be considered if forests were deliberately created in order to bring about a change in the climate."[80] Although the Ministry of the Occupied Eastern Territories had experts like Dr Wetzel, it did not have any power. The anthropologists whom he sent out found closed doors almost everywhere.[83] The SS ruled. This may also explain the lack of influence of the most important and popular 'race-investigators' of the period before 1933, Professor Günther and Professor Clauss. Both were men of letters, trained initially in the humanities, who had attended Fischer's lectures on anthropology when he was still in Freiburg. Both had been extraordinarily productive authors. But neither had access to those in power.

Professor Clauss, who had been a student of Husserl*, believed that he had discovered that individuals of different races could never understand each other because of differences in their 'racial souls', even when they spoke the same language (German, for example). Only bold investigators, like Professor Clauss himself, presumed to believe that they could bring even a fleeting light to bear on this abyss of ignorance. Professor Clauss was involved in a scandal, when it was revealed during his divorce proceedings, in 1941, that he had been living since the 1920s with his Jewish collaborator, Miss Landé, and had protected her. It did not help him to maintain that on her death bed, Miss Landé's mother had told her daughter that she had an Aryan father. The 'Reich Kinship Bureau' had declared Miss Landé to be fully Jewish. Professor Clauss had to undergo a party disciplinary procedure. He explained to the party court on 20 December 1941: "I am interested in Jewry as a physician is interested in disease. I set an anti-bacillus against a bacillus. Only by being part of Jewry, can one track down every last Jew. I cannot live with Jews—that is too much to expect of me. I could live as a Bedouin among Bedouin, but not as a rabbi among rabbis. I cannot share a ghetto-existence. Miss Landé finds it difficult, but she can do it. And if I want to continue to use my method, I need someone who can live in this way. If I have to let her go, I will need someone else. I must have someone of this kind, just as the police need informers. I would not say it was exactly the same thing, but the comparison helps us to understand. Of course, the informer abuses the trust of other people, but I would not ask this of Miss Landé. If you take this exception into account, the comparison is appropriate. If I give her up, I will need someone else and I will be in exactly the same situation as before. I must ask the Party, therefore, to allow me to continue to employ her under these conditions. . . . She is not only my instrument, she is also my favourite object of study. I study how she reacts to people, how she constructs speech in an oriental, Arabic, manner and seeks a term or an expression. In short she is an instrument, an object of study, an assistant."[84] He had previously written to the party court on 23 October 1941: "I do not give up hope that one day an institute will be set up to investigate Jews using the methods of psy-

---

* Edmund Husserl (1859–1938) was a philosopher and the father of phenomenology. He was born in Moravia of Jewish parents. He taught at the University of Freiburg from 1916. Heidegger, a former student of his, who was Rector in 1933–4, forbade his retired teacher the use of the university library.

chology and physiognomy."[84] Professor Clauss was expelled from the Nazi Party on 21 January 1943 and shortly afterwards dismissed from his position at the University of Berlin.[84]

His former student, Dr Beger, had in the meantime pursued a career in the SS. In June 1943, he had selected "79 Jews, 2 Poles, 4 Asiatics, and 30 Jewesses" in Auschwitz from the vast mass of prisoners.[85b] With the help of Dr Fleischhacker, an assistant of Professor Gieseler (Tübingen), he made the relevant anthropological measurements in Auschwitz.[85b] Two months later, these 115 prisoners were sent to the concentration camp of Natzweiler, near Strasbourg, to be killed at the request of the anatomist Professor Hirt, who was interested in building up a representative collection of Jewish skeletons.[85b] Professor Hirt had additional research interests. One of them was to study the action of mustard gas (chlorodiethyl sulphide, a poison gas used in World War I) on about 150 prisoners in the Natzweiler camp. His assistants at the time were Dr Wimmer and Dr Kiesselbach.[85b] Dr Beger himself was mainly interested in skulls of Asiatics. He assembled a collection for his mentor, Professor Schäfer of the Research Foundation of the SS [Stiftung Ahnenerbe].[85b] Dr Beger supported his teacher and wrote to Himmler on his behalf: "Like Clauss, I take the view that the complete extermination of the Jews in Europe and, beyond that, in the whole world if possible, will not mean that the spiritual elements of Jewry, which we encounter at every turn, are fully eradicated. The important role of research on racial souls stems from this fact. Working tools, such as the one which Professor Clauss developed in the person of the half-Jewess, Landé, are indispensable for this research, since they form bridges to racial souls which are alien to Germanic individuals."[85a] Professor Clauss wrote to Himmler in similar vein. As a result, Himmler asked him to take up his research again and, as a member of an SS-unit, to observe 'the races in battle', first in the USSR and then in Yugoslavia, reporting his observations. Professor Clauss accepted this mission and made his reports.[85a]

While extermination was the only task of the RSHA, racial selection or evaluation were the tasks of the Race Bureau of the RuSHA. SS-Colonel Professor B. K. Schultz was promoted from acting head to permanent chief of the 'Race Bureau' on 1 January 1943. As one of his first official steps, Professor B. K. Schultz tried to extend the activity of his Bureau to a previously unexplored field, the assessment of quarter-Jews.

Dr Gross had proposed previously, at the time of the Frankfurt conference, that all half- and quarter-Jews who had escaped deportation should be sterilized.[64] This plan was extensively discussed by representatives of the SS, the Party and of various ministries. After some deliberation, the experts realized that, for the time being, this project was impracticable for technical reasons and, in addition, that it would cause an undesirable state of unrest in the German population. But it was here that Professor B. K. Schultz saw an opportunity for the RuSHA. In an expert report on "race-biological assessment of quarter-Jews", Professor Schultz wrote: "It is proposed that quarter-Jews should not be included in the same category as persons of German blood *without exception*, but that they should first undergo a racial classification. Every quarter-Jew, in whom Jewish racial characteristics are clearly prominent, as judged from external appearances, should be treated in the same way as half-Jews [i.e. as Jews]."[86] Professor Schultz seems to have forgotten that the large number of human genes and chromosomes makes it unlikely that any quarter-Jews would manifest these 'Jewish' traits in concentrated form. Professor B. K. Schultz's 'expert report' was passed to Himmler* by his chief.[86] In this context, it is of some interest to note that Professor Schultz did show some common sense in an expert opinion which he gave later. It concerned the question of whether the existence of a Jew nine generations back(!) would tarnish Germanic blood. Professor Schultz answered "no" without ifs or buts.[86] His colleague Professor Astel (Jena) challenged this opinion in a 'comment' and argued with feeling: "If such a young man were to ask for my daughter's hand in marriage, I would not simply advise against it, I would forbid it."[86]

---

* Himmler liked the 'proposal' made by Professor B. K. Schultz that quarter-Jews be investigated. The problem was that such a study was not within his authority. So he turned to Bormann: "Dear Martin, I refer to the brief conversation we had about part-Jews. I am enclosing a proposal from my collaborator, the well-known race-investigator, Professor B. K. Schultz, the Chief of the Race Bureau of the RuSHA. I regard such investigations as being absolutely necessary, perhaps not only in quarter-Jews but also in persons with even less Jewish blood. We must follow a similar procedure to that which is used in breeding plants and animals, but this must remain between us. For several generations (at least 3 or 4), the offspring of such mixed families must be racially examined by independent institutes, and, if racial inferiority is shown, they must be sterilized, and thus prevented from passing on their traits further . . . Perhaps you will let me know what you think about this. Heil Hitler! Your HH.' Himmler to Bormann 22.5.43, cited in *Reichsführer!* H. Heiber, ed., p. 268. Munich, 1970.

The RuSHA found itself in constant conflict, over racial evaluation and selection, with those SS agencies whose task was extermination. However, the RuSHA did win the right "to conduct, after 'successful separation' of individuals of foreign stock, a further racial selection designed to establish potential for Germanization."[87] In other words the negative, coarse, selection was to be the task of other SS agencies, while the positive, delicate, selection, when of course Jews and other undesirables might still be discovered, was to be the task of the RuSHA.

The population of the occupied territories was divided into four categories I, II, III, and IV. Persons assigned to Group I were Germans, while those assigned to Group IV were Jews or others who were either to be exterminated straight away or worked to death. The criteria for assessment were worked out in the 'Race Bureau' of the RuSHA. The 'Race Bureau' was also responsible for training the staff involved in the selection process. For example, Professor B. K. Schultz organized a course in which the basic facts of genetics and anthropology were taught.[88] This course for the staff doing the selection ('aptitude-testers') seemed far too intellectual to his chief, Hofmann: "I am absolutely convinced that the Reichsführer-SS will hit the ceiling when I submit this set of lectures to him. He has already explained to me in detail that he does not need scientists for this work, but practical men with a breeder's eye!"[89] Nevertheless, the course took place as planned. The 'aptitude testers' were trained and put to work. In Zamość [Poland], between 27 November and 31 December 1942, the RuSHA 'aptitude-testers' divided the population into categories as follows: "5147 persons in Group III, of interest only in so far as they are able to work"; "1534 persons in Group IV to be sent to the work camp at Auschwitz."[90] The children and old people of Groups III and IV were deported to empty villages ('retirement-villages'), and there abandoned to the freezing cold and to starvation. The adults of Group III went to Germany, the men and the women separately. Dr Gollert had recommended this treatment in a memorandum sent to his minister, Rosenberg.[91] He discussed three possibilities for a 'solution to the Polish question': "(a) The first possibility would be to Germanize the fifteen million Poles. Quite apart from the fact that there would be great practical difficulties, the Germanization of fifteen million people is entirely undesirable ... (b) A second solution would be to eradicate these fifteen million people. This solution, too, is to be rejected. Recourse to such radical measures can be justified before the court of history on biological grounds; just such measures were necessary, for example, in the case of the Jews. But to do away with a foreign people of fifteen million, in *this* way, is unworthy of a civilized nation." So he also proposed a division of the Poles into groups, similar to that which the 'aptitude testers' were undertaking.

Dr Gollert may have thought that this attitude towards the Poles showed benevolence on his part. They, however, saw the situation quite differently and, wherever they realized that they had nothing more to lose, they started resistance movements. This alarmed the administrators. For example, Medizinalrat* Dr Wilhelm Hagen wrote to Hitler from Warsaw: "My Führer . . . We learnt from the Chief of the 'Department of Population Organization and Welfare', Oberverwaltungsrat† Weinreich, at a Government conference on the campaign against tuberculosis, that it was intended (or at least being considered) that during the resettlement of 200 000 Poles to the eastern part of the Generalgouvernement, one-third of them (70 000 old people and children) should be dealt with in the same way as the Jews, that is to say they should be killed. . . ." Dr Hagen's letter,[92a] in which he went on to describe the possible consequences of such an act, reached Himmler's desk. Himmler ordered that Dr Hagen be sent to a concentration camp. Dr Hagen, helped by high-ranking friends, fled to the Wehrmacht and remained unharmed.[92e] But other letters of protest, even in the end one from Governor-General Frank himself,[93] had some effect. At least the problems that such policies could cause began to become apparent and it was realized that it would be unwise to make enemies of the *entire* Slav population.

The 'aptitude-testers' needed no higher academic qualification for their anthropological field-work. However, from 9 March 1943, a licence to practise medicine was required of those making the 'selection' which took place on the railway ramps (see p. 77) and of those supervising the killing process in Auschwitz and other extermination camps.[94] Pharmacists could be co-opted for these tasks. For example, Dr Capesius had been the guest of a Hungarian-Jewish family in December 1943, when he was working as a travelling salesman for IG-Farben, and had presented himself as a cultured man, an opponent of National Socialism. Six months later, he 'selected' his host's wife, Dr Perl, on the ramp in Auschwitz—but he directed her to the right, that is to say to work rather than immediate death.[95]

---

* A civic title which roughly translates as Medical Councillor.
† Councillor, a middle-ranking civic official.

Auschwitz resembled the psychiatric institutions for extermination in that physicians were in charge of the 'selection' and killing. They had won these rights and were unwilling to have them taken away by others.[96]

The Chief of the Police and SS in Lublin, Globocnik, as organizer of the extermination for the area, claimed that he had been ordered to make a report to Hitler. He said this to two visitors, Professor Pfannenstiel (Marburg) and an SS-officer, Gerstein,* to whom he was explaining the method of extermination. Gerstein noted down the conversation afterwards.[97] "Professor Pfannenstiel asked "And what did the Führer say?" Globocnik, now Chief of the Police and SS in the Adriatic Coast Region, Trieste, replied: He said "Faster, get the whole thing over with faster!". Then Ministerial Director, Dr Herbert Linden of the Ministry of the Interior asked "Would it not be better to burn the corpses rather than bury them? Perhaps another generation will think differently of the matter . . ." Globocnik then replied "But, gentlemen, if a generation coming after us should be so cowardly and so corrupt as not to understand our deeds, which are so beneficial and so necessary, then, gentlemen, the whole of National Socialism will have been in vain. Rather, we should bury bronze plates with the corpses on which we should write that it was we who had the courage to accomplish this gigantic task!" Hitler then commented, "Yes, my dear Globocnik, that is the truth of the matter. I entirely agree with you.""

The inhabitants of the territories occupied by the Germans were reduced to being slaves and had no rights; the police disposed of them as they wished. Within the Reich, there still existed a system of justice for its own citizens which sometimes even afforded them a remnant of protection. However, from the very beginning of the war, work was proceeding apace in the Ministry of the Interior on a draft law,[98] which had long been under consideration, and which was to replace the whole system of justice. It was to be called 'the law against social misfits [Gemeinschafts-

---

* SS-Captain Kurt Gerstein, who plays a central role in Rolf Hochhuth's play *Der Stellvertreter* [The deputy], was something of an enigma. His sister-in-law had been killed during the euthanasia programme and he was so shocked by her death that he resolved to expose the entire machinery of extermination. To this end, he joined the concentration camp services of the SS. Between 1942 and the end of the war, he made the exact nature of the system known to influential figures in the German churches and passed the information on to the Vatican and to Sweden. As a devout Christian, he led a double life in the SS, where he was employed as supply officer for the hydrocyanic acid crystals (Zyklon B) used in the gas chambers. He was either murdered or, more probably, committed suicide in a French prison soon after the end of the war.

fremden]'. These 'social misfits' were to be sterilized after rulings which would be made by doctors, and punished by internment in a camp or by death after rulings made by police officers. This dream of power was shattered, however, by resistance from the conventional ministries, which saw their very existence threatened. 'Social misfits' included anyone who would not or could not submit unconditionally to the state. Not only psychiatrists, like Professor Rüdin,[20] but also the physician and investigator of animal behaviour, Professor Lorenz (Königsberg),[99] had been busying himself with this problem: "Any attempt at reconstruction using elements which have lost their proper nature and characteristics is doomed to failure. Fortunately, the elimination of such elements is easier for the public health physician and less dangerous for a supra-individual entity than such an operation by a surgeon would be for the individual organism. The main technical problem lies in the *recognition* of such elements. In this, the proper cultivation of our own inborn patterns can help us a great deal. A good man can very easily feel with his deepest instincts whether another is a scoundrel or not. From this some provisional advice follows, which may perhaps sound strange coming from the mouth of a causal–analytical investigator of nature; we should rely on the unanalysed and deeply rooted reactions of our best individuals to define the type-model of our people, for which we should be striving. At the same time, the causal–analytical investigation of human inborn patterns must naturally remain our chief aim and must be pursued with vigour." So the 'main technical difficulty' was not 'recognition', since for that one could rely on the 'reactions of our best individuals'.

Professor Kranz and Dr Koller[100] estimated the number of German 'social misfits' to be at least one million. Registers were set up on a regional basis. "The distinction between those to be eliminated and those worthy of advancement in our society is of the utmost importance if we wish to safeguard our hereditary endowment and our race. It is desirable that such registers be set up throughout the Reich so that we may combat asocial mentality with all the means at our disposal", wrote Professor von Verschuer in his journal *Der Erbarzt.*[101]

The hundred thousands of half- and quarter-Jews to be sterilized and the million of 'Gypsies' must, of course, be added to the asocial individuals. The 'Gypsies' were the subject of Dr Ritter's research. But 'research on Gypsies' was also pursued at the KWI of Anthropology, Human Heredity, and Eugenics,[41c] and at some university institutes. In 1935, Dr Ritter, who was at that time an assistant in the psychiatric clinic of the University of Tübingen under Professor Gaupp, had solicited support for his 'research on Gypsies' from the NDW (renamed the DFG in 1936).[102a] The records both of the NDW and of the DFG have been preserved, so it is possible to follow the progress of this research. An application to study the 'Gypsies' of Württemberg was warmly supported and approved by Professor Rüdin. In 1937, Dr Ritter moved from Tübingen to the Reich Department of Health in Berlin to take over the direction of the 'Section for Research on Race-hygiene and Population Biology'. Between 1937 and 1944, Dr Ritter was generously supported by the DFG; for example, his project 'Studies on asocial individuals and on the biology of bastards' (Gypsies, Jews) was allocated funds of 15 000 RM in 1938. Dr Ritter and his co-workers pursued genealogical and anthropological investigations on *all* Gypsies. Some 30 000 individuals had to be registered and investigated. For this purpose, they travelled to the Gypsy campsites and, when the Gypsies were interned in camps and concentration camps, they followed them there too. The results of this work 'confirmed' the hypothesis which Dr Ritter put forward in 1935 that most of the 30 000 'Gypsies' were not really Gypsies at all, but were rather "the products of matings with the German criminal asocial subproletariat". In a 'progress report' which Dr Ritter prepared for the DFG in January 1940 he wrote: "Through our work we have been able to establish that more than ninety per cent of so-called native Gypsies are of mixed blood. It has been demonstrated that Gypsies in their racial crosses in our homeland have mated predominantly with non-Gypsy nomad Yenish [Jenisch] and with asocial and criminal elements and that this has led to the formation of a Yenish-Gypsy lumpenproletariat which costs the State enormous sums in welfare costs. . . Further results of our investigations have allowed us to characterize the Gypsies as being a people of entirely primitive ethnological origins, whose mental backwardness makes them incapable of real social adaptation. . . The Gypsy question can only be considered solved when the main body of asocial and good-for-nothing Gypsy individuals of mixed blood is collected together in large *labour camps* and kept working there, and when the further *breeding of this population of mixed blood* is stopped once and for all. Only then will future generations of the German people be really freed from this burden. *The Section for Research on Race-hygiene is today already in a position today to give an expert opinion on the proportion of Gypsy blood and on the hereditary value of each so-called Gypsy. Thus, obstacles to the introduction of race-*

hygienic measures no longer exist. . . ."[102b] He expressed similar opinions in a publication in 1939.[103] A summary of the data from these investigations on Gypsies was published in 1941.[104]

In his capacity as an administrator used to dealing with Gypsies, Dr Portschy, the leader of the provincial government of the Burgenland, had previously, in a memorandum written in 1938, demanded sterilization and forced labour for all Gypsies.[105] The Attorney-General of Graz made a similar petition to the Minister of Justice in 1940.[106] Thus, it is not surprising that state secretary Pfundtner of the Reich Ministry of the Interior wrote on 24 January 1940 to the 'Head Office of the Security Police', "I am still convinced that a definitive solution to the Gypsy problem can only be achieved by making Gypsies and part-Gypsies infertile."[107a] On the other hand, the RSHA wrote in a publication intended for the general public: "A total separation of bastard Gypsies [Zigeunerbastarde] from the German population has not yet been possible because, due to a shortage of time, it has not been possible to establish the proportion of Gypsy blood in some individuals."[107b]

The German Gypsies were arrested at the beginning of the war and deported to Poland. At first they lived partly in camps and partly in relative freedom. The 'racial analysis' which Dr Ritter had made was disconcertingly similar to that which 'race-investigators', such as Günther, had made of the Jews: "an oriental racial admixture with an asocial European component."

This explains why Heydrich, who had been entrusted with 'the final solution of the Jewish question' on 31 July 1941, shortly after the German invasion of the USSR, also included the Gypsies in his 'final solution'. In the minutes of a discussion on 10 October 1941 dealing with the solution of the Jewish question, with Heydrich as chairman, it says: "The Gypsies to be evacuated can be handed over to Stahlecker, whose camp is administered on the model of Sachsenhausen."[108a] This arrangement was to apply to the Gypsies of the annexed territories of Czechoslovakia. The Einsatzkommandos, which began their work shortly after the assault on the USSR, received the order to kill all Jews, Gypsies and mental patients. These massacres were soon extended to the Balkans. On 25 October 1941, a diplomat from the German Foreign Office, who had just returned from Belgrade, noted, for example: "The male Jews will be shot by the end of this week and so the problem raised in the Embassy's report has been dealt with. The rest of the Jews, some 20 000 (women, children, old people), as well as around 1500 Gypsies (also after the men have been shot), will be collected together in the so-called Gypsy quarter of Belgrade, which will serve as a ghetto."[108b] In the autumn of 1942, Staatsrat* Dr Turner was able to report to General Löhr: "In the interests of keeping the peace, the influence of the Jews on the public, on the Serbian administration, and on the management of the economy was first eliminated; the Jewish question, and the Gypsy question as well, were then settled. (Thus, Serbia has become the only country where the *Jewish* and *Gypsy questions* are solved.)"[108c] The Senior SS-officer and Chief of the Police for the East, Dr Landgraf, in Riga, informed Rosenberg's Reich Commissioner for the East, Lohse, of the inclusion of the Gypsies in the 'final solution'. Thereupon, Lohse gave the order, on 24 December (!) 1941, that the Gypsies "should be given the same treatment as the Jews".[108d]

What was to happen now to the German Gypsies, who had been deported to Poland in 1939, but had begun to return? At a conference, in which Dr Ritter participated, the gentlemen of the RSHA discussed taking them out on ships and drowning them in the Mediterranean Sea.[109a] Probably in order to shorten the distance the Gypsies need be transported, they then discussed the possibility of turning them loose from trains into the open countryside, somewhere in the East, in the depths of the winter of 1941–2 and allowing them to freeze to death in temperatures below minus twenty degrees centigrade. Dr Ritter successfully resisted these proposals with the argument that, so far, only two-thirds of the Gypsies had been included in his anthropological investigations and registered. It was important to complete the study not only for purely scientific reasons but also to register the few Gypsies of pure race, who carried Indo-Germanic hereditary material, so that they could later be settled on a 'reservation'. So argued Dr Ritter in his presentation to the gentlemen of the RSHA. In his 'application and report' to the DFG dated 14 March 1942, he spoke of "about 15 000 Gypsy cases completely studied."[102c]

The German Gypsies gained a year's reprieve. On 16 December 1942, it came to an end when Himmler gave the order that all individuals of mixed Gypsy blood be sent to Auschwitz. On 29 January 1943, the RSHA released the regulations which governed the implementation of this order[110] and, shortly thereafter, the majority of German Gypsies were taken to Auschwitz. At the same time, Dr Ritter wrote in a report to the

*A very high civic rank first introduced by the National Socialists, Councillor.

DFG, dated 23 March 1943:[102c] "The registration of Gypsies and part-Gypsies has been completed, roughly as planned in the Old Reich and in the Ostmark* despite all the difficulties engendered by the war. Our studies are still in progress in the annexed territories. The number of cases clarified from the race-biological point of view is, at the present time, 21 498. Following our examination, over 9000 part-Gypsies have been assembled by the police in a special camp for Gypsies in the Sudetenland . . . Our collaboration with the Institute of Criminal Biology of the RSHA continues without friction, for the centralized direction of the two institutes ensures that duplication of work is avoided."

The Gypsies and part-Gypsies who were exempted by the regulations governing the implementation of the Auschwitz deportation decree (for example, those with Aryan spouses) were offered the choice between 'voluntary' sterilization and a concentration camp by the local German police stations, acting on instructions from the RSHA. Those who did not choose the way out provided by sterilization were sent to Auschwitz. To preserve a semblance of legality, the requests for sterilization by consent were referred to the Reich Commission for the Registration of Severe Disorders in Childhood, whose real task was the provision of expert reports on mentally abnormal children and adolescents to be killed (see p. 44). One of the experts signed the requests.[109b] The police stations were obliged to report to the RSHA that the sterilizations had been performed.

Dr Ritter's institute provided 'scientific' data as an aid to the decision-making process in these cases and in newly discovered residual cases. Dr Ritter wrote in his 31 January 1944 report to the DFG: "As before, countless official enquiries, affecting the safeguarding of our hereditary endowment, were answered from the Gypsy archives of our research section. This required very considerable effort."[102c] In the same report, Dr Ritter mentions 23 822 Gypsy cases as being conclusively clarified. This number is some fourteen per cent higher than the number of Gypsies registered in Auschwitz (20 943).[111] However, the Gypsies of East Prussia were not included in these registers. They were decimated by hunger and disease, in a camp near Bialystok, during their first internment. Late in March 1943, when they arrived in Auschwitz, the survivors were sent straight to the gas chambers, without registration, in order to prevent epidemics.[111] A survey

---

*Pre-war Austria was known as the Ostmark after its union [Anschluss] in 1938 with Germany, the Old Reich.

of a sample of the fragmentary collection of index cards preserved in West German archives shows that Dr Ritter and his co-workers found that some ninety per cent of the Gypsies should, in principle, be subjected both to sterilization *and* to internment in camps, having been labelled as being 'of mixed blood'. The total number of Gypsies sent to Auschwitz is in good agreement with the results of Dr Ritter's classification.

Of the 20 943 Gypsies registered in Auschwitz, 3461 were transferred to other camps. The rest died by starvation, disease or gas. After 2897 children, women and men (including former soldiers of the Wehrmacht) were driven into the gas chambers on the night of 2–3 August 1944, there were no more Gypsies left in Auschwitz. The 'Gypsies' were dead but the anthropological records on them survived the war. Dr Ehrhardt, once a collaborator of Dr Ritter's and now a professor at the University of Tübingen, continued to work on the material she gathered from the East Prussian Gypsies (those who came, dying, from the camp at Bialystok to Auschwitz).[112] In 1966 she applied to the DFG for financial support for further work on this material. The referees apparently liked the proposal since she was awarded her grant for 'population studies on Gypsies'. However, after unfavourable press coverage of this decision and a complaint by the Central Council of the Sinti and Roma Gypsies, Professor Ehrhardt had to deposit the material which she had collected in the Federal Archives in Koblenz. Dr Ritter prudently destroyed the correspondence between the various agencies which had been involved in the deaths of the Gypsies. A legal action brought against him ended with his suicide in 1950.

How did the academics see the situation? First, I quote Professor Fischer writing in a newspaper article which appeared in March 1943.[113] "It is a rare and special good fortune for a theoretical science to flourish at a time when the prevailing ideology welcomes it, and its findings can immediately serve the policy of the state. The study of human heredity was already sufficiently mature to provide this, when, years ago, National Socialism was recasting not only the state but also our ways of thinking and feeling [Weltanschauung]. Not that National Socialism needed a 'scientific' foundation as a proof that it was right (ideologies [Weltanschauungen] are formed through practical experience and struggle rather than created by laborious scientific theorizing) but the results of the study of human heredity became absolutely indispensable as a basis for the important laws and regulations created by the new state." Professor Rüdin had written in similar vein in an article which had appeared a few months earlier.[114] "The results of our science had earlier attracted much attention (both support and opposition) in national and international circles. Nevertheless, it will always remain the undying, historic achievement of Adolf Hitler and his followers that they dared to take the first trail-blazing and decisive steps towards such brilliant race-hygienic achievement in and for the German people. In so doing, they went beyond the boundaries of purely scientific knowledge. He and his followers were concerned with putting into practice the theories and advances of Nordic race-conceptions . . . the fight against parasitic alien races such as the Jews and the Gypsies . . . and preventing the breeding of those with hereditary diseases and those of inferior stock."

What did specialists in Gypsy affairs do now that their victims had been deported or killed? They looked for something new. One such new research area, again supported by the DFG, was a 'prognostic review of asocial adolescents'. Dr Ritter's co-workers now turned to investigating these young people, who had come within the scope of new regulations making them liable for punishment, from the anthropological, psychiatric, and genealogical points of view, just as they had done in the case of the Gypsies. Dr Ritter's investigations were intended to serve as a 'model' and to show that whole families could be condemned to sterilization and to concentration camps, just as the Gypsies had been. This new investigation overlapped with an earlier 'applied' programme which provided for the 'criminal–biological' investigation of asocial adolescents by psychiatrists. The aim of the investigation was to identify those who were to be killed immediately (some in the mental hospital and extermination centre in Hadamar which was still functioning) and those who might be curable and were, therefore, to be sent to concentration camps. Thus, for example, Professor Heyde wrote to the Minister of Science, Education, and National Culture on 24 April 1942, saying that psychiatric facilities for adolescents existed in Würzburg and that criminal–biological investigations were possible: "On the one hand, personality types which lead to asocial or antisocial development, and which, from the very beginning, are not amenable to training because of fundamental defective elements in their biological constitution, must be recognized in order to avoid major expense, but on the other hand . . ."[115]

To return to the 'technical' problem of mass sterilizations. The surgical sterilization of women was too labour-intensive. Three possible substitutes for surgery were discussed and tested. The first was sterilization by X-rays. Dr Lang, who was on the staff of the KWI of Psychiatry until 1941, claimed in a statement made to allied interrogators on 10 May 1945, that even before the war, Professor Rüdin and his co-workers had discussed X-irradiation which would escape the patient's notice and that collaborators had conducted such experiments outside the institute during 1940.[116] It is possible that these were the experiments of which Brack wrote in his letter to Himmler on 28 March 1941.[67] I have found no other evidence for this supposition but it is fact that Professor Rüdin's investigations were supported in 1939 by a grant of 30 000 RM which came from Heydrich's budget.[117] The reports, for which Heydrich asked, have not survived. In any case, the method was never sufficiently well developed to be put into practice. In Auschwitz, the former director of an extermination centre, Dr Schumann, and Professor Clauberg (Königsberg) both attempted to develop it for large-scale use. Professor Clauberg also tried out his own method for rapid sterilization by intrauterine injection of formaldehyde. Finally, a Viennese physician, Dr Pokorny ("spurred on by the thought that the enemy must not only be vanquished but must also be exterminated, I feel an obligation . . .") called Himmler's attention to a plant poison whose effects were similar to castration.[118] Dr Tauboeck, a plant physiologist working for IG-Farben, found the idea feasible at first, but later he had misgivings having explored its background.[119] The project did not progress beyond a few attempted sterilizations (in Auschwitz?),[120] since the botanists involved were not able to grow enough plants.[119]

All the extermination centres had not been closed down by this time nor had all the doctors participating in the euthanasia programme yet been sent to the Eastern front. Those centres which were still functioning began to be used for other purposes. On 10 December 1941, Himmler issued an order[121] that medical boards should visit all concentration camps to 'sort out' all those prisoners who were unfit for work, ill, or were psychopaths (meaning Communists). Those 'combed out' in this way (those who were ill were not examined and their documents sufficed) were then brought to the nearest functioning extermination centre and were killed there with carbon monoxide. This campaign, which was led by Professor Heyde and Professor Nitsche and in which Dr Mennecke also participated, as did eight other doctors, claimed some tens of thousands of concentration camp prisoners. The doctors had taken a further step forward. Any of the following diagnoses was sufficient: old, ill, Jewish, priest, Communist, Social Democrat. The campaign continued until Pohl, worried at losing too many workers to these doctors, wrote to the camp commandants on 27 April 1943: "After the problem had been brought to his attention, the Reichsführer-SS and Chief of the German Police ruled that in future only mentally ill prisoners should be picked out for programme 14 f 13* by the medical board appointed for this purpose . . . All other prisoners who are unfit for work (those with tuberculosis and bedridden cripples) are to be excluded from the programme on principle; sick prisoners are to be set appropriate work which can be accomplished in bed."[122]

The background to these instructions includes the retraction of an order which Himmler had given earlier for the extermination of *all* Poles with tuberculosis,[123] and Pohl's exertions to force slave labour into the war effort.

What now happened to the long-term patients of the mental hospitals who had survived the 'euthanasia programme'? Forced labour ('work therapy') was envisaged as an important component of the reformed programme of treatment. But a person needs to eat at least a minimum in order to be able to work. However, the Government had reduced food supplies to the hospitals to levels which caused widespread malnutrition and, in addition, had cancelled coal allocations for the winter. Thus, the real situation in these hospitals was that death from starvation, illness, and the cold were common. In many hospitals, such deaths were hastened by injections or by phenobarbitone. Because these deaths occurred on a massive scale, there were always places for patients sent from hospitals in the towns exposed to the danger of air raids.

"One of the essential requirements for carrying out euthanasia is that it should be as unobtrusive as possible . . . In the first place, the surroundings should be unobtrusive . . . Orders for euthanasia must be given and executed entirely within the framework of the normal activity of the ward. Thus, with few exceptions, it should be difficult to distinguish euthanasia from a natural death. This is the goal towards which to strive. The fact that a few active psychiatrists with progressive attitudes have been practising medical euthanasia in their hospitals and that today a hospital can carry out medical euthanasia, even in a Catholic district, for long periods without attracting attention shows that this goal can be achieved," says a report written in 1942.[124] "I am very often astonished," writes a doctor who was

---

* 14 f 13, used as a code name, was the index reference of the file on the Inspector of Concentration Camps in Himmler's office.

practising euthanasia,[125] "by the contrast between the negative attitude which some directors have towards helping their patients to die and their clear approval of the reductions in rations for mental patients, which in some hospitals take really unpleasant forms. They refuse to end the suffering of their patients by administering drugs but they are happy to accept the fact that patients, who are by then really famished and emaciated, will one day take the road which could earlier have been made so much easier for them by a little assistance."

How large was the number of German mental patients killed? A January 1942 statistic gives details of the numbers killed by gas.[126] "The total number of beds for mental patients (including those which are now being used for other purposes) is 282 696. Of these, 219 407 are in public hospitals while the remaining 63 289 are maintained in religious and private institutions. A count of beds used for other purposes shows that only 42 982 are in state hospitals while 51 539 beds in religious and private institutions are so used. These figures show convincingly that the programme involved the religious and private institutions to a much greater extent than the public hospitals and asylums."[127] If we assume that there were no discharges, we can deduce from these figures that the approximate total of those killed was 94 000. Figures given by a T4-official in August 1941 indicate a total of 70 273 killed by gas.[128] Those mental patients who were shot in Pomerania and in West and East Prussia are excluded from this figure, as are the children killed in other ways, together making up a total of at least 5000 persons. The number of those who starved to death in 1942–5, after the euthanasia programme had ended, can be estimated from the Kaufbeuren mental hospital's mortality figures. The percentages of patients who died in the years 1933, 1941, 1942, 1943 and 1944 were respectively 3.1, 5.8, 14.0, 11.2 and 25.5.[129] The estimate derived from these figures of 100 000 as the number of patients who starved to death in German mental hospitals after the end of the euthanasia programme roughly agrees with the number given for those who survived the war, which was 40 000.[130a] About 40 000 psychiatric patients died from hunger in French mental hospitals during the same period. The French followed the German example without being ordered to do so.[130c]

The Use of Those Who Had Been Deprived of Their Rights as Material for Anthropological and Psychiatric Research

The massive killing of mental patients, Jews, Gypsies, Slavs, and aso-cial individuals opened up new perspectives for psychiatric and anthropological research. As far as psychiatry was concerned, neuro-anatomists, in particular, were faced with the problem of whether or not to investigate the brains of murdered mental patients. The Departments of Brain Anatomy of the KWI of Psychiatry and of the KWI of Brain Research had no scruples about working with the brains of murder victims. A research report of the KWI of Psychiatry reads as follows: "The number of post-mortems on children in the mental hospital in Haar has risen substantially. As a result it has been possible to obtain much rare and valuable material pertaining to the problems of brain injuries in early infancy and to congenital malformations . . ."[131] Nor was Professor Haller-vorden from the KWI of Brain Research inhibited by scruples. He wrote in a report to the DFG on 8 December 1942: "This material is constantly being added to by the post-mortem department of the mental hospital in Görden, which is directed by Dr Eicke, who is also an assistant at this institute. All the cases examined there are investigated further by me and a written report is deposited. In addition, during the course of this summer, I have been able to dissect 500 brains from feeble-minded individuals and to prepare them for examination"[132a] On 9 March 1944, Professor Haller-vorden wrote to Professor Nitsche, who was at that time in charge of the euthanasia programme: "Dear Colleague; I have received 697 brains in all, including those which I took out myself in Brandenburg. Those from Dösen* are also included in this figure. The greater proportion of them have already been studied, but whether I will be able to make a histological study of them all, only time will tell."[132b] The mental hospital in Görden where Professor Hallervorden had formerly worked as a morbid anatomist became closely connected to an 'extermination centre' in 1940 when a carbon monoxide gas chamber was brought into service in the old jail in the town of Brandenburg, which is nearby. Professor Hallervorden visited the extermination centre and talked to the physicians who supervised the killing. On one occasion he himself took out the victims' brains immediately after they were killed.[133] He provided the 'killing centre' with a technician from his institute and invited one of its physicians, Dr Bunke, to join his institute for a few weeks to do some research and to learn techniques.[133]

Professor Hallervorden later said to his American interrogating officer,[134] "I heard that they were going to do that and so I went up to them: "Look here now, boys, if you are going to kill all these people at least take the brains out, so that the material could be utilized." They asked me: "How many can you examine?" And so I told them an unlimited number—"the more the better". I gave them fixatives, jars and boxes, and instructions for removing and fixing the brains and they came bringing them like the delivery van from the furniture company . . . There was wonderful material among those brains, beautiful mental defectives, malformations and early infantile diseases. . . . One was the case of a severe athetoid disorder which developed in the child of a mother who had suffered accidental carbon monoxide poisoning when she was five months pregnant." Professor Hallervorden published this 'interesting case' in 1949,[135] as he continued to use these brains for his research. The collection belonged now in part to the University of Frankfurt and in part to the MPG. It was destroyed in 1900.

As a histologist, Professor Hallervorden was interested only in the brains of those killed. Professor C. Schneider (Heidelberg) had a weightier project in mind. With Professor Heinze, he wanted to create research centres in the mental hospitals of Wiesloch (near Heidelberg) and Görden in which patients could undergo thorough psychological and physiologi-

* A mental hospital near Leipzig where covert euthanasia was carried out.

cal investigations before being killed. For their time, these projects, as approved, were on a very large scale. The Reich Research Council, that is to say the DFG, helped to finance them.[136a] The projects ran into considerable difficulties. Firstly, a separate house had to be made available in Wiesloch. The patients were finally transferred in November 1942, and the ward began to function in December 1942 with five assistants and fifteen patients when it first opened.[136b] Dr Mennecke came to Wiesloch as a visiting investigator from the nearby Eichberg mental hospital, where the patients were to be killed.[137] Only two months after this work had begun Professor Schneider wrote to Professor Nitsche: "Dear friend . . . We would now like to make our first applications to the Reich Commission for the Registration of Severe Disorders in Childhood. For the sake of good form, I am sending you a carbon copy in case you can intervene on our behalf. I very much hope that the Reich Commission will support this application. Then the best thing would be for transfers to be made to Eichberg with full instructions to return the brains to us."[138a]

In the summer of 1943, after the Soviet victory at Stalingrad, all the medical assistants from Heidelberg who had been participating in the Wiesloch project were conscripted, with the exceptions of Dr Rauch, Dr Schmieder, and Dr Wendt. Among those who had to leave was Dr Suckow. By that time more than 30 patients had been investigated in Wiesloch. Professor Schneider had no choice but to close the ward in Wiesloch and to continue the research, on a smaller scale, in his Heidelberg clinic. Even this smaller project ran into all kinds of difficulties. Some of the patients who had been investigated and then transferred to other hospitals were discharged, and some perished in air raids, together with their documents.

By that summer, 1943, either no decision at all, or perhaps an unfavourable decision, had been made on Professor Schneider's applications by the Reich Commission which was charged with considering whether the killings were justified. However, Professor Schneider, and the other academics concerned, continued to press the matter untiringly and to demand a limited resumption of their work. In August 1943, they made some progress. "You will remember", Professor Nitsche wrote to Professor de Crinis, "that when we were both with Professor B. [Brandt] at the end of June, I made a firm proposal concerning the question of E. [euthanasia]. I have not been able to let you know before now that he accepted this proposal. On the strength of this, and with the consent of Mr Blankenburg, I invited a specially selected group of practising psychiatrists to my house on 17 August for a discussion (but I have just noticed that I have already told you this, in my letter of 25 August). As I wrote then, you can obtain further information through Dr Borm if you wish (his telephone number is 223582)."[139]

The age limit for patients, which had previously been four years, became more flexible, and was raised to puberty. The following letter shows that the decision reached on Professor Schneider's applications had been, at least in part, favourable. "Right from the beginning, I had allowed for the possibility that we would lose one-third of the idiots we had investigated", Professor Schneider wrote to Professor Nitsche on 2 September 1944.[138b] He then continued: "As you know, the children who had been under our care were transferred to Eichberg by the [euthanasia] transport company. Now the people in Eichberg claim that they knew nothing about these patients ever having been with us, even though we had taken all the necessary steps and all the arrangements had been made . . . They maintain that they knew nothing about our experiments being continued, even though one of our collaborators had been going there from time to time. A few days ago, when he was in Eichberg, Dr Rauch, at my suggestion, once again raised the whole question of sending the brains and it turned out that our containers were there all the time. They had been hidden and the director had been told that none had arrived. It also seems that there was insufficient formaldehyde in Eichberg, so the brains were spoilt. A number of the children had not been dissected. For whatever reason, we will not receive the brains of about ten of the idiots we had investigated. Another group has been lost, partly because they were not transferred and partly because they do not fall within the scope of the procedural definitions recently drawn up by the Reich Commission. So, I have to reckon with the fact that only half the idiots we have investigated here will be available to us for a full examination. This is a pity, but nothing can be done about it now."

Professor Schneider had not given up his hopes of continuing his research. The letter continues as follows: "Because of this, my main interest naturally lies in being able to continue to collect more material and I should be pleased to be given permission to proceed in the way which I proposed to Mr Blankenburg. Currently, the problem is as follows: There are children now available from the mental hospital in Herten. Mr E. Schneider, who works in the ministry in Karlsruhe, has promised me that he will transfer to Eichberg those patients who are in the appropriate age groups and who are of an appropriate degree of idiocy. But before this can be done, Eichberg must get authorization from the Reich representative for mental hospitals and nursing homes, and must be given the resources to set up a children's ward of 30–40 beds for long enough for us to be able to finish investigating these idiots. Even then, there are many other difficulties in Eichberg. There are no proper facilities for dissection since our colleague Schmitt [actually Schmidt] has too few doctors . . .".[138b]

Professor Schneider fled from Heidelberg as the American army advanced and had himself admitted as an in-patient of the psychiatric clinic in Erlangen.[140] The Americans showed less consideration than the pursuers in Fritz Lang's film, *Dr Mabuse*.* They arrested him and interned him in a camp. He committed suicide when he was called as a witness during the trial of Dr Mennecke. The Heidelberg clinic's Chief Physician, Professor Zucker, who had been an expert witness during the euthanasia programme, was also a psychiatric in-patient at that time, in what had been his own clinic. No charges were ever brought against Professor Zucker or any of the assistants at the clinic. How could this be? Professor Rauch explained to me (see p. 180) that he and his colleagues had known nothing about Professor Schneider's plans to kill his own patients.

Professor von Verschuer, who had succeeded Professor Fischer on his retirement as Director of the KWI of Anthropology, made use of the enormous possibilities offered by Auschwitz. Originally planned as a slave-labour camp, specifically for IG-Farben, Auschwitz became an extermination camp in 1943. The operating capacity of the crematoria (4756 persons a day from June 1943)[141] and the railway which ran right into the camp complex, determined the rate of extermination. The exterminations were carried out in sealed gas chambers by means of hydrogen cyanide, in the form of Zyklon B, supplied by Degesch,[142] a company which was 42.5 per cent owned by IG-Farben.† The change from using gassing-vans for the killings and then burying the corpses afterwards, to killing in gas chambers and then burning the corpses, was intended to avoid any difficulties in the way of separate peace negotiations with the Western Allies if the corpses

* Dr Mabuse was the chief character in two films directed by Lang. He was a criminal mastermind who, when finally cornered, was discovered to be a raving maniac.
† Zyklon B had been developed during the First World War by Professor Haber and his colleagues. It was a by-product of his activities in developing chemical weapons and was originally intended for pest control. Degesch stands for Deutsche Gesellschaft für Schädlingsbekämpfung [German Company for Pest Control].

were to be discovered. The SS-leadership must have considered the possibility of a separate peace when the war situation was deteriorating after the Soviet victory at Stalingrad.

As for Professor von Verschuer, we must appreciate that opportunities for research in the Reich itself were increasingly restricted. The twins Professor von Verschuer had been investigating were dispersed all over the Reich and it was no longer possible for him to make unlimited trips in order to investigate those affected by rare hereditary diseases before their euthanasia. So it seemed a piece of good fortune when Professor von Verschuer's former assistant from his Frankfurt days, Dr Mengele, was transferred to Auschwitz as camp doctor on 30 May 1943,[143a] after a short posting to the RuSHA in Berlin, where he had been using his spare time as a visiting researcher in his teachers' institute.[144] Dr Mengele's first duty as camp doctor was to control the epidemic of typhoid brought in by the Gypsies who had been transferred from Bialystok in March of that year. He 'selected' several hundred of the sick and sent them to the gas chambers.

His Auschwitz project needed more money than Professor von Verschuer could obtain from the KWG, so he turned to the DFG, i.e., to the Reich Research Council for support. There were two special projects which his assistant, Dr Mengele, would pursue in Auschwitz. They were called 'specific proteins' and 'eye colour'. The applications were approved by Professor Sauerbruch on 18 August 1943 and 7 September 1943,[143b] and Professor von Verschuer's laboratory in Auschwitz received the equipment it needed, an incubator, microscopes, and a table-centrifuge as well as the relevant journals. That familiar little plate 'On loan from the DFG' was probably attached to each piece of apparatus.

The nature of the scientific work Dr Mengele carried out in Auschwitz can be reconstructed from the report of his Jewish slave-assistant Dr Nyiszli, and from the accounts of other prisoners. The German Gypsies were sent to Auschwitz at about the time Dr Mengele arrived. These Gypsies had already been subjected to a thorough anthropological investigation by Dr Ritter and his co-workers. Dr Wagner of the KWI of Anthropology had made a special study of twins with the help of Dr Ritter's research section and in 1943 he obtained his doctorate with a thesis entitled *Race-biological observations on Gypsies and Gypsy-twins.*[145] In the course of this work, he had found two families with hereditary anomalies of the eye (partial discoloration of the iris).[146] He reported on further eye anomalies in a paper which was submitted to the *Zeitschrift für Morphologie und Anthro-*

pologie, but did not appear because of the progress of the war. Dr Nyiszli describes in his book how he had to prepare the heterochromatic* eyes of four pairs of twins Dr Mengele had killed by intracardiac injections, and to send them to the KWI of Anthropology in Berlin-Dahlem.[147a] An entire family of eight was killed in this way so that their heterochromatic eyes could be sent to the Dahlem institute.[148] Dr Magnussen, the investigator of the KWI of Anthropology involved in the eye project, received these eyes and submitted a manuscript on the subject for publication in the *Zeitschrift für Induktive Abstammungslehre und Vererbungsforschung.* The referee for this paper, Dr Melchers, suspected at the time that the eight members of this family had met an unnatural death.[149] The paper did not appear in print since, by then, the end of the war was approaching.

The enormous possibilities which Auschwitz offered Dr Mengele were never more apparent than at the time of the 'selection', which was made by doctors and anthropologists. This 'selection' on the railway ramp[†] consisted in dividing the groups of as many as 10 000 Jews who arrived at Auschwitz every day into two: children, with their mothers, and old people to the left (to Birkenau) to be gassed and those fit for work to the right (to Monowitz) as slave-labour for IG-Farben. Here, Dr Mengele collected over 100 pairs of twins and about the same number of families of dwarfs and deformed individuals. The twins and dwarfs were measured and analysed in every possible way. They had to undergo psychological tests such as: "All animals die. Napoleon died. Was Napoleon an animal?" They were tested serologically for typhoid and many proved positive. After they died from infectious disease, starvation, or lethal injections, they were dissected by Dr Nyiszli. "I had to keep any organs of possible scientific interest, so that Dr Mengele could examine them. Those which might interest the Anthropological Institute in Berlin-Dahlem were preserved in alcohol. These parts were specially packed to be sent through the mails. Stamped "War Material—Urgent", they were given top priority in transit. In the course of my work at the crematorium I dispatched an impressive number of such packages. I received, in reply, either precise scientific observations

---

* This term covers various anomalies of eye colour: total heterochromia where the irises are of different colours and segmental where there are segments of different colours in the same iris.

† The ramp was in a siding on the main Cracow to Vienna railway line. Passenger trains passed through the camp complex every day.

or instructions. In order to classify this correspondence I had to set up special files. The directors of the Berlin-Dahlem Institute always warmly
thanked Dr Mengele for this rare and precious material."[147b] When Dr
Nyiszli writes about "Directors of the KWI", he probably means the Director of the KWI of Anthropology, Professor von Verschuer, and some
department or group heads. Those who received these packages may have
included Dr Stroer, a Dutch physician appointed to the institute by von
Verschuer, and Dr Grebe, appointed to a chair at the University of Rostock
in 1945, a specialist on dwarfism. Dr Mengele went to Berlin several times
to report to his teacher on the progress of his work. While the work of Dr
Mengele so far described was more or less supplementary to projects being
pursued at the institute, in 1944 he began his own project on twins, a project which was of great interest to Professor von Verschuer. Were there
reproducible racially determined differences in serum following an infectious disease? On 20 March 1944, in his first interim report to the DFG,
Professor von Verschuer wrote about the project on 'specific proteins'.[150]
"My assistant, Dr Mengele, has joined this part of the research as a collaborator. He is employed as an SS-Captain and camp doctor in the concentration camp of Auschwitz. With the approval of the Reichsführer-SS,
anthropological studies have been carried out on the very diverse racial
groups in this camp, and blood samples have been sent to my laboratory
for processing." In a follow-up report, he writes on 4 October 1944: "Further research is being carried out with Dr Hillmann, a colleague from the
KWI of Biochemistry." Hillmann was working in Professor Butenandt's
institute in Dahlem on a scholarship from the DFG, although Professor
Butenandt himself had just moved to Tübingen.[150]

Dr Mengele infected identical and fraternal, Jewish and Gypsy twins
with the same quantity of typhoid bacteria, took blood at various times for
chemical analysis in Berlin, and followed the course of the disease.[151]
According to Dr Nyiszli, he also worked with tuberculous twins. It may be
of significance in this connection that, in his report of 4 October 1944 to
the DFG, Professor von Verschuer wrote:[150] "Our research on tuberculous
twins is being continued. Further material is being collected. . . . " The epidemics 'raging' in Auschwitz, which had already been used to explain the
simultaneous deaths of entire Gypsy families and families of dwarfs, also
served as an explanation for the deaths of these twins. Dr Mengele's letters
and reports to Professor von Verschuer were probably destroyed by von

Verschuer.[152a] However, passages from two letters to his colleague in Frankfurt, Professor de Rudder, are written in very explicit terms. On 4 October 1944, von Verschuer wrote to de Rudder thus: "Precipitates have been prepared from the plasma of more than 200 individuals of various races, some twin pairs, and some families. Abderhalden's method has been used and supplemented by a method newly discovered by Hillmann (who has joined us as a collaborator). So we can begin our real research very soon. The aim of our various efforts is now no longer to establish *that* the influence of heredity is important in various infectious diseases, but rather how hereditary factors act and what kind of events take place in their action."[152b]

Right up to the last moments of the war, Professor von Verschuer was still hoping for a major breakthrough. On 16 November 1944, he gave a lecture in the Academy of Sciences entitled: "On the action of genes and parasites in the human body." The abstract of his talk[153] concludes as follows: "The task of future research involves the analysis of all those parts of the defence mechanism which are genetically determined. Individuals with a particular defect in this mechanism could be supplied with a factor identified in such experiments." As late as 6 January 1945, he wrote to Professor de Rudder:[152c] "You will be interested to know that my research on specific proteins has finally reached a decisive stage now that we have overcome some considerable methodological difficulties, with the help of one of Butenandt's collaborators, Hillmann, who is a protein chemist." A few days later Dr Mengele left Auschwitz. Hillmann, Dr Mengele, and Professor von Verschuer did not solve their problem. The Red Army liberated Auschwitz and Berlin. Professor von Verschuer and Dr Mengele fled to the west. The collapse of the Third Reich must have come as a surprise to Professor von Verschuer, for even as late as November 1944, he wrote: "We are facing, today, a serious threat to the racial survival of the entire European population from the onslaught of Bolshevist Russia. After the victorious conclusion of this war and the guarantee of the racial survival of Europe which will accompany this victory, the future story of race and of heredity will depend on two factors: 1. the reproduction of a few nations and the migratory movements to which this will give rise and, 2. selective processes within individual nations."[154]

Dr Mengele had used the opportunities which Auschwitz provided not only to further his scientific career but also, in all probability, to become very wealthy. He had installed his dissecting room and laboratory in one of the crematoria.[147a,c] Thus, each day he entered a veritable gold mine. Here the gold teeth and wedding rings of the victims, as well as diamonds, money, and gold, which many of them had concealed on their persons or in their clothing, provided a rich source of booty for the ruthless. In South America he may have been protected from retribution and from the law both by the money and by the 'scientific material' of which he had robbed the victims of Auschwitz. Much embarrassment might have been caused if he had revealed where he had sent this human material.

On the Role and the Self-image of Some Anthropologists

I have reached the end of my presentation of the facts. I have tried to show in the preceding account how the scientific practice of psychiatry and anthropology gradually developed into the mass murder of anyone who was different or thought or acted differently. What kind of position did anthropologists and psychiatrists hold in National Socialist society? They had no power. Yet as scientists, they helped by justifying robbery and murder. They gave a scientific gloss and tidiness to the Nazi programme. The middle and upper classes were allowed to take part in this programme and to profit from it. The military hoped for, and got, rearmament and a war which was, at least initially, successful. Industrialists hoped for, and achieved, the break up of democracy and of the workers' movement. At first, they had reservations about the fake socialist propaganda of the National Socialists. On the other hand anti-Semitism did not worry them at any time, because from its very beginning it destroyed their competitors and later it provided slave-workers.[142,155-6] At his trial in Nuremberg Alfried Krupp said: "When I was asked about the anti-Jewish policies of the Nazis and what I knew of them, I answered that I knew nothing of the extermination of the Jews and that, furthermore "When one buys a good horse, one must put up with a few defects." "[157] Almost all other citizens profited from the anti-Semitic measures. The irksome competition that doctors, lawyers, and merchants had experienced now disappeared, and the property of those who had been expelled could be acquired cheaply. The posts of the professors and assistants who had been driven out opened up career prospects for students and assistants who would have had no such chances in the past. Anthropologists and psychiatrists hoped for an enormous expansion of their research, since they had helped to invest the National Socialist myth with an aura of scientific respectability. But this myth of 'necessary' murder only needed an aura of scientific respectability for the purposes of propaganda in the early stages; later, it needed technical advances.

The anarchic–polycentric form of rule of National Socialism also helped to cloud any insight the academics might have had into their own positions and indeed those of others, for it was never entirely clear who was making the decisions. Their experience was that everyone denounced everyone else. An inspection of the documents shows that professors denounced their fellow professors, assistants denounced other assistants, or their own professor, janitors denounced professors and professors denounced janitors. On one occasion, Professor von Verschuer told the police that the janitor of his institute was a saboteur because the tyres of the institute's bicycle were flat.[158] Everyone was everyone else's enemy and everyone had a right to claim that, despite their best efforts to serve the regime, they had at one time or another fallen into disfavour or had even experienced danger. I would like to demonstrate this briefly using Professors Lenz, Fischer, and Loeffler as examples.

Although he had a few reservations, Professor Lenz had pinned his hopes on Hitler as a potential champion of a vast eugenic programme, some two years before Hitler rose to power in 1933. He wrote in his textbook, in 1931: "We must of course deplore the one-sided 'anti-Semitism' of National Socialism. Unfortunately, it seems that the masses need such 'anti' feelings ... we cannot doubt that National Socialism is honestly striving for a healthier race. The question of the quality of our hereditary endowment is a hundred times more important than the dispute over capitalism or socialism, and a thousand times more important than that over the black-white-red or black-red-gold banners."[159] Later he took up a position in favour of compulsory sterilization and euthanasia but, without really noticing how it happened, he came into conflict with Himmler. On 15 June 1937, the Ministry of the Interior hosted a conference on the status of illegitimate children.[160] Professor Lenz expressed his long-held opinion that illegitimate children were undesirable from a race-hygienic point of view. Himmler was of a different opinion: "I will resist with might and main any legal steps or even attempts to influence public opinion towards imposing excessive moral restrictions on relationships between men and women. Of course, this is not a personal point of view; on the contrary I am acting in full agreement with the Führer, to whom I have often spoken about this matter. Everything which we do to restrict these relationships has the undesirable effect of encouraging homosexuality ... Heil Hitler!" Opposing the Reichsführer-SS on scientific grounds increased this academic's feelings of self-esteem, but it also caused him anxiety. The dispute between the SS and the eugenicists, like Professors Lenz and Loeffler, over illegitimate children and later over polygamy, lasted until the end of the war. It is true that this did not in any way inhibit Professor Lenz from submitting a memorandum in 1940 to the RuSHA of the SS about the settlement of German peasants in Poland;[161a] its main thrust was to advise that only Germans who were racially irreproachable should be settled there.

It cannot have escaped Professor Lenz that this demand for 'quality of the hereditary endowment' would be at the expense of those in assessment category IV (see p. 58), particularly as he was a speaker at a working conference of the RuSHA in January 1941 where new 'aptitude testers' were to be briefed. Professor B. K. Schultz gave a lecture with slides about 'European and non-European racial mixing'.[162] The confusion felt by these 'aptitude testers', simple members of the SS doing their job in doctors' white coats, can be appreciated from their later correspondence. It was no easy task to decide who should be Germanized and who belonged in a concentration camp on the basis of a single lantern slide lecture about individuals of mixed blood.

In a second memorandum written in 1941,[161b] Lenz proposed tax allowances which would have the effect of encouraging families with four children to resettle. Himmler's verdict on Lenz's proposal was: "Many good ideas, but they cannot be implemented now while the war is on."[163] A report on the activities of the KWG states: "The independent Department of Race-hygiene (Eugenics), under the direction of Professor Lenz, has been looking into the feasibility of a race-hygienic population policy in the post-war years; it has also been working on a rural population policy and on the methodology of research on human heredity."[164] So it was that, in 1942, Professor Lenz advised Rosenberg's Ministry of the Occupied Eastern Territories on the suitability of the Crimea for settlement by German peasants.[80] What would happen to those who were driven out was not his problem. In 1943, he published a paper: "On the racial assessment of an individual"[165] through 'the information service of the Race-policy Bureau of the Nazi Party'. It begins with the sentence: "The momentous events of the present time have enabled us to address the question of how we should recognize the racial quality of an individual and his racial value to our people." When the war ended, Professor Lenz fled from Berlin to Göttingen. In 1946, he was appointed to that university's chair of genetics. He wrote nothing more of any substance, apart from an article attempting to cover up his past.[166]

Professor Fischer also felt himself superior to most, if not all, National Socialists on matters of a theoretical nature. After all, he was a scientist and so he understood anthropology, the study of human heredity, and eugenics, which were the main pillars of National Socialist ideology, better than "these young people" did. On 1 February 1933, when Hitler had just become chancellor of the Reich, Fischer gave a lecture to the élite of Berlin, in the KWG's Harnack House. It was entitled "Racial crosses and intellectual achievement", and in it he contradicted the popular version of National Socialist ideology on two points: "It is untrue that persons of mixed blood are always intellectually and morally inferior." Two decades earlier, he had written a book in which he had stated that he considered Negroes to be inferior.[167] The German Jews, however, were not necessarily inferior, they were 'different'. "It should make an enormous difference whether matings occur with offspring of old-established cultured Jewish families or with Jews whose families are recent immigrants from the East. For all that, in both cases a racially alien element is introduced by such a mating and what would result, after several generations of matings of this type, is entirely uncertain."[168] Professor Fischer's scholarly anti-Semitism was too mild for the National Socialists. The professors of the University of Berlin elected him Rector even though the National Socialists voted against him, but, the race-hygienists of Munich (among them Professors Lenz, Mollison, Rüdin, Dr Bonhoeffer, Dr Spatz [a brother of Professor Spatz], and Dr Stumpfl)[170a] stripped him of the presidency of the German Eugenics Society. Nevertheless, Professor Fischer continued to hold these opinions. In his inaugural lecture as Rector, he praised the new regime but did not deviate from his previously stated views.[169] Letters denouncing him and his institute were sent to the Ministry of the Interior by his colleagues[170a] and his assistants.[170b] Professor Fischer stood by his department heads, Dr von Verschuer and Professor Muckermann, who were also under attack. Why should it not be possible to find places for these two academics in the new order? Since even Dr von Verschuer's opponents conceded that he was a nationalist and anti-Semite, the reproach that he was liberal in his views hardly justified his dismissal. The Jesuit, Muckermann, could also be integrated. In the case of Dr von Verschuer, Professor Fischer succeeded, in that of Professor Muckermann, he failed.[170c] Attacks in the press increased; Professor Fischer was said to be a friend of the Jews. Professor Fischer wrote a memorandum,[171] for the Ministry of the Interior, in which he explained that he had been an anti-Semite since his youth but he was also a scientist and, therefore, could not change his statements at will. He relied on 'science'. Professor Abel told the story[82] of how, as an assistant in the institute, he turned down a gentleman who wanted to bribe him to give a more favourable expert opinion on his ancestry. Shortly afterwards, Professor Fischer received a letter from the Führer's Chancellery, signed by Bormann. His assistant could not treat one of the most important industrialists of the land in this way. It was a scandal and, in such a case, he should have been more lenient and understanding. After speaking to his assistant, Professor Fischer replied saying that leniency and understanding were political, and not scientific, concepts. Thus, Dr Abel and Professor Fischer acquired a reputation for being incorruptible and objective scientists, albeit at times incomprehensibly stubborn. This gave them freedom to formulate their expert opinions as they wished. After all, who else knew the laws of inheritance of dermal ridges, nasal bridges and auricles? Fraud, if there was any, would never be revealed since the opinions of other experts on the same cases were rejected as being unnecessary and inadmissible (see p. 139).

Neither Professor Fischer nor Professor von Verschuer applied to join the Nazi Party until 1940, after the German victory in France. Perhaps they felt then that everyone should pull together in time of war. Himmler had already given much thought to the question of whether these stubborn scientists (Professor Lenz had made his application in 1937) should be allowed to join the Party. "On the question of membership for Professors Fischer and Lenz, having read the report sent to me by the chief of the Race-policy Bureau of the Party, as well as your own letter, and on the basis of my own personal knowledge, I am convinced that through their scientific work, they have both made a considerable contribution, in the last few years, to the theoretical basis and the scientific recognition of the racial components of National Socialist ideology. Although some doubts certainly still exist, I am convinced that Fischer and Lenz can be allowed to join the Party. In fact I believe that their enrolment is a matter of political necessity, since we can hardly use the talents of these two men to provide scientific support for our ideology while rejecting them as members of the Party."[172]

Shortly before he retired, Professor Fischer had published with Professor Kittel, who was a New Testament scholar, a lavishly illustrated book entitled *World Jewry in antiquity*. In this publication, Professor Fischer compared old portraits with photographs which one of the assistants from his institute had taken during a 'research trip' to the ghetto in Łódz´, where he had the help of his former collaborator Dr Grohmann, who had since become the head of the race section of the public health service there. In March 1940, Dr Grohmann had helped to select the patients to be killed in the local Kochanowsky asylum.[173] In Łódz´ he was probably helping to spot 'typical' Jews in the ghetto. A single example of Professor Fischer's anthropological analysis will suffice:[174] "As for the women, we can give figures 96, 97, 106, 108 and 113 the short and highly unscientific description of "common Jewish hussy" which refers not so much to their coarse physical features as to their facial expressions. On the other hand, figures 98, 100–2, 105, 114–15, and 117 illustrate rich Jewish ladies, who are often so much like those we used to see ten years ago on the Kurfürstendamm* that they remind us of people we know." The book appeared in a series financed by Rosenberg, *Researches on the Jewish question*, in which Professor von Verschuer had also published. It is entirely understandable, therefore, that Rosenberg should invite Professor Fischer to be one of the chairmen at an international 'Anti-Jewish Congress' which was to take place in Cracow in 1944. Professor Fischer answered: "Dear Reichsminister! That you intend to create a scientific front line for the defence of European culture against the influence of Jewry, and to call together for that purpose scientists from all the nations fighting Jewry, seems to me a very good idea and absolutely necessary, if I may allow myself to express such opinions. It is high time that this was done, since Jewry has been conducting its campaign against us for decades, not only on the political front but also as part of their historical spiritual struggle. I am delighted to accept your invitation to attend this congress and to take part in the discussions. I am also prepared to participate in a workshop, especially one on race-biology. It is an honour for me to be invited to serve as chairman of the workshop and I will gladly do my best to justify your trust . . . Of the French, I would invite Professor G. Montadon. As I am sure you know, he is a professor at the School of Anthropology in Paris, a co-editor of *Ethnie Française*, a strongly anti-Jewish monthly journal, and the author of a very fine little book entitled *Qu'est-ce qu'un Juif?* [What is a Jew?]"[175]

* A fashionable shopping avenue in Berlin.

Professor Fischer suggested, in addition, that Professor Loeffler be invited. The organizers also invited Professors Mollison, Reche and Sauerbruch.[176] Professor H.F.K. Günther had declared that he was prepared to speak at the congress on the subject: "The encroachment of Jewry on the cultural life of the nation." The high point of the scientific programme was to be an address by Minister Rosenberg on "Biological humanism". Furtwängler was to conduct *Fidelio*, and an Aryan brothel was to provide relaxation for the distinguished guests.[177] But the congress did not take place.*

Professor Fischer's home-town, Freiburg, was bombed. He heard a false rumour that his friend, Professor Montadon, had been killed in Paris and fled from his beautiful home to a small room in a distant village. There he began to work on a book intended for the victors. On 20 January 1945, he wrote to Professor von Verschuer, "I would like to call it something like "The Biological Basis of Racial Politics". What do you think of that? It is not really political, still less National Socialist (though probably still based on those principles). I will write it so that anyone, Japanese or even Jewish, can practise race-politics, each in his own way. The work is most enjoyable."[178] He was back at his old task, giving advice to rulers. His student, Professor Günther, was not allowed to continue his scientific work. On 24 November 1944, he appealed to Rosenberg without success: "I must interrupt the work which I have begun, and on which I have already made a lot of progress, since I have been ordered to present myself tomorrow morning, ready to march with a company of the Volkssturm†".[179]

That Professor Lenz and Professor Fischer were in conflict with the Nazi Party and the SS, could, superficially, be regarded as an example of the conflict which often occurs between science and the powers of an expansive state. On the other hand, the clash involving Professor Loeffler was without question one between science and destructive forces hostile to science.[180]

Professor Loeffler, once Professor Fischer's assistant and a member of the Party from 1932, had refused a chair in Frankfurt (the chair which von Verschuer later accepted) because Frankfurt with its large Jewish population seemed to him beset by too many problems. He subsequently accept-

---

* In June 1944, Hitler banned the congress for the duration of the war.

† People's Companies, a home guard which towards the end of the war consisted mainly of elderly men and adolescents.

ed a chair in Königsberg. There he became chief of the local Race-policy Bureau. Shortly before he had used his influence within the Party to prevent the distribution of a bizarre and amateurish book written by a Dr Gauch, *New fundamental problems of racial research*.[181] In it Dr Gauch had stated: "Non-Nordic Man occupies an intermediate position between Nordic Man and the animal kingdom, in particular the great apes . . . we could also call non-Nordic Man a Neanderthal; however, the term 'subhuman' is better and more appropriate."[182]

Professor Loeffler became involved in a dispute with Streicher* over an expert opinion in a paternity case. Streicher had previously published the following statement: "For those in the know, these are established facts: 1, The seed of a man of another race is a 'foreign protein'. During copulation, the seed is, in part or in whole, absorbed by the woman's fertile body [literally Mutterboden, mother-soil] and thus passes into the blood. A single act of intercourse between a Jew and an Aryan woman is sufficient to pollute her for ever. She can never again give birth to pure-blooded Aryan children, even if she marries an Aryan. Their children will be bastards, in whose breasts two souls dwell, and who reveal their mixed race by their physical appearance . . . 2, The originator and promoter of this commerce and its concealment is the Jew! He has known the secrets of the race-question for centuries, and, in this way, he methodically pursues the destruction of superior nations. Science and the 'authorities' are his instruments of forcing his so-called knowledge onto us and suppressing the truth. . . ."[183] In a paternity case which concerned an illegitimate child, the lawyer acting for the Jew who, according to Professor Loeffler, was the probable father, had made the plea that the mother of the child had already had two illegitimate children by his client. But, recently, the mother had also had intercourse with a non-Jew. According to Streicher's theories, the Jewish-looking child could well have been his. Professor Loeffler was then asked to present a fresh expert report on the case,[184] in which he proved, conclusively, that Streicher's statements were not consistent with the scientific facts, and must therefore be false. When Streicher learnt of this expert report he shouted to his entourage: "If that snotty-nosed little upstart were

---

* Julius Streicher was the Gauleiter of Middle Franconia and was based in the administrative centre of the Gau, Nuremberg. He was the publisher of the violently anti-Semitic newspaper Der Stürmer [The Storm-Trooper]. It was noted for the pornographic and obscene tone of its anti-Semitism.

here, I would kill him with my dog-whip." The situation did not look good for Professor Loeffler. His friends in the Party and the SS backed away, withdrawing their support. Finally, Dr Gross arranged that the conflict should be resolved by a debate between the protagonists. The debate took place in the garden of Streicher's villa in the presence of his bodyguards and two professors pale with fear. Professor Loeffler was well prepared. He led Streicher into a trap by bringing the discussion round to the topic of vaccination. Streicher, who also disapproved of vaccination, immediately began to rave against it. But Professor Loeffler countered: "If anyone talks against vaccinations after the outbreak of war, I will have him shot." And then he explained that Dr Grawitz, the Chief Physician of the SS, had said this to Hitler when he was called in to resolve a dispute between Dr Grawitz, who maintained that vaccination was beneficial, and Himmler, who claimed that it was harmful. Streicher did not know what to say next and so he gave up the fight.[180]

Like Professor Loeffler, many believed that what they were doing was simply serving and protecting science, even though from time to time they risked their lives. Perhaps because of this, they did not see that only small islands of rationality remained in a foaming sea of unreason and that these islands could no longer protect them from being engulfed by the great flood of destruction. Injustice breeds unreason. If injustice becomes monstrous, reason and science perish together with all else.

Germany capitulated on 8 May 1945 and the rule of the Nazis ended, but life went on. Professors Astel, de Crinis, Hirt, and Kranz, and Dr Gross committed suicide, and so, later, did Professors Clauberg, Heyde*, and C. Schneider, when charges were brought against them. Those who had been politically active from the beginning, like Professor Loeffler who had joined the Race-policy Bureau of the Nazi Party, and like Professors Abel and Schultz, who had joined the SS, found it the hardest to regain a footing in university life. But it was different for the purely 'apolitical' academics. This, more or less strictly maintained, separation of the 'good', 'pure' scientists and the 'wicked', 'political' scientists, had various consequences. Thus, the 'pure' scientists, who had been ensnared into crime, were threatened with the destruction of their scientific careers, if they were ever to tell the truth or attempt to understand what had really happened. So the dis-

---

* Heyde took the alias of Dr Sawade after the war and worked as a legal psychiatric expert until he was unmasked in 1959.

semination of half-truths flourished. The 'pure' academics once again appreciated how advantageous it was to be an objective, apolitical, pure scientist. This applied equally whether, like Professors Hallervorden and von Verschuer, their own ends had been served by the large-scale murders, or whether, like Professors Fischer, Lenz, Mauz, Panse, Pohlisch, and Rüdin, they had done no more than act as advisers and expert witnesses to the machinery of murder, or whether they had simply pursued their research peacefully and blindly. They had known nothing and could say nothing. And so they once again became a part of the scientific establishment. "We cannot tell, from the evidence available to us, to what extent Dr Mengele himself was aware of the abominations and murders perpetrated in Auschwitz during the period under discussion, that is when the blood samples were being sent." Such were the findings, in 1949, of a committee of professors, among them Professor Butenandt, later President of the MPG, who reported on Professor von Verschuer's work.* Their report ends with the following sentences: "We believe that it would constitute a pharisaical attitude on our part if, in the light of the situation today, we were to consider a few isolated events of the past as marks of some unpardonable moral defect in a man who, in other respects, had honourably and courageously pursued his difficult path, and who had often enough shown evidence of his high-minded character. We, the undersigned, unanimously believe that Professor von Verschuer possesses all the qualities appropriate for a scientific researcher and a teacher of academic youth."[185]

They made a cult out of their silence and of the 'incomprehensible mysteries' of National Socialism. Professor Fischer, for example, wrote in a draft of a letter to his old colleague Professor Muckermann, who took over as Director of the KWI of Anthropology in 1945/6, "I confess that I am very deeply shocked by what has been revealed. I believed, steadfastly and honestly, that I was serving the same ideals and that I was faithful to the same responsibilities as I always had been. And right up to the end I suspected nothing of the enormity of what happened. But this cannot be discussed here. . ."[186a] In 1946, Professor von Verschuer, writing one of his first letters after the war to a foreign scientist, Professor Adrian, began: "Allow

---

* If they had only read Weinreich's book *Hitler's Professors* (New York, 1946) they would have known better: "Dr Joseph Mengele . . . was known to be particularly severe and sometimes used to send whole transports to the gas chambers immediately on their arrival" (p. 198).

me to remain silent about all the frightful things which now lie behind us."[186b] Between themselves, they were more light-hearted. Thus, Professor von Verschuer wrote, to his old colleague, Professor de Rudder, now the Dean of the Faculty of Medicine in Frankfurt, where he hoped to return to take up his old chair: "I thank you very much for the 'Persilschein'* (a very good term!) which you sent me."[186c]

Even Professor Muckermann, who had been dismissed in 1933, but who was now honourably reinstated in his profession, was able to view his colleagues in a charitable light. In the preface to his first report as Director of the Institute of Anthropology he writes: "Today Eugen Fischer is back in his home town of Freiburg im Breisgau, where he is continuing his life's work as one of our foremost anthropologists. Otmar von Verschuer, to whom twin research is indebted for many great advances, left Berlin-Dahlem in 1945. Today, as Professor of Human Genetics, he directs a newly founded institute dedicated to its study at the University of Münster. Fritz Lenz, whose contributions to shaping the study of human heredity, and its applications, are very highly valued, also left Berlin-Dahlem in 1945. Today, he directs an institute for the study of human heredity in conjunction with his teaching at the University of Göttingen. Hans Nachtsheim stayed at our institute right up to the end. Today he directs the Institute for the Comparative Biology and Pathology of Heredity within the German Research University and in conjunction with a chair of General Biology and Genetics at the Free University in Berlin-Dahlem."[187] And what did Professor Muckermann's colleagues study at the institute which had been renamed Institute for Anthropology in the Sciences and Humanities? The subjects had not changed: "Investigations of somatic and mental development in offspring of European-Negro matings."[187] Professor Abel's[22] old results were approvingly cited. The article ends with the ominous sentence: "There can be no doubt that these children are dominated by their sexual urges and that certainly presents some dangers." They were right back where they had started from in 1932.

None of the anthropologists or psychiatrists involved have written an honest history of their science during those years. If anything at all is writ-

---

* Persil was a well-known brand of washing powder in Germany long before the trademark was established internationally. It had been developed by Henkel, a family-owned chemical company, at the beginning of this century. The connotation, of course, is that of whitewashing.

ten about the period, it reveals a complete lack of understanding, or else is virtually silent about these events.[188] The only comprehensive book, Weinreich's *Hitler's Professors: The part of scholarship in Germany's crimes against the Jewish people*, has never been translated into German. The university library in Cologne does not possess a single copy. None of those involved has publicly questioned even the component parts, let alone the fundamental basis, of his science. The only critical book about the anthropology of those years, *The race-theory of National Socialism in science and propaganda*,[189] was written by Dr Saller. When the Nazis came to power he was a Privatdozent in Göttingen. He had welcomed the new sterilization laws but later had difficulties and disagreements with Dr Gross about his 'unorthodox' conception of race. In addition, some of his friends had aroused the suspicions of the Gestapo. He lost his position at the University of Göttingen in 1935. His book was considered to be in the nature of a personal revenge and made him all the more of a pariah. After it was published, in 1961, he was shunned by most of his colleagues in West Germany. On psychiatry, apart from Platen-Hallermund's short book, *The killing of mental patients in Germany*,[190] only one comprehensive book (Dörner *et al.*, *The war against mental patients*[56]) had been published, until a fundamental book, *'Euthanasia' in the National Socialist state: The 'destruction of lives unworthy to be lived'*,[191] was written in 1983 by the journalist, Klee.

No one has written any genuine memoirs. There is a book by a psychiatrist, Professor Geyer, *On stupidity*.[192] This former member of the SS, and former assistant to Professor Lenz, found stupidity especially common among the Americans, who had interned him. He wrote that, after 1933, he had Karl Marx's *Das Kapital* on his bedside table, and that once, when he was asked to give an expert opinion, he pronounced in favour of sterilization because the unfortunate individual was so frightened that he interpreted a picture in which a man was knocking a child over: "This man is surely a Jew."

The memoirs of Professor Fischer[193] are revealing in their way. It is a remarkably colourless book with every trace of reality filtered out. Not a word appears in it about his fatally wounded son, about the Third Reich, or about the dead Jews. Some of the anecdotes, however, do have a certain significance. In one, he describes how, in 1935, he gave an anthropological expert opinion on the recently disinterred (and later reinterred) skeleton of Henry the Lion* (whose reincarnation Himmler believed himself to be). He gave his opinion that the unmistakable deformity of the hip of the skeleton was due to an accident which occurred when the Duke was out hunting. However, Professor W. Lenz, the son of Professor F. Lenz, told me[194] that subsequent investigations had revealed that, in reality, the pelvis of a woman with a congenital dislocation of the hip had been examined. Professor Fischer had reinterpreted reality, according to the exigencies of politics and in the service of a higher truth, that of Himmler (see p. 124). Another story is remarkably illuminating. This is the story with which Professor Fischer ends his book. He had travelled to Tuscany to make inquiries based on Rosenberg's suspicions[195] that the Etruscans were related to the Jews. According to Rosenberg, the Etruscans had been just as destructive and as dangerous as the Jews. Professor Fischer examined Etruscan sculptures and paintings and came to the conclusion that the Etruscans were a distinct race and unrelated to any other.[196] He even found individuals of Etruscan type in the present-day population. As an example, he had photographed a young man who seemed to him to typify 'a real Etruscan'. He then described how he was sitting in a café when the young man came to join him. During their conversation, he gave his name as "Aloisio Breitenmoser". Although he had been born in Tuscany, his father had been a Bavarian who had been a prisoner of war and had remained in Italy after the end of the First World War. "An enormous disappointment seized hold of me, and then I woke up." Professor Fischer had dreamt the encounter. The real Etruscan was an Italian. "We were happy about the *real Etruscan*," he concludes his memoirs.

Professor Fischer's subsconscious mind had shown him that the racial theory about the Etruscans was a fraud. He had spoken in Rome[197] about the necessity for racial laws, but were they not also based on a similar scientific fraud? However, Professor Fischer's conscious mind successfully prevented him from admitting this. But he must have brooded over this Etruscan anecdote for a long time, for why else would he have given the story the significance which it had in his memoirs? Wherever the truth lies, in his own way he deluded everyone. I have asked all his surviving students whether Professor Fischer was an anti-Semite. With one exception, they all said "No. Whatever else, he was not that." And yet he was to have been one

---

* Duke of Saxony and Bavaria (1129-95), so called because of his fearlessness, colonized the whole of northern Germany as far as the Elbe.

of the chairmen of the Anti-Jewish Congress in Cracow. What are we to make of it?

Here we should note that there are good reasons for supposing that Hitler himself did not believe in the biological basis of his ideas on race. Shortly before his death, he dictated to his closest confidant, Bormann, as part of a sort of political testament: "The Jew is the quintessential outsider. The Jewish race is, more than anything else, a community of the spirit. In addition, they have a sort of relationship with destiny, as a result of the persecutions they have endured for centuries . . . And it is precisely this trait of not being able to assimilate, which defines the race and must reluctantly be accepted as a proof of the superiority of the 'spirit' over the flesh . . ."[198] If this was Hitler's deepest conviction, then he used those scientists who thought in biological terms as misguided, but useful, accomplices to murder.

After the war, those who returned to university life were, at first, proving to each other that they had known nothing and done nothing. The anthropologists never looked at themselves or their colleagues with the eyes of an anthropologist, and the psychiatrists never looked at themselves or their colleagues with the eyes of a psychiatrist. They never doubted their science. They took comfort in the fact that almost all psychiatrists and anthropologists in other countries saw events in Germany as a terrible and regrettable aberration caused by a few individuals, or as the work of agents of capitalism, who of course treated human beings with contempt. Almost no one stopped to think that something could be wrong with psychiatry, with anthropology, or with behavioural science. The international scientific establishment reassured their German colleagues that it had indeed been the unpardonable misconduct of a few individuals, but that it lay outside the scope of science. The pattern of German anthropology, psychiatry and behavioural science continued essentially unchanged, and it will continue so, unless a substantial number of these scientists begin to have doubts and to ask questions.

Nine Questions

Now that we have examined some of the facts, we must address some questions, if we wish to understand the mystery and the enormity of the destruction. Not just one question but several. I suspect that my explanations and answers will not satisfy. "Too speculative", people will say. But mass murder is a reality which cannot be explained simply by the introduction of terms such as 'genocide', 'Final Solution', or 'Holocaust'. The involvement of professors cannot be explained away as typifying the limited outlook of narrow-minded specialists. Nor do the key-words of the Marxists, 'private property' and 'capital', suffice as an explanation. I will be grateful to anyone who calls my attention to defects or gaps in my arguments.

1 Why was it that the mass murder of Jews, Gypsies, asocial individuals, Slavs, and mental patients took place under German Fascism rather than elsewhere? Why did German psychiatrists and anthropologists participate, as propagandists and organizers, in the extermination of their clients and patients? Why was there no comparable extermination taking place in other fascist countries such as Italy or Spain? Why were there no comparable developments in democratic countries such as France, England, or the USA? I believe the answer to be as follows: Germany was once one of the leading countries in the world, both in science and in industry. At that time, its psychiatry and its anthropology were the greatest and the best. But after Germany suffered a humiliating defeat in the First World War, German science and industry slowly lost their pre-eminence. German professors and their assistants were full of resentment and hatred for the realities of the democracy of the Weimar Republic. In their opinion, the Jews and the Communists bore the guilt for the defeat and for the capitalistic democracy which was undermining everything. When Hitler came to

power, psychiatrists and anthropologists were enthusiastic, since they saw in him someone who would realize and give due prominence to their ideas. And so, from the early days, they placed themselves at his disposal as scientific propagandists. The laws which were passed or planned, and which required the sterilization of 'schizophrenics', 'psychopaths', and 'social misfits' [Gemeinschaftsfremden], which forbade 'Jews' and 'schizophrenics' to choose their lovers freely, which required the killing of 'schizophrenics', all had their origins in the proposals and demands made by these learned specialists. But these were men with orderly minds. The people classified as 'inferior' had to be catalogued, so that the measures to be taken (sterilization, forced labour, death) should be applied 'correctly'. The actual process of extermination, which was planned next, also needed the apparatus of modern science and technology. At any one time, a small group of scientists, doctors, and technicians was needed, and, within this group, the less able and the less willing could be, and were, constantly replaced by others. As documents and my interviews show, anyone who wanted to do so succeeded in escaping the 'honourable' task of participating in the extermination process. This was possible because there were other experts pushing forward to take their places.

Scientists espouse objectivity and spurn value judgements. But pure objectivity leads to regarding everything as being feasible. The killing of mental patients? If it is objectively necessary on economic grounds, and if it can be objectively organized, why not? The use of mental patients, the Jews, and the Gypsies as experimental animals before or after their necessary deaths? If the authorities allow it, why not? The division of labour during the scientific process also reinforces its objectivity. The medical expert did not make a report on his own patients which might lead to their death. Nor did the expert who gave the opinion carry out the killing to which it led. If he gave no opinion at all, then others would give it, perhaps with fewer scruples. Thus, the expert plays a part in extermination, but can do so without facing up to the end results. Professors C. Schneider and von Verschuer did not kill anyone themselves in order to obtain the eyes, blood, and brains which they wanted. Others did it for them. Even their assistants, who did the scientific work, did not do the killing. In this respect, Dr Mengele was an exception. For these scientists, objectivity opened the door to every conceivable form of barbaric practice. These German scientists and physicians lived in a world without values. Jewish values were not theirs. Neither were Christian values upheld by their peers. The values of the Age of Enlightenment* and of the French Revolution had never become popular with them. Thus, these scientists and physicians were ready to do anything at all, motivated by their belief in pure objectivity.

Scientists sublimate their sexuality by striving for knowledge and their destructive urges in its analysis. Anthropologists and psychiatrists had already begun to act out their death-wishes before the advent of National Socialism. The proscription and branding of others (the insane, the Jews and so on) was a goal which had already been attained, or at least declared. Now these scientists were no longer casting aside just ideas but people. The next step in the process of acting out their death-wish was sterilization, a symbolic threat of murder. The final solution was release pure and simple, mass murder. Why were they prepared to follow a path which led to acting out their death-wish? Whence came the hatred and resentment in these middle- and upper-class individuals (for they were all the sons and daughters of the middle and upper classes)? What made it so easy for them to take the path towards the extermination of those whom they did not understand? Was it a product of German history? Is it international?

2 Where did anti-Semitism come from? There had been anti-Semitism in Germany for a long time. For example, Freiburg, which later produced Professor Fischer and his students Clauss and Günther, had closed its gates to the Jews between 1424 and 1852.[199] It is impossible for me to survey or to give a detailed account of anti-Semitism in the Germany of the end of the eighteenth and of the nineteenth centuries. It appears in its most terrifying form where it would least have been expected. Kant advocated the 'euthanasia of Jewry' by conversion to "pure moral religion stripped of all laws and rituals".[200] When the Jews obtained civil rights during the French Revolution, Fichte† recommended that "their heads should all be cut off in one night and replaced with others which did not contain a single Jewish idea".[201] Fichte is not dear to me. But at the time Lichten-

* The Age of Enlightenment [Die Aufklärung] was an intellectual movement in 18th-century Germany (although the term is often applied to a similar period in England and France) for general education and culture, and away from prejudice, convention, and tradition.
† Johann Gottlieb Fichte (1762–1814), a German professor of philosophy and nationalist.

berg* called the Jews "vermin-like"[202], and this cuts deeper for I honoured and loved him.

It is the belief and the hope of all anti-Semites that the Jews themselves provoke anti-Semitism. The suggestion that anti-Semitism results from a more or less justified jealousy is of the same ilk. Professors Clauss, Günther, Fischer, Mollison, Reche, and von Verschuer had no particular reason to be jealous of the Jews. I should like to propose an alternative explanation. The image which the anti-Semite has of the Jew (sensual, cowardly, deceitfully clever, greedy for power, in one word 'inferior') corresponds to the image which many European men had of women, an image which can first be found in the works of Aristotle,[203] and continues in those of Albertus Magnus.[204] The way in which anti-Semites view the Jew is as a substitute for the image of woman. Sons who submitted to their tyrannical fathers and who learned to despise their mothers, along with everything else which is weak and feminine, but who had to conceal this hate and scorn from the world, could take the Jews as a substitute hate-object.† Weininger was probably the first to compare the 'inferior' female with the 'inferior' Jew fully and in detail, finding them to be surprisingly similar, in his widely-read *Geschlecht und Charakter* [Sex and character] (16th edition. Vienna and Leipzig, 1917). H. F. K. Günther wrote in his first book: "The author of this book is indebted to him [Weininger] for his illuminating synthesis of many isolated phenomena."[205] In his table-talk, Hitler called Weininger "the only decent Jew."[206] Weininger, himself a Jew, had correctly described women and Jews, and Hitler and Günther probably thought that it was to his credit that, having drawn the appropriate conclusion, he committed suicide.

But the mother, the German woman, could not *be* inferior, so there must be other inferior individuals who had tainted her. Hitler confessed in his autobiography that he had vacillated for a long time over 'the Jewish question.' Then he made the acquaintance of a Jewish pimp. "When I saw the Jew for the first time in this role of an ice-cold, shameless, efficient manager of this disgraceful and vicious commerce amongst the dregs of

---

* Georg Christoph Lichtenberg (1742–99), a German professor of physics and satirical writer.

† Fischer gives a good example of this in the story about the Etruscans on p. 93. What name does his unconscious give to the 'real Etruscan'? Breitenmoser, which sounds like breite Möse meaning large cunt. Thus, he shows the similarity between his hatred directed towards the Jews, represented in this case by the Etruscans, and towards women.

the city, a chill ran up my spine. Then everything exploded inside me. I no longer shrank from discussion of the Jewish question; on the contrary, I actively sought it out."[207] This was the fundamental experience which led Hitler to support Streicher and his newspaper, *Der Stürmer* (see p. 88), in spite of criticism from many of his National Socialists.

If hating and exterminating Jews has its origins in ill-comprehended aspects of sexuality, it becomes much easier to understand why the extermination of Jews, Gypsies and mental patients took on a ritual uniformity, whereas the Slavs were to be exterminated by working them to death. The sexuality of mental patients and of the Gypsies had alarmed and frightened the specialists for a long time. Although psychiatrists had very successfully neutralized the sexuality of female mental patients by segregating the sexes in their institutions, many of them still advocated and carried out ritual sterilizations. As I have already described, sterilized Gypsies and asocial individuals were not intended to live in freedom, but were to be concentrated in camps where the sexes were separated. The fact that anthropologists and psychiatrists wanted to allow the marriage, after sterilization, of a few 'distinguished' individuals with hereditary defects can well be understood as an act of self-preservation. For it could very easily happen that they, and others like them, would fall within the scope of the laws on hereditary health.*

3 What made doctors especially liable to become the apostles of destruction? Minor destructive procedures have always been a normal part of medical practice. Doctors amputated limbs or aborted preg-

---

* When I was looking through the German manuscript as it was about to go to press and when it was too late to make significant changes, I discovered that I had suppressed mention of an entire group of persecuted persons, the homosexuals. As a group they were different from the others, since they could not easily be seen as sharing common genetic traits. They had to be identified as individuals and not as members of families. In fact some psychiatrists, like Professor Rüdin, were against criminal prosecution and punishment of homosexuals (see p. 130). But from what I have written, it is entirely understandable that anti-Semites of Hitler's and Himmler's ilk, profoundly disquieted by homosexuality, demanded Draconian penalties. Sentences of penal servitude, castration, commitment to a concentration camp, and death were all part of an attempt to outlaw that which made them so uneasy. It is also understandable that young scientists eager to make a career took up these themes (see Jensch N., *Untersuchungen an entmannten Sittlichkeitsverbrechern* [Investigations on castrated sexual offenders]. Leipzig, 1944). Jensch, a Dozent at the University of Strasbourg, writes in the introduction to his book: "To find our probands, who were in custody, we turned to jails and concentration camps . . ." It appears from the text that, among these 'probands', or index cases, of his study, 37 percent were homosexuals and 10 per cent exhibitionists.

nancies on social or genetic grounds. They also wrote expert reports which determined whether an individual would or would not receive a pension. Professor V. von Weizsäcker discussed this destructiveness in a lecture which he gave in Heidelberg during the summer semester of 1933, lamenting that "only an incomplete theory of extermination" was available. "A policy of extermination thought out to its logical conclusions and implemented nationally would prove not only feasible but very constructive."[208] In the same lecture he called schizophrenics "inferior," an opinion which was common among psychiatrists at that time. If these were not just empty phrases was it not clear who was to be exterminated? Later, Professor von Weizsäcker profited scientifically from the euthanasia programme: his institute in Breslau regularly received the brains of those who had been murdered in the mental hospital in Lubliniec.[209] Back in Heidelberg after 1945, he wrote about the problem again. Previously the idea of 'extermination' had fascinated him, now it was the idea of 'sacrifice'. He 'discovered' that both for physicians and for the mass of ordinary people living under National Socialism "the ethos of sacrifice which pervaded its measures for eradication and extirpation was perhaps its most dangerous strength . . . and . . . that the concept of sacrifice represents a fusion of killing and redemption."[210] As an example of human sacrifice, he singled out: "Abraham sacrificed his son." But, of course, this was not so. Abraham actually sacrificed a ram and not his son. Professor von Weizsäcker now disseminated the idea of "sacrifice by common consent." However, it was not and still is not a question of sacrifice by common consent, but rather one of symbolic sacrifice.

Psychiatrists and medically trained anthropologists were able to make excellent diagnoses of mental illnesses and racial traits. However, as far as therapy was concerned they were helpless. Until the end of the 1920s, there was no known therapy for the major mental illnesses schizophrenia and depression. The most sophisticated therapy that psychiatrists could offer in the 1930s consisted of various methods of inducing a partial loss of memory. That these psychiatrists considered the major mental illnesses to be hereditary, just as anthropologists considered racial inferiority hereditary, handicapped them even further. But they were no more helpless than the general practitioners, who, without the benefit of antibiotics, were powerless in the face of many infectious diseases.

Psychiatrists had achieved the isolation and separation of their patients in 'secure' institutions some time previously. On the other hand, the segregation of German Jews and Gypsies in ghettos was a new Utopia for anthropologists. It is, therefore, easy to understand why the killing of their patients weighed less heavily on psychiatrists than the killing of Jews and Gypsies did on anthropologists, who had first to come to terms with the initial step in the process. The limited number of effective therapeutic measures may well also have been a reason why psychiatrists allowed such an extraordinary relationship to develop between them and their patients. Thus, Professor Bürger-Prinz wrote in his memoirs that, while under the influence of mescaline, he saw his patients in his Heidelberg clinic as "enormous worms." On the other hand, their nurse looked to him like "a skeleton."[211] The jurist Professor Binding, who with Professor Hoche wrote the book *The sanctioning of the destruction of lives unworthy to be lived,*[212] found that "incurable idiots . . . inspire terror in almost everyone." "Horror in the face of mental patients and of Jews" was the principal message of the writings of SS and party physicians. They probably did feel real horror at the sight of mental patients and of Jews. What is this horror? An extreme form of loathing, repulsion which turns into a desire to destroy its object. However, deeply hidden within this loathing is the desire to be close to the hated object. Every investigator had encountered such individuals whom he wished to protect from destruction. Dr Robert Ritter wanted to save a tiny group of German Gypsies from sterilization and the camps. As Himmler once remarked bitterly, every German had "his own Jew" who was different and whom he wanted to protect. Professor Heyde did not want to exterminate all asocial children but wanted to save the less afflicted. More than one anthropologist affirmed to me that a Jew or a half-Jew was his best friend, or was the only person with whom he had discussed the past.

I want to ask once again the question I have asked before, but in a somewhat different way. Why was it the physicians who so particularly took it upon themselves to become the theoreticians and priests of the cult of extermination? Why did doctors trained in anthropology stand on the railway ramp in Auschwitz and carry out the process of selection and killing? Why were doctors trained in psychiatry prepared to kill their patients or allow them to starve to death? It was the result of a long historical evolution. The traditional role of the priest (whether Protestant or Catholic) was divided up during the eighteenth century into three new, secular spheres of activity: the role of the enlightened philosopher (and teacher), the role of the natural scientist (and engineer) and finally the role of the biological anthropologist (and physician). The geneticists amongst the physicians believed that they had only to understand the genes, the psychiatrists believed that they had only to understand the fine structure of the human brain, the behavioural scientists believed that they had only to understand animal behaviour, and then they would understand themselves, mankind, its society and its history.

But this was all a great mistake. They had not proved that mental illnesses such as schizophrenia were inherited nor had they proved that racial mental traits were heritable. They had stepped out of their role as physicians and into that of priests long before the advent of National Socialism. They were flattered and delighted to be allowed to expand their role under National Socialism. "He [the physician] should go back to his origins, he should again become a priest, he should become priest and physician in one," the Chief Physician of the Reich, Dr Wagner, had proclaimed in a speech in 1937.[213] The professors of anthropology and psychiatry did not believe in a literal interpretation of the writings of Hitler, the founder, and of his disciple Rosenberg,[214] just as modern Christian theologians do not believe in a literal interpretation of the Bible. They could even claim that they had never read these writings. That was also a part of their secret. They were prepared to make up regulations about sacrifice, and to put forward theories about sacrifice, for anyone who would let them. Thus, professors of anthropology, of psychiatry, of behavioural science became the theologians of the new cult of Baal, and practising physicians became its priests. These anthropologists and psychiatrists said that their scientific problem was the biology of Man. For these theologians of the cult of destruction, 'the different, the other' man (the Jew, the schizophrenic, the Gypsy) became a seemingly insoluble riddle. The total and final solution of this riddle was mass murder, which literally 'dissolved' the riddle. The white coat was their priestly garment. Physicians with anthropological and psychiatric training had acquired, on 9 March 1943, the right and the duty to carry out the selection and killing of the victims. They fought hard to retain this right,[96] and sacrificed millions on their altars, the ovens which they had erected everywhere. The corpses of the sacrificed returned to the womb of the ovens. Their souls departed as smoke from the chimneys. Auschwitz was their greatest shrine.

We can now understand why these medical men chose mental patients and Jews as their victims. The mental patients and the Jews, who would forever think, feel, and act differently, were chosen for the role of animal sacrifices in the new cult of Baal.[227] These physician-priests would even have destroyed those whom they pretended to love. They would have sterilized Beethoven because he was deaf. They would have gassed Hölderlin because he was a schizophrenic and Nietzsche because of his general paralysis, though probably not without making further enquiries.* They were serious in their intent. The Jews, whether they practised their religion or not, were members of the first European monotheistic cult, and, as such, the ancient enemies of these new priests of Baal. Destructive hatred was directed towards the Jew, destructive rage towards the mental patient. The religions of Moses and of Christ were the religions of the oppressed. By the 1930s Marxism had also developed into a universal religion of the oppressed, although it represented much else besides. The religion of National Socialism, on the other hand, was unmistakably the religion of oppressors and of despots.

Philosophers and teachers were given no opportunity to help in shaping the ideology of German fascism. Perhaps this was in part because philosophers had taken this role upon themselves in the much hated Soviet Union. Thus, Professor Heidegger's attempts to make himself the principal philosopher of National Socialism was doomed to failure from the outset. Physicists, chemists and engineers did not at that time regard it as any part of their role to explain the sense of human life. And at that time the general public was unwilling to give up its opinions and to regard itself as a mere cog in a machine supervised by scientists. So it was that biological anthropologists and psychiatrists gave form to the new ideology, or better religion, which at the time seemed to offer such promise for the salvation of the Fatherland and of capitalism.

4 Why was the extermination of the Jews and of mental patients a secret? The fascination, which extermination held, melted away for most people when they saw corpses piled up in heaps. Only a few indi-

---

* Johann Christian Friedrich Hölderlin (1770–1843), the poet and neo-Hellenist, is said to have manifested the symptoms of severe schizophrenia in his early thirties.

Ludwig van Beethoven (1770–1827), the composer, was troubled from the age of 28 by increasing deafness which became a tragic and pervasive theme in his attitudes, thoughts, and writings.

Friedrich Nietzsche (1844–1900), the philosopher, is said to have suffered from general paralysis of the insane at the time of his death, presumably as a late result of syphilitic infection.

viduals were so strongly attracted by extermination that they were willing to serve as priests in the Holy of Holies of German fascism, Auschwitz. For the rest, the secrecy was necessary. Everyone knew that the Jews and the mental patients were being killed, but no one was allowed to say so. The highest, most sacred principle of German fascism, extermination, was an open secret and had to remain so. Hitler was the oracle of extermination. Whoever wanted to understand him, understood him. Just as man should not speak the name of God, so man should not speak the name of extermination.

Hitler came to power because he made it possible for German citizens to think of their dreams of destruction as a science with a biological basis. Dr Benn, a poet and physician, was won over by him in 1933, for just that reason. As the dreams of destruction became reality, people like Dr Benn were no longer needed. Even the physician and writer Céline, "The Führer and I are the only true anti-Semites," would not have been allowed to depict Auschwitz.

Hitler allowed the German people to satisfy their desires for extermination while still being able to say that they were forced into it all, and that they had known nothing. He turned them into small children again, small children who forget so quickly that they really can say that they know nothing. In this respect he was like those psychiatrists who try to take their patients back to the state of young children who no longer remember anything.

'Secret' also meant for the professors of anthropology and psychiatry that what was then a secret should remain a secret today. Thus, the past crimes of anthropologists and psychiatrists cannot and should not become research topics for anthropologists and psychiatrists today. Anthropologists and psychiatrists did not see themselves through anthropologists' and psychiatrists' eyes. Surely, when Plato wrote in his *Politeia* [The rights and conditions of citizenship]: "Race-hygiene [to use the modern term] is not a science at all but a Phoenician myth . . . . it is a fraud of which it is necessary to make use in order to dominate the masses and it must remain an occult doctrine," he was telling the truth.[214b]

Hitler's 'high-priest' was Himmler and he had his own ideas on the subject: "We Germans, who, alone among nations, have the proper attitude towards animals, will also adopt a proper attitude towards these beasts in human form . . . take care that these sub-humans always look up to you, they must always look their superiors in the eye. It is just the same as for an animal. As long as it looks its tamer in the eye, it does nothing. But always bear clearly in mind that you are dealing with a beast. This approach has enabled us to get the better of the Russians; this approach will always give us the mastery over the Slavs . . . just as we did not hesitate on 30 June 1934 (see p. xviii) to do our duty as ordered and to put those comrades who had failed us up against a wall and shoot them, so we did not speak about it afterwards, nor will we ever speak about it. Thanks be to God that the discretion which has become second nature to us has stopped us talking about such things, even among ourselves. It sent a shudder through every one us, but it was still perfectly clear to each of us that he would do the same again next time, if he were ordered to do so and if it were necessary . . . Most of you know what it means when a hundred corpses are lying next to each other, or five hundred, or a thousand. To have endured this and, apart from a few inevitable examples of human frailty, to have remained decent men, that has made us hard. This is a glorious page in German history, which has never been written down and is never to be written."[215] What did their parents, their teachers, the world, do to these children, to the little Himmler, to the little Hitler that they became such monsters? "Only he who has been the most vulnerable and sensitive can become the coldest and the hardest . . ." said Goethe[216] in a conversation with Riemer.* How does a man become the coldest and the hardest?

5 Was there a 'plan' from the beginning for the extermination of mental patients, the Jews, the Gypsies, and the Slavs? I believe that I have shown that this question is inappropriately phrased. The desire to exterminate Jews, Gypsies and mental patients was more important than any 'total plan'. This desire led to smaller-scale planning. The deportation and concentration of Jews in camps and in special zones, for example, led to hunger and filth. Filth led to epidemics. Epidemics cried out for solutions. But how is an epidemic to be controlled when there are no hospitals and no medical supplies? Dr Mengele chose a very successful method to combat an epidemic of typhoid in Auschwitz when he sent all the patients to the gas chambers. Hitler unleashed the forces of destruction in Germany. He encouraged both latent and overt amateurs of extermination. Each of

---

* Friedrich Wilhelm Riemer (1774–1845) was the literary amanuensis of the poet Johann Wolfgang Goethe (1749–1832).

them did whatever was within his powers and whatever he had the opportunity to do: drafting regulations, laws, expert opinions or plans, or turning a hand to actual murder. To collaborate in the extermination no one needed to know the goal. It was sufficient to believe in it.

Hitler was blinded during the First World War. Professor Bumke, a psychiatrist from Munich, is said to have examined him at the time and to have diagnosed hysterical blindness. Hitler had seen the horrors of annihilation in the large-scale massacres of the First World War and had not been able to endure the sight. When he regained his sight, "he decided to become a politician", and to turn annihilation against its alleged originators, the Jews. In the last sentence of his testament, he was still calling on the party to observe the racial laws. The only murder he even came close to carrying out with his own hands was that of his mistress, whom he had married just before he killed himself. A frustrated matricide, he directed his transcendent intelligence and fantasy towards war and towards the extermination of others, 'woman-like' individuals in particular.

6 Could National Socialism happen again in Germany or anywhere else? West German anthropologists and psychiatrists have been on the defensive since 1945. Their oft-repeated claim "to have known nothing" guaranteed them their chairs, but did not exactly make them attractive as academic teachers. Who can feel attracted by scientists who are always saying that they were the only ones who did not know what everyone else knew and that, in any case, this is not a subject which they want to discuss? The last of this generation are now retiring. Paradoxical though it may seem, by occupying their chairs, these disabled former ideological and bureaucratic pioneers of National Socialism have guaranteed that there would be no revival of a new National Socialism. It was precisely their 'discretion' (to quote Himmler) which rendered them and their students, who emulated their teachers, incapable of taking action. Will these students, now that they are alone, show the same 'discretion' or will they, freed from the burden of the old murders, with their eloquent and sharp tongues restored, one day renew the call for segregation, sterilization, euthanasia? I suspect that, with the retirement of these academic cripples of the older generation, the period of tolerance in West Germany is coming to an end.

The biological anthropology of West Germany is no longer where it used to be in the early 1930s—at the forefront of scientific endeavour. The techniques of modern genetic analysis of DNA with restriction enzymes and Southern blotting are unknown fields for many German anthropologists. Those who have mastered and now understand the new techniques often have no interest in anthropology. The imaginary or real possibilities for manipulating *Man's* genetic material are not at the centre of scientific interest today, in either the USA or Europe. But that could change.

The figure of a new Hitler on whom all wishes and impulses towards destruction are reflected and concentrated is lacking. But I consider it possible, although by no means inevitable, that given all the problems of foreigners' and Turks [guest workers in West Germany], destructive forces in West Germany or elsewhere in Europe may once again choose the same old road. Perhaps the people of the western democracies are already beginning to feel that they are merely insignificant cogs in a gigantic bureaucratic industrial machine the management of which is best left to experts. If so, the forces of destruction, marching under the banner of science and technology, may once again gain the upper hand.

7 Are the experimental studies of Professors Hallervorden and von Verschuer, mentioned in this book, to be rejected because they constitute 'bad science' or were 'unscientific', or because they were carried out on inappropriate experimental subjects, i.e., on human beings who had been deprived of all their rights? In retrospect, these studies, like so many experimental studies, seem much less significant now than they did at the time when they were performed but it would be wrong to condemn them as bad experiments if they had been carried out on mice. The fundamental defect of these investigations is that they were carried out on human beings who had been deprived of their rights. In carrying out his investigations, Professor Hallervorden showed no reverence for the murdered victims. When Professor von Verschuer began to use Dr Mengele as an assistant in his programme of research in Auschwitz, he probably did not realize that the experiments would be performed on individuals who were completely without rights. It will probably remain a secret how much Dr Mengele told him of the reality of Auschwitz, although we do know that Dr Mengele confided to Professor von Verschuer's wife, among others, that Auschwitz was a dreadful place (see p. 128). However that may be, Professor von Verschuer supported these experiments right up to January 1945. Later, he always asserted, to be sure, that he had known nothing, that Dr Mengele had not been an assistant in his Berlin institute[144] and, therefore, that he could not have collaborated with him.

Academics cannot simply be divided into two groups, the blameless and the criminals. Not only murders, but lesser crimes also, are reprehensible. Charlatans like Dr Rascher (who began by fabricating harmless results, and, through this fraud, obtained a scholarship from the DFG, and who ended up as a mass-murderer) have always existed. What is more terrible is the complete silence of the professors who listened at a scientific meeting as Dr Rascher gave a lecture with slides describing experiments in the concentration camp at Dachau which led to the death of the human subjects.[217] Assistants and prospective professors such as Dr Mengele must be seen against the background of professors like Hallervorden and von Verschuer. Professors Clauberg, C. Schneider, and Hirt, all first-class scientists, who avoided trial, and with it an analysis of their crimes, by committing suicide, had resolutely advanced even further along the path Professors Hallervorden and von Verschuer had trodden before them. They often, and knowingly, brought about the death of those whom they were investigating. But even their investigations could not have been judged 'bad science' if they had been carried out on mice. Thus we begin to understand why the traditional restraints of a scientific administration run by scientists failed and failed of necessity. The scientists who were in control regarded some human beings as a special kind of experimental animal. The DFG at that time was smaller than it is today, but it was not constituted differently in so far as it relied on peer review of projects. Professor Sauerbruch's approval of Dr Ritter's genocide project and of Professor von Verschuer's Auschwitz project showed that control by the peer review system was not working. Nevertheless, the peer review system seems, in general, to be the best possible system. There are no other safeguards.* There

---

* I should like to give just one example out of many which I could have presented: 'Professor Friedrich Deinhardt of the Institute of Hygiene of the University of Munich indicated that perhaps the most difficult question he had faced was the justification of experiments with the hepatitis virus, carried out ten years earlier in homes for mentally handicapped children and which had already become classics . . . In these controversial experiments, children in homes in which various forms of liver inflammation were prevalent were infected with hepatitis virus, in order to obtain more detailed data about the illness, and to facilitate the development of a vaccine. This investigation was approved by two ethical committees. The justification presented was that children, once admitted to these homes, would very probably contract hepatitis, and would then suffer from a far graver form of the disease than they would in well-supervised experiments.' Behrends, M. Medizin und Ethik [Medicine and Ethics], *Frankfurter Allgemeine Zeitung*, 6.1.82. See also Krugman, S., and Giles, J. P. Viral hepatitis. New light on an old disease. *The Journal of the American Medical Association*, **212**, 1019–29, 1970.

is only one hope, and even this may be a vain hope; it is absolute openness and the absence of any secrecy in science. Only thus can we hope that the scientists who succeed will be those who do not confuse exceptional human beings with experimental animals. And, furthermore, this means that we must think and speak about destruction in order to be able to hold it at bay. There can be no pleasure in wanting to understand those things which we reject and never want to use. Dealing in destruction harms and defiles. But to repress it and to consign it to the unmentionable blinds and lames.

8 Now comes the most important question of all. Let us regard the scientific activities of anthropologists and psychiatrists documented here as a large-scale experiment which failed. Let us now trap these scientists with their own logic. What can we learn about anthropology and psychiatry from the massive experiment of the National Socialist anthropologists and psychiatrists? I believe that I have made it clear that we are not dealing here with defects in the character of a few individuals, but rather with defects in psychiatry and anthropology as a whole. Every science at its beginning builds on mythological foundations. As it processes, those parts which can no longer be integrated into the whole are dropped. I have shown that the mythology of psychiatrists and anthropologists in the Third Reich revealed itself to be entirely evil, that is to say unjust, malevolent, destructive, and, in the last analysis, stupid. Many of the psychiatrists and anthropologists whom I have named showed themselves to be traitors to their science, in that they made blood sacrifices of innocents to their myths. It would be the greatest triumph for these psychiatrists and anthropologists, and for their faithful disciples, if their opponents were to reject science as a whole and make emotional demands for the promotion of anti-science.

The volumes of German psychiatric journals for 1933–45 must be studied thoroughly. The textbooks and monographs which were published in those years must be critically reviewed. It would need a separate book to analyse the scientific charlatanism of the psychiatry of that time. The brain biopsies of old people which were regularly taken in the institute run by Professor de Crinis, Professor Heyde's watershock treatment, electroconvulsive therapy as a routine treatment for a variety of general disorders, the castration of homosexuals followed by hormonal implants; all these 'unbalanced excesses' reveal the mythological basis of this speciality, which is equally prevalent today. To remember the past requires an active effort and remembering is a prerequisite of mourning. All psychiatrists and every student of psychiatry should make this effort and, in doing so, should also give thought to the phrase: 'In the case of a science where it can be said "this is no longer true", nothing is true.'[218]

I suspect that even this process of cleaning up these sciences, psychiatry, anthropology, and psychology, will not be sufficient. There are many things about individuals who are investigated by psychiatrists, anthropologists or psychologists which can only be understood through basic science. The exact nature of the chromosomal anomalies, and of the changes in the anatomy, physics, and chemistry of the brain, which characterize Down's syndrome [mongolism], for example, can only be studied by scientific methods. Even if we come to understand Down's syndrome in detail when these investigations are completed, it will be of little help to the affected individuals. And this is even more true in the case of mental patients. In schizophrenia, for example, despite intensive investigations, no alterations in the brain have been found. It seems to me that to reduce other people to the status of depersonalized objects is of no help to them whatsoever. The 'scientific' psychiatrists does not console those in despair, he calls them depressed. He does not unravel the tangled thought-processes of the confused, he calls them schizophrenic. If he speaks to those in despair, to the confused, to those who think slowly, as a wise, friendly person speaks to another person, then he is no longer considered to be an objective scientist but a . . . well, what would he be? We have no appropriate word to describe such persons. When we envisage them, we must admit that their training could not and cannot take place within any of the existing university specialities. I am not speaking of an anti-science or an anti-psychiatry, but rather of a field which does not yet have rules. Similar considerations apply to the other 'human sciences'. Could it not be that as anthropology and psychiatry advance, the patient, the 'other person', continually becomes more remote and less significant? Is this whole style of investigation, together with its predictions, anything more than an ever more marked degradation of the individual until he becomes a mere cipher? It seems to me that the inexorable encroachment of science, which began in the eighteenth century during the Age of Enlightenment, on activities more properly belonging to the human individual who speaks and gives signs, has had unforeseen and devastating effects. In science all that really matters is getting interesting, accurate results as quickly as possible; there is simply no time to talk to patients. Moreover, the language of the experts is a restricted, unelaborated jargon, composed of perhaps a maximum of a thousand words and is suitable only for communication among themselves. This 'pidgin' language is considered sacred and lay people are not allowed to use it. But it would be of no use to the patients to be able to speak it, since it does not describe reality as they would see it, but, rather, abstractions of abstractions. So conversation between patients and experts is increasingly difficult, if not impossible. And the introduction of machines in no way eases the situation, for the more expensive and complicated the machines, the more the investigator distances himself from the person who is being investigated. This attitude reduces the person to a subservient depersonalized object. Such a process formed the bond which held the psychiatrists, anthropologists, and Hitler together.

9 The last question is whether there were anthropologists or psychiatrists in Germany who did not conform, and who would not fit into the picture which I have sketched here. As far as the anthropologists and human geneticists are concerned, I believe that I can say with certainty that none differed in any important respect from those whom I have named. There were outsiders such as Professor W. Scheidt who, rejecting the concept of race which his colleagues held, switched his research to the field of biological psychology. He left the writing of expert reports to his assistant. But he too remained silent after 1945. I have not, however, named everybody. This does not mean that I could not have quoted the others. I have named those who stand out, so as not to be accused of spending time on second- and third-rate scientists. But it should not be forgotten how much smaller German universities and the KWG were then than they are today, and that there were fewer universities then than there are today. The institutes which did exist were substantially smaller. University departments of anthropology or race-hygiene contained one professor and two or three assistants. The DFG helped, but even its help was tiny when measured by today's standards.

Of the psychiatrists, I know less. Professor Kurt Schneider succeeded in retaining a compassionate attitude. Professor Ewald spoke out in public against sterilization and euthanasia. And the others? Any letters of protest which may have been sent to Dr Linden at 4, Tiergartenstrasse [T4 in glossary] have presumably been burnt, or have simply disappeared. Those who participated in discussions of the forms which destruction should take because they had an honest desire to apply restraints, only succeeded in giving the killings a scientific gloss. Professor Villinger's contribution to a discussion on whether there was any need for a law on asocial individuals, if the law on sterilization were broadly interpreted, is an example of a fundamental conceptual mistake; the stream of destruction could not in any way be channelled. Another example is the proposal made by Professor Mauz that schizophrenics should be killed only after five years of observation, rather than the two which were laid down (see p. 43).

I have found no written testimony against euthanasia from a psychiatrist. Ernst Klee, who has studied all the records connected with euthanasia prosecutions, names one psychiatrist in a mental hospital, Dr H. Jaspersen, who denounced the euthanasia programme, and who tried in vain to persuade the heads of the university departments of psychiatry to make a collective protest.[219] I know of no psychiatrist who was suspended or dismissed because of such a protest. I know of only one psychiatrist, Dr J. Rittmeister*, who belonged to the resistance movement. Professor Bonhoeffer, whose son Dietrich also belonged to it, had retired in 1938 and he kept silent, perhaps to protect his son. No German psychiatrist accompanied his patients on their last journey. They were no martyrs. It seems to me that the best of them considered themselves to be eye-witnesses who rejected what they saw in silence, and who would never speak about it. Their colleague, Professor Heyde, meant more to them than their patients.[†]

I have come to the end of my account. I have tried to describe the actions and behaviour of psychiatrists and anthropologists in their own words. I have used the language of a science which also became the language of destruction. I have spoken of asocial individuals, products of racial mixing, idiots, persons of mixed blood, non-Aryans, schizophrenics, and Gypsies. None of these individuals called themselves by these names. You will not hear the screams of children as the chloroform injections reached their hearts in my sentences. Nor will you hear the cries of the

---

* Dr Rittmeister, a neurologist and psychoanalyst, was executed in 1943 as a member of the Communist resistance. His work in the German Institute of Psychotherapy, which was directed by Reichsmarschall Göring's cousin, Professor M. H. Göring, was, however, far removed from the events of the euthanasia programme.

† Professor Heyde practiced under the alias Dr Sawade between 1950 and 1959 in Flensburg, West Germany. That Dr Sawade was Professor Heyde was known among West German psychiatrists and the local legal establishment.

resisting patient: "You will rue this with your blood", as the door closed behind him.[220] I have not spoken of those who blew up the crematorium in Auschwitz and who were executed immediately. Who hears the cries of the last of these men hanged in front of fellow prisoners: "Comrades, I am the last."[221] Any hope there was for mankind was not to be found in German scientists but in their resisting victims. The staring eyes of the murdered rest on us. I have no inhibitions about calling murderers murderers, even when the West German Supreme Court gives rulings such as "manslaughter excluded by the statute of limitations", as in the case of Dr Borm, the director of an extermination centre. Murder remains murder even when the law shows itself to be totally impotent and the courts are unable to punish even one single person for the genocide of the German Gypsies. All indignation is in vain if it is not based on knowledge of the facts and if it does not endure. "If I do not stand up for myself, who will stand up for me? If I am only for myself, who am I? If not now, when then?"[222]

A warning

"When will all this extermination cease?" Dr Nyiszli asked Dr Mengele in Auschwitz. And Dr Mengele answered: "My friend! It will go on, and on, and on."

Conversations

Miss Gertrud Fischer, *the daughter of Professor Eugen Fischer*

I step into one of the big old houses in the Schwimmbadstrasse in Freiburg, where prosperous townspeople and professors live. Miss Fischer receives me at the door. She shows me into the living room. A small table is laid. There are glasses and cakes. Miss Fischer offers me the choice between two bottles of Baden wine.

Miss Fischer is now, she tells me, seventy-eight years old. When her father worked in Berlin, she was in church-service in Kassel in the seminary of the Evangelical Charitable Society. She tells me that she has no professional training, and that she first helped her father with his correspondence when he was already very old.

A beautiful landscape in the style of Altdorfer hangs on the wall, and, over a table, a portrait of Eugen Fischer, reminiscent of Kokoschka. I ask about the landscape. "It's by the elder Bühler. One day Bühler came to visit my father, and told him that he must study anatomy with him. He had been asked to paint a picture of Prometheus in the university auditorium and he couldn't do it without some knowledge of anatomy." I remember it, a large painting, somewhat too large in fact, with naked male figures. "That day a long friendship began between them. Later on, Bühler's son also came to work in the institute."

"My father was a true Freiburger. He came to Freiburg when he was three years old, when there still weren't any houses on the River Dreisam. He didn't want to leave Freiburg, ever. He was a student of Wiedersheim, the anatomist. It was only by good luck that he was able to stay in Freiburg. How often have I heard about it. He simply didn't have enough money. "I will open a practice," he often used to say. But then he had his great success with his book on the Rehoboth bastards."[167]

I interrupt "It's strange that he didn't once explain Mendelian segregation of physical characteristics, let alone mental traits, in that book. Did he ever discuss with you whether he had doubts about this?"

"No," she says, "I know that for certain. He never doubted that everything had been properly explained." "Did he ever have doubts about National Socialism?" I ask further. "My father was a completely apolitical person. Early in life, he was a Catholic, but later he left the Church. He was no National Socialist. He was a nationalist and a conservative, but they all were at that time, that's not a matter of politics. He joined the Party late, when pressure was brought to bear on him." About 1938, she thought.

"Was your father an anti-Semite?" I ask. "No, no," she says. "He worried a lot about what happened to his Jewish colleagues and their wives." "Did you discuss the persecution and extermination of the Jews with him, either during the war or afterwards? Did he ever question himself about his involvement?" "No," she says, "we never spoke about that. I didn't know anything about it during the war. Von Verschuer and he must have known. But we didn't ever discuss it. It's an entirely new thing that people talk about it now. After the war, there wasn't anything like the television film about the Holocaust. At the time we thought only about reconstruction. In any case, why are you picking on him in particular? They were all guilty. He didn't do anything special."

"When he retired, he went to live in a village. I lived there with my parents until 1950. He never complained. It was a very hard time for him. It's difficult for you to understand. It was only in 1950 that the French left my grandparents' home and we were able to move back here. Both my mother and he lived to be over ninety. In their last years, both of them were confined to bed. I looked after them myself. My father was a kindly man. So sensitive. He was brave too. And unassuming. A piece of sausage, a roll, and a glass of wine, he wanted nothing more."

"At the age of eighty, he went once more to Venezuela, and gave some lectures. He was clear-headed right up to the end. At ninety, he was dictating to me from his bed. He thought a great deal about the history of the white man in Africa. It became lonely for him. Heidegger visited him now and then. His students all stuck by him. Abel also came to visit him; he was the only member of the SS among his students." "What were the others really?" "Bühler was a convinced National Socialist," she says.

I ask about von Verschuer. "My father had a special relationship with von Verschuer. He loved him like a son. Von Verschuer was his successor, of course. He was a member of the Confessional Church.* I made the acquaintance of Niemöller through him. I met Niemöller again a year ago in Majorca. I said to him, "You don't recognize me any more, but I met you in Dahlem." And then he did recognize me. Von Verschuer went to church

---

* The Pfarrer-Notbund [Pastors' Emergency League] was created in 1934 under Martin Niemöller, in protest against Nazi attempts to incorporate the German Evangelical Church Federation and other Protestant churches with the pro-Nazi 'German Christians'. This led, in 1934, to the creation of the Bekennende Kirche [Confessional Church]. In 1937 the Confessional Church was banned and Pastor Niemöller was arrested. He survived the war in concentration camps, mainly Dachau.

every Sunday." "Was von Verschuer an anti-Semite?" "No, certainly not. He was just like my father. He never said "the Jews are bad," he said "the Jews are different." " And she smiled at me. "He supported the segregation [Trennung] of the Jews. You know what it was like, when we came to Berlin in 1927. Cinema, theatre, literature, it was all in their hands. He was for segregation. But he wasn't an anti-Semite."

We talk about the death of von Verschuer. "The von Verschuers were on a trip at the time. He went to post a letter. Mrs von Verschuer heard the screeching of the car that ran over him. He was unconscious in intensive care for eleven months. Sometimes he opened his eyes. But he never spoke again."

Miss Fischer gives me a list of her father's publications. "Saller is there too as a co-author," I say. "Yes, Saller," says Miss Fischer. "He was making trouble for himself in those days. He was a doctor in Badenweiler later. He wasn't a good man. My father also broke with Gottschaldt. He attacked von Verschuer in East Germany. That wasn't nice of Gottschaldt. My father supported von Verschuer."

"It's curious," I say, "that he called his memoirs *The Memoirs of an Anatomist*.[193] His reputation was in human genetics and anthropology." "He saw himself as an anatomist. He felt at home as one," she says. "He was already old when he came to Berlin. He was a very special father, you know."

Time is up. I take my leave.

Professor Widukind Lenz, *Director of the Institute of Human Genetics at the University of Münster, the son of Professor Fritz Lenz*

In the corridor in front of the Director's office, pictures of the great men of genetics were hanging on the wall. Muller and Morgan next to Fischer, Lenz, and von Verschuer. A strange juxtaposition.

We begin to talk about von Verschuer. "He was a believer. God's will was manifest to him in world history, and obedience seemed to him to be one of the principal virtues. So, he believed in God and in his viceroy, the Führer. Later, he spoke of God in his lectures on occasions which seemed quite inappropriate to me. He had a split personality. He was a member of the Confessional Church, but, at the same time, he was bewitched by National Socialism." "Did he know about the mass exterminations in the East?" I ask. "I rarely discussed the past with him, and then only briefly. I had the impression from what he said that he knew little or nothing of the planned mass exterminations, even though I have no precise recollections of those conversations. The one thing I can remember clearly is that von Verschuer protested vigorously against the reproach made by Nachtsheim, that the Dahlem institute had arranged for the eyes of Gypsies who had been murdered in Auschwitz to be sent in, so that research on hereditary cataracts* could be pursued. Nachtsheim considered von Verschuer an opportunist, pure and simple. We had many discussions about this (naturally we did not include von Verschuer), and this characterization always seemed a somewhat one-sided rationalization to me. I don't believe that he was a calculating opportunist."

"Did you know about the extermination of the Jews in the East and about euthanasia in Germany?" I ask. "My father knew about the destruction of 'lives unworthy to be lived'. We had neighbours whose son perished in this way." "Did your father ever tell you that he participated in an advisory role in the formulation of a law on euthanasia between 1939 and 1941?" (see p. 43). "No, I don't know anything about that." "And about the extermination of the Jews?" "We only knew about isolated cases of killing Jews in the East. That is to say, neither the whole truth nor the whole extent. That was all kept secret. Do you know of any public references to the mass exterminations?" "Rosenberg informed representatives of the

* Actually eye colour (see p. 77).

German press at a reception on 18 November 1941 that the final solution had started. He ordered them not to write about it in detail, but to use certain specific stock phrases to refer to the mass extermination of the Jews. 'Definite solution' or 'total solution of the Jewish question' were terms which could be mentioned in this context. So that must be why von Verschuer used the term 'total solution of the Jewish question' in his textbook." "No one could be expected to understand these hints; they were ambiguous," says Lenz. "That's true, if one closed one's eyes and ears, but even ordinary people knew about the murders committed by the Einsatzgruppen," I say. "That reminds me of Nietzsche, "I did not do that, says my memory. I could not have done that says my pride. Finally, memory gives in"," says Lenz. (Back at home, I discover that his memory had altered the quotation. It goes: "I did do that, says my memory. I could not have done that, says my pride, and remains adamant. Finally, memory gives in.")

Lenz continues, "Old Ploetz went one day to see Frick in Berlin. He protested against the killing of the Jews in the East, which he had heard about, and gave his party card back. That wasn't race-hygiene as he had conceived it." "But he must have visited Frick before the time of the final solution," I say. "Ploetz died in 1940."*

The conversation turns to the early years of National Socialism. "During its first years, the Nazi Party was an anti-capitalist, anti-individualist, unliberal party. It was extremist in its demands. Its basic thesis was "the common good takes precedence over the individual good." The most important point of its programme was "breaking the chains of bondage to vested interests."" "You are forgetting anti-Semitism, which was expressed in the Party programme in 1921,"† I say. "I didn't remember that." He continues: "Certainly, Hitler read Chamberlain, but he also read Baur-Fischer-Lenz.[37] My father never corresponded with Hitler, nor did he ever talk to him. He learnt from Hanfstaengl, or from someone in the Lehmann publishing house, that Hitler had read his book during the time when he was imprisoned in Landsberg. For example, there is that long passage about syphilis in it. That was one of my father's obsessions too."

---

* A file-card indicating that Ploetz was a member of the Nazi Party has been preserved in the Berlin Document Center, but nothing more.

† Point 4 of that programme stated, "Only our fellow countrymen can be citizens. Only those of German blood can be fellow countrymen, without regard to creed. Therefore no Jew can be a fellow countryman."

"Ploetz met Hitler in the twenties. I don't know what they talked about at all. But my father told me that Hitler had become annoyed on that occasion, and had said that professors and intellectuals understood nothing of what was going on, and that he could not depend on them. They were both obstinate men. The hope that everything could be solved by a theoretical analysis was widespread at the turn of the century. Just think of Marx, or Freud. They set too high a value on their theoretical solutions. Just as Hitler set too high a value on this racial business. But people believed in it. That's why the Nazi leaders' ideas about race became more and more muddled. For example, Ley wrote somewhere or other, "The Jew isn't of any race, but is rather the antipode of all races. Because of continuous miscegenation and incest among this bastard people, the molecules and atoms that are components of their blood have been split up, and can now only fashion fragmentary remnants of their previous form and nature.""

"In your memory, how do you picture your father as a scientist?" I ask. "My father was entirely a theoretician and, as such, was a mixture of the scientist guided by knowledge and the unworldly Utopian. However, he thought of himself as a pragmatist, in the sense of English and American pragmatism, to which he liked to refer. Thus, he saw himself as an adherent of a theory of values which holds that the practical consequences of an action are more important than the correct opinions, or, rather than commitment to particular opinions. He liked to quote the English advocate of pragmatism, F. C. S. Schiller, and his book *Cassandra, or the Future of the British Empire*. He shared Schiller's pessimism and also his illusion that eugenics could protect us from decline and ruin. Making a distinction between himself and two of his colleagues, he once said: "Astel's father was a policeman, and Astel will arrange everything according to orders and regulations. Stengel-Rutkowski's father was a pastor, and Stengel-Rutkowski will work by means of homilies and by faith. My father was a farmer and I am more in favour of letting things grow!" He believed, like so many others, that the race was going to rack and ruin, and that the National Socialists were the ones who could stem the tide."

I ask about his father's views on the law on the restoration of the professional civil service. "When was that?" "April 1933," I say. "We didn't ever speak about it. That wasn't an important programme from his point of view. Please don't make a moral issue out of it." "But, all the same, the expulsion of the Jews from German universities and research establishments was an act of some significance," I say. "I wish that I could give you a clearer answer, but I was fourteen years old at the time, and all this happened fifty years ago. In any case, I can't remember that my father ever discussed the law in favourable terms and I do remember that he was perplexed and saddened by every injustice and by the individual suffering which resulted from it. It's true to say, and we can't spare him this reproach, just as we can't spare many others, that he didn't feel that he shared any responsibility for the law, and that he didn't foresee all the developments to which it would later lead."

I ask about his father's attitude towards Jewry and anti-Semitism. "He had nothing against the Jews. He wasn't an anti-Semite. Anti-Semitism resulted from an exaggerated form of nationalism which was widespread at the time, and which we can no longer understand today. But still, we do see similar things today. The present legal situation of the Palestinians is comparable to that of Jews in the Germany of 1933. I am, of course, expressly excluding later developments in Germany from this comparison." "Was your father a member of the Nazi Party?" I ask. "At one time, around 1937, Gütt pressed my father to join the Party. My father didn't want to join. But he was sharply attacked from various quarters. He received a very rude letter from Himmler, because he had spoken against encouraging the birth of illegitimate children. "You professors will never understand what this is all about," Himmler wrote."

Then we began to talk about Fischer. Lenz says: "His fame is based on his book about Rehoboth.[167] In it, he didn't prove Mendelism. In a population like that, it wasn't actually possible to do so. At a time when anthropologists in general understood nothing of genetics, he believed that he understood something of the subject." I ask why none of his colleagues had pointed out later that Fischer hadn't demonstrated Mendelism. "People probably thought," says Lenz, "that he was basically right, even though he didn't demonstrate the details. It was a curious claim to fame. In the introduction, he writes that it's a work of the most infinite significance. Infinite was not big enough for him! And then the cruelty of it. He was actually a mild-mannered and timid man. In his book he writes, however, that the Hottentots and the racially mixed population of German South-West Africa should only be allowed to live as long as they were doing useful work." "Later, that became the concept on which Auschwitz was based," I interject. "The theories of Social Darwinism were widespread at the time," Lenz continues. "In American history books, too, the prevailing view was that God and evolution exist so that the better individuals should prevail because of their greater commitment to democracy and justice, while the inferior should go under."

"Fischer did one thing which was scientifically very wrong, and, from the layman's point of view, grotesque and laughable. You know that Himmler considered himself to be the reincarnation of Henry the Lion. The bones of Henry the Lion were disinterred, and Fischer was to write an expert report about them. But the skeleton showed a dislocation of the hip. And they couldn't possibly admit that Henry the Lion had suffered from any hereditary disability. So, Fischer invoked an honourable hunting accident (see p. 93). Subsequently, the matter was investigated further. It was incontestably a congenital dislocation of the hip, which, at that time, was widely regarded as a hereditary malformation. And, do you know the best part of the story? It was actually the skeleton of a woman. Of course, after all the propaganda surrounding the affair, this couldn't be revealed. Fischer couldn't have failed to have realized the real truth of the matter."

Finally, the conversation comes round to the KWI of Anthropology in Berlin-Dahlem, directed first by Fischer and then by von Verschuer. "Not much came out of the Berlin institute," says Lenz. "Their research methods weren't up to date."

I ask how history will view the guilt of Fischer, Lenz, and von Verschuer. "Your question about guilt is phrased in such an all-embracing manner that it can't be answered with a simple yes or no. Guilt for what? Guilt on account of what pronouncements, what actions, what silences, what omissions? After the fact that these dreadful events had taken place had been revealed, I believe that everyone was obliged to ask himself whether and how he had been an accomplice. Basically, everyone can only answer such a question of personal conscience for himself. A person standing on the outside to whom this whole period and the individuals involved aren't known through personal experience should be very careful how he judges it. I know that my father, like myself, felt a sense of complicity and suffered from it, even if he claimed otherwise. But, all the same, your question about guilt seems to me to be somewhat different from an attempt to understand this whole development from the historical point of view. To do this, I believe, we should start from what Fischer, Lenz, and von Verschuer knew about, and what they understood of these scientific, biological, and political questions, as well as from what they held to be desirable, given that they were children of their culture, their time, and their class. It seems clear, to me at least, that in many cases, our present perceptions of malicious intentions are simply based on a faulty understanding of the reality of situations where intentions had, in fact, been basically good. I have never been able to recognize, in what these three men said or wrote, any path which might lead towards the hate, fanaticism, and sadism which made Auschwitz possible. As far as I can see, those responsible for Auschwitz never called on any of these three men to provide a justification of their brutality. Rather, they looked for models, or supposed models, in quite a different direction, where, in those years, the preaching of implacable antagonism, hate, and a fight to the death against opponents was the norm."

"I am sure that you would have arrived at a fairer assessment of my father if you had known him personally and hadn't just looked through his published views for whatever can be used against him. Since the end of the war, I, at least, have spoken about my father with many people who knew him, and who often distanced themselves in a critical fashion from his prejudices and his system of values, but I haven't ever encountered any view of him which resembles yours. Of course, I won't deny you the right to appear as a prosecutor and a preacher dedicated to a cause. Every man is subject to the moral judgements of others, especially when his views or actions involve the public. There must be prosecutors and advocates, but prosecutors are, by the very nature of their tasks, one-sided. You're performing a very important function in society, but you shouldn't set yourself up as a judge or a historian. When a prosecutor usurps the power of a judge, justice must suffer."

Dr Helmut von Verschuer, *the son of Professor Otmar von Verschuer*

He lives in Brussels in a beautiful detached house, and works as an official of the European Economic Community. A sporting type, fifty-six years old.

"I've been told," I begin the conversation, "that your father was a very religious man." "Yes, that's true," he says. "As soon as they arrived in Frankfurt in 1935, my parents started looking for a congregation which they could join. They rejected the local congregation of Dornbusch which was led by a minister of the German Christian Church (see p. 118). By chance, they met Otto Fricke, Pastor of the Confessional Church, which was already under surveillance at that time. A close friendship developed between them and the Frickes. My father always made excuses for me when the Jungvolk* met on Sundays, because we were attending the church service. Catholics, who have masses in the early morning and in the evening, didn't have this problem. After our move to Berlin-Dahlem in 1942, my father joined Niemöller's congregation. Niemöller himself was in prison at the time. There, we often met Adam von Trott zu Solz. Sometimes he also visited our house in Dahlem. I cherished a great admiration for this much older cousin of mine. No one suspected his involvement in the resistance movement. For the rest, I took part in the activities of the youth circle of the congregation, which were led by Pastor Mochalsky and which were formally prohibited."

"What was your father's position on anti-Semitism?" I ask. "At home, there wasn't ever a trace of any such thing. We never spoke about Jews. When I was at our family house in Solz as an eight- or nine-year-old, a soldier, belonging to a tank corps on manoeuvres, gave me some money and asked me to fetch cigarettes for him. I went to the store where we always did our shopping, which belonged to a certain Isidor Katz. When I came back with the cigarettes, the soldier said: "My boy, you shouldn't buy things in Jewish shops." I didn't know what Jews were, and I asked my parents. Later on, it became clear to me that the so-called Jewish question had something to do with my father's scientific field. But I don't remember my father making any anti-Semitic remarks in our house."

"How about your father's party membership?" I ask. "I have a recol-

---

* The junior section of the Hitlerjugend, the Hitler Youth.

lection that, when we lived in Frankfurt, my father had to decide whether to be drawn into the Party, together with the other members of an organization to which he belonged, or to resign. Obviously, he didn't do the latter. After that, there weren't any more talks in our family circle about his party membership. I also don't remember him wearing the party badge." "Did he ever tell you of his leading role in the student Freikorps in Marburg and of the workers they shot while they were 'trying to escape' from the custody of that corps?" "No, he didn't. He occasionally spoke of von Selchow's* importance as an historian."

"My father often said: "Render unto Caesar the things which are Caesars, and unto God the things which are God's." That was one of his precepts. Under the influence of Adam von Trott's participation in the events of 20 July 1944,[†] I refused to take part in a demonstration of loyalty to the Führer in our village, Solz. My father didn't show any understanding for this attitude, steeped as he was in the Prussian-Protestant tradition of loyalty to authority, and condemning, as he did, political assassination. In addition, an attempt to overthrow the regime seemed irresponsible to him at a time when the country was at war."

"My father favoured a strict separation between 'pure' science and politics. That was also one of his precepts. He selected his co-workers on the basis of their professional qualifications, and not their political ideas. Some of his co-workers were active party members, others not. I remember a Jewish assistant, Dr Kahle,[‡] in Frankfurt, who was able to emigrate to

---

* Von Selchow, a former army officer, headed a student Freikorps [a right-wing-paramilitary unit] at the University of Marburg which supported an attempt to overthrow the German government in March 1920, the Kapp Putsch. After this failed, they arrested some workers and killed fifteen of them, alleging that they were trying to escape. Von Verschuer was the right-hand-man of von Selchow, who took responsibility for the killings. The murders were brought to trial, but all the students involved were acquitted.

† An attempt, which nearly succeeded, to kill Hitler with a bomb which Count Claus von Stauffenberg placed under the table during a conference at Hitler's war headquarters in East Prussia. The rebellion was put down: von Stauffenberg, von Trott zu Solz, Erwin Planck (the son of Max Planck), and many others were executed.

‡ This is in fact Dr O. H. Kahler whom I later met. He had a Jewish great-grandmother. He served as an army doctor on the Russian front during the war. He showed me the affidavit which he had written on behalf of Professor von Verschuer after the war. In it he affirmed that von Verschuer had never been a Nazi. Dr Kahler told me that he had heard from a reliable source that Mengele and Professor von Verschuer had met after the war. Mengele had asked his teacher whether he should kill himself; Professor von Verschuer had refused to advise him.

America in time. My father maintained friendly contacts with Muckermann, who, early on, was forbidden to go on working. I remember many
visits to him in our Berlin days, right up to 1935. We children were taken
along, and it was always an enjoyable outing."

I ask about the expert report written by his father in Frankfurt in a
race-dishonour trial (see p. 38). "Perhaps a co-worker wrote it," he says. I
answer: "But not the letter to the Minister of Justice." "Perhaps not, I did-
n't know about this incident before. To my knowledge, my father helped
some Jews with his expert reports. After the war, he once mentioned that
he had received a letter of thanks from America." I say: "But Mengele wrote
that expert report and most of the others. It was he who was thanked for
the "lenient expert report"." "My father didn't ever speak in more detail
about this matter at home in the presence of his children."

"Do you remember Mengele?" I ask. "Of course. Above all, from our
time in Frankfurt. I remember him as a friendly man. In the institute, he
was called "Papa Mengele" by the ladies on account of his kindliness. Like
the other assistants, he sometimes used to come to tea in our house with
his young family. I don't recollect any meetings in Berlin. But, in any case,
I was often away from home at that time. My mother told me that when
Mengele was asked during a meal in Berlin whether what he had to do was
hard, he answered: "It's dreadful. I can't talk about it." I wonder myself
whether he didn't deliberately keep my father in the dark about the context and background of Auschwitz, so that he could continue his scientific
collaboration with him."

"The fact that your father destroyed his correspondence with Mengele
indicates that he wasn't totally in the dark. Did he ever talk to you about
that?" I ask. "No. During his time in Münster, I heard about the slanders
spread by Nachtsheim and Gottschaldt. But my father thought it best not
to respond. He maintained silence about everything which he thought to
be slander. He was disappointed that Nachtsheim, whom he had housed
along with his whole family in his official residence in Dahlem, when they
were bombed out, and Gottschaldt, who found temporary shelter, together with other co-workers and with material from the institute, in our home
village in Hesse, had attacked him in this way."

"Your father considered these attacks by Gottschaldt and Nachtsheim
to be slanders," I say. "But these attacks by his former colleagues seem to
me to have been based, in large part, on a correct interpretation of the
facts. For example, Mengele sent the eyes of individuals whom he had

killed in Auschwitz to the institute. Your father applied to the DFG for a grant for his collaboration with Mengele. When you speak of slander, I understand you to be quoting your father rather than expressing your own opinion based on the facts. But I agree that there is no doubt that your father was rather roughly attacked." "You're right in so far that I can't really form my own opinion about this matter, since these events weren't known to me at the time and weren't explained to me later by my father. I only know from my own experience that the motives which underlie past events are on occasion very difficult to fathom, and that even the opinions of those who were present at the time of the events aren't necessarily reliable. Do you know the story of the attempted theft of the institute's material in Frankfurt? One day, two lorries arrived with an authorization to take away the material. At that time, it was stored in a shed in Rajewsky's institute. The caretaker showed great presence of mind, and first talked to Rajewsky about it. It turned out that the order came from East Berlin. So the drivers had to turn around and leave without accomplishing their mission."

"Was this before the article in *Die Neue Zeitung?*"* I ask. "I think so." "Why didn't your father write any account of his life, any memoirs, after the war?" I ask. "I think that a public admission on his part of his culpable involvement in the events of the time would have been helpful, and would have relieved him from a great burden. But he couldn't bring himself to do it despite much urging on the part of Trott's relatives. Nachtsheim's attacks probably made things even more difficult for him. In addition, he was convinced of his own scientific integrity. His talk to the Prussian Academy of Sciences in 1943, "The foundations of heredity as destiny and duty", appeared to be a relatively courageous one for the time. The review of his activities by Professors Adolf Butenandt, Max Hartmann, Wolfgang Heubner, and Boris Rajewsky in 1949 bears witness to many diverse facets of his personality (see p. 90). Were people aware of the inevitable ambiguity of every action of persons in positions such as his? And are we any more aware of it today?"

---

* An article appeared in *Die Neue Zeitung*, the daily newspaper of the American occupied zone, on 3 May 1946, accusing Professor von Verschuer of obtaining eyes and blood samples from prisoners in Auschwitz, with the collaboration of Dr Mengele.

Professor Edith Zerbin-Rüdin, *the daughter of Professor Ernst Rüdin*

Mrs Zerbin-Rüdin is a psychiatrist, just as her father was. And just as he did, she is investigating the inheritance of schizophrenia. She took the opportunity afforded by a psychiatry congress in Bonn, and an associated visit to relatives in Cologne, to come to talk to me in the Institute of Genetics in Cologne, where I work. She is already sitting in my office when I arrive. She had come an hour too early due to a misunderstanding. I had been unwell at home with a temperature, and first I must speak to some students. To fill the time, I give her the manuscript to read. When I return, I say to her that she will probably have discovered my critical attitude from reading the manuscript, and I begin my questions. "How old were you in 1933?" "Twelve. In 1945, when I finished my studies at medical school, I was twenty-four years old." I ask about sterilization. "My father was convinced of the importance of sterilization. There was an international eugenics movement at the time. He never took his duties in the appeal court which dealt with hereditary health and sterilization lightly. When a patient claimed, as a prosecution witness in the proceedings against my father before the Denazification Tribunal that he had been unjustly sterilized, it was an embarrassment to the members of the Tribunal, so feeble-minded was he." I raise objections concerning the propriety of the legal procedures for sterilization. "Yes," she says, "when my step-mother, who was a teacher, saw the questions to be answered on the forms, she also said: "Mere school-test questions which don't test intelligence." My father, for example, had one person who answered: "A herring without a head" to the question: "Who was Bismarck?"* Quite clever, considering his condition. But the questions were altered later." "Did your father have any second thoughts about sterilization later on?" I ask. "He was always in favour of sterilizing those with hereditary defects; he was never in favour of sterilizing others, like psychopaths, for example." "He supported the legalization of such sterilizations many times," I say. "That can't be true," she says. "In addition, he wasn't in favour of sterilizing homosexuals." "That I can corroborate," I say. "He only wanted to punish homosexuals when they assaulted minors," she says, and continues "He wanted persons who had been sterilized to be allowed to marry and to choose their marriage part-

---

* Bismarck herring is sold without the head.

ners freely. In so far as Jews and Gypsies were concerned, he hoped that all that would come to an end, once the war was over. The only alternative to full collaboration which he could see was emigration. But he decided against that because, as he said to the Denazification Tribunal: "Emigration would have been desertion." That's the way he saw it." "And his vehement article in favour of the racial measures of National Socialism?" I ask. "Around the end of 1942, or the beginning of 1943, he wrote it as a neutral statement at first, then he rewrote it. It was like that in those days. What should he have done? He would have sold himself to the devil, in order to obtain money for his institute and his research."

I ask: "What did he have to give to Heydrich, to get 30 000 Reichsmarks from him?" "I don't know anything about that." I tell her that a former co-worker of Rüdin, Theo Lang, had told the British Secret Service, while the war was still going on, that Rüdin was involved in a project on mass sterilization by X-rays. "That's not right. Lang is not a good witness. He was a member of the Party early on. Then he left. However, he maintained his contacts in the inner circles of the party. Because of this, he got money to continue his researches on goitre in Switzerland, even during the war. He attacked my father very unjustly. During the time of the Third Reich, Lang threatened to denounce him in *Das Schwarze Korps*, and then, after 1945, he denounced him as a Nazi. The least harmful accusation was that my father had misappropriated funds given to him for official expenses. The fact is that my father paid for all that out of his own pocket. After the war, Lang was the director of a mental hospital. But he didn't do well there. There was an epidemic of tuberculosis, and he was dismissed. He then had a practice in Munich but he couldn't make a go of that either." She smiles faintly. "Then he committed suicide. Not a good witness."*

"Did your father know about euthanasia?" I ask. "My father protested to Dr Linden that he was not asked and not informed. Dr Linden replied that his attitude towards the question of euthanasia was known, and that they had not wanted to involve him in the programme. I looked for the letters, with my father's secretary, before the Denazification Tribunal proceedings." I ask: "Were your father's papers preserved?" "No. They were

---

* On 20 January 1941, Dr Theo Lang called on Dr M. H. Göring, the cousin of Reichsmarschall Göring, at the German Institute of Psychotherapy in a courageous, but unsuccessful, attempt to persuade him to sign a petition against the killing of mental patients in the euthanasia programme.[130b]

stored in various places and, because of this, some of them were lost. Those which stayed in the institute were soaked because of a burst pipe. It was there that we found the letter from Dr Linden in which my father was first informed of the euthanasia programme in September 1940. In the end, my father was classified by the Denazification Tribunal as a fellow-traveller*."

"He spoke of murder to Luxenburger. He also told him that he intended to get a motion adopted against euthanasia at the next congress of the Society of Neurology and Psychiatry. But there wasn't another congress before the end of the war." "That's true," I say, "but there is no public or written evidence that he ever made a protest. I find it difficult to believe that your father put up any firm opposition to euthanasia. In the autumn of 1941, he wrote to Nitsche[223] that he found the film *I accuse* "moving"†. He named a colleague who wanted to mobilize the Society of German Neurologists and Psychiatrists against the film, and said: "I myself am naturally against such an attempt."" I tell her about the draft of the law which was to regulate the killing of mental patients and I quote the proposed formulations for various parts of the law, including that by Professor Lenz suggesting killing "by medical means of which the patient remains unaware . . . ,"[50b] (I forgot to mention her father's name on a memorandum advocating covert euthanasia.[58]) "But that just wasn't so," she says, "that was the terrible thing about it. Römer told my father that a review commission had come to his hospital in Illenau, and that the patients clung to the nurses as they were taken away. They knew very well what was going on."

"Was your father an anti-Semite?" "No, not at all. My best girl-friend was half-Jewish. My father even tried to keep Kallmann." "But he wasn't even employed in your father's institute?" "Yes, that's so, but he was working there as a visiting scientist. When Kallmann wasn't allowed to give a lecture in Dresden in 1935, my father let Bruno Schulz give it. Kallmann

---

* The Denazification Tribunal classified those who appeared before it into five categories war criminals; major offenders; activists, militarists and profiteers; fellow-travellers; non-offenders.

† The film "*I accuse* [Ich klage an]" was made in 1940. It advocated euthanasia. In it, the wife of a professor of medicine is suffering from disseminated sclerosis. She asks her husband to kill her, and he does so. The film portrays the professor as a hero. Many in the medical world thought the example of disseminated sclerosis badly chosen and disapproved of the film.

did much to exonerate my father before the Denazification Tribunal. As you know, Kallmann continued his research on the inheritance of schizophrenia in the USA."

"Was your father a National Socialist?" "No, certainly not. He only joined the party in 1937 under the pressure of the conditions prevailing at that time. He was denounced twice. Once, because in his institute "Good day", and not "Heil Hitler!", was used as a greeting. But that passed off without trouble. A denunciation by one of his assistants, Dr Riedel, who was an SS-doctor—he is now in Düsseldorf; he had no problems after the war—was worse. He said that my father was spreading defeatist propaganda. That was really much worse. There were three groups within the institute, first the SS, Dr Riedel and Miss X, then the harmless individuals, like Stumpfl, Harrasser, and Thums, and finally those disposed to be critical of the Nazis, like Schulz and Miss Juda—she passed the Aryan descent test despite her name."

"Did you speak about sterilization, euthanasia, and the final solution at home after the war?" I ask. "Only a little. There weren't many opportunities in any case, because of my father's frequent absences on account of internment and illness. We had our own problems. For example, the entire family of some friends of mine, father, mother, children, had been murdered by the Russians in Königsberg. Both sides committed wrongs."

"Did your father ever consider writing an autobiography?" "No. He was far too modest. For example, he didn't want any ceremonies on the occasion of his sixtieth or seventieth birthdays.* Only his own assistants made speeches, no one from outside. But as is the custom at festivities, a laurel bush was placed next to the speakers. He was a scientist, not a politician. Politics is a dirty game. Then just as now."

---

* On the occasion of his sixty-fifth birthday, 19 April 1939, Professor Rüdin was awarded the Goethe medal for art and science by the Führer himself, and was honoured by a telegram from the Reich Minister of the Interior, Dr Wilhelm Frick: "To the indefatigable champion of racial hygiene and meritorious pioneer of the racial-hygienic measures of the Third Reich, I send my heartiest congratulations."[224]

Mrs Susanne Lüdicke, *Professor Fischer's medical technician, and Dr Lore von Kries*

Visit to Mrs Lüdicke in the home for retired gentlewomen near Göttingen. A high-rise apartment block in a village. A room with a view over the forest. The leaves stir, but she doesn't see them any more. She is almost blind and very deaf. Dr Lore von Kries, who obtained her doctorate in March 1933 in Fischer's institute, is also present.

Mrs Lüdicke begins her story: "I became Professor Fischer's medical technician in 1918, 'a maid of all work'. First in Freiburg, when he was still in the old anatomical institute, and then in the new building. After that I went with him to Berlin in 1927 to the KWI of Anthropology, Human Heredity, and Eugenics. I was able to take part in building up the institute. It was a big and harmonious community. We never spoke about politics. Professor Fischer took good care of his people. Once, he sent me to Merano when I was completely exhausted by overwork. The caretaker in the KWI of Botany was the person who had to make out a certificate of political reliability. I got it immediately; it was that simple."

"Was there any anti-Semitism?" I ask. "No, no. There was only one Nazi in the whole institute," says Mrs von Kries. "Neese, who came to the institute in his SA uniform. But, one day, he fell from a window on the fourth floor of the Gestapo headquarters building in the Prinz-Albrecht-strasse. He was mixed up in some corruption scandal." "When was that?" I ask. "I don't remember any more exactly when it was," says Mrs von Kries.

I ask again about politics and anti-Semitism. "Naturally, we went to the May-day demonstrations, but we went as a big family. That didn't have anything to do with politics," Mrs Lüdicke says. Mrs von Kries supplements her account. "I didn't take part with the institute in the May-day demonstration in 1933. No pressure was put on me to go. Nor was I forced to join the Party or the National Socialist Women's Organization. I was neither a member of the Party nor did I belong to any of its organizations. No one in the institute used "Heil Hitler!" as a greeting. That was so at least as long as I was in the institute, that's to say until the spring of 1933 when I left. Once, I brought a Jewish friend, who was Thannhauser's assistant, to the institute, and introduced him to Fischer. No, there wasn't any anti-Semitism in the institute. Fischer stayed with my parents when he went to Dortmund to give a lecture; my father was Professor of Gynaecology there. Fischer wasn't an anti-Semite. We would have noticed if he had been."

I mention the Nuremberg laws, which had Fischer's approval, and say: "But by then, if not before, people must have known what was going on." "No, people only understood the Nuremberg laws after 1945," answers Mrs von Kries, and continues: "It would be a lie if I didn't admit that I, too, was swept along with the tide at that time. My relationship with Thannhauser's assistant ended then. But not because of the Nuremberg laws. We still write to each other today. I got a letter from him only last Christmas. He lives in England now. Even the most stupid person could see that, after Stalingrad, the war couldn't be won any more."

I tell them that Fischer accepted a chairmanship at the International Anti-Jewish Congress in Cracow. "And you say that he wasn't an anti-Semite. But that can't be right." Mrs Lüdicke smiles: "Every man has his secrets." Then she becomes serious: "That was 1944. Fischer was a broken man. His son had died of a severe wound while he was being taken to Freiburg." "Did you write expert reports at that time?" I ask Mrs Lüdicke. "I helped," she says. "Were the expert reports always correct, or was there a bit of cheating?" "No, no, they were always meticulously correct. Fischer said again and again that we must make them meticulously correct because people's lives depended on them. No, there was never anything falsified in them." "What did you do after the war?" I ask Mrs Lüdicke. "I was a technician with Professor Spatz in Giessen." "Did you know Hallervorden?" "Yes, a small, cheerful man." "What did you do after the war?" I ask Mrs von Kries. "I was Professor Lenz's secretary in Göttingen from 1950. He wrote expert reports in paternity cases, and published on problems connected with that subject." "It's strange that he never wrote about the past," I say. "Did you ever ask him about it?" "I?" she says. "That would have been like asking the Himalayas."

Professor Wolfgang Abel

Mondsee.* He picks me up in a restaurant. A hale and hearty old man in long leather trousers, heavy clothes and a fur cap. He drives me in his car along the Mondsee. The snow lies deep on the ground. I tell him about my scientific career. "Dear God, how beautiful it is here," I say. "Humboldt† called this region one of the three most beautiful in the world," he says. "And what were the other two?" I ask. "Rio and Istanbul," he says. We are driving along the lake right by the water's edge. In front of us there is a little spit of land. He turns into a side-road covered with snow and ice. "This is where my, our, kingdom begins." He drives at great speed along the steep, narrow road, or, rather, path, through a wood. Then the path becomes less steep, and leads through meadows until we stop in front of two rustic houses. A sheepdog welcomes us. Professor Abel leads me into the house. The dog comes with us, even though ordered to stay outside. "He protects the wife," he says. We go inside up some steep wooden steps. There are beautiful paintings everywhere, landscapes, animals, flowers. The living-room, on the first floor, is in rustic style with old carpets. Fine old furniture. Rows of old books, Goethe's amongst them. He sits on a sofa covered with carpets. I sit in an easy chair. His wife brings coffee and cakes.

He begins to talk. "I wanted to become a painter. My father forbade it. My mother advised me to study medicine. So, I studied medicine, biology, and painting, in Vienna. My special interest in zoology was kindled by observing animals as a painter, the way their musculature changes and adapts with alterations in their mode of life. I chose this as the subject of my doctoral dissertation, with Professor Versluys, a zoologist. Whilst I was salvaging the skeletons after a fire in the Institute of Zoology, I acquired an intimate knowledge of each individual bone. That was how I came to accept a position as a demonstrator with Professor Weniger, an anthropologist, in order to classify his zoological collection and display it. In this job, I also classified the collection of skeletons of individuals of mixed Hottentot, Bushman and Negro ancestry, which Dr R. Pöch had brought to Vienna from South Africa. While doing this, I realized that jaw-size and tooth-size were inherited independently, so that the big teeth of Negroes could be found in the small jaws of Bushmen, and the small teeth of Hottentots

---

* A lake in Austria, near Salzburg.
† Baron Friedrich Heinrich Alexander von Humboldt (1769–1859), a German naturalist and traveller.

in the large jaws of Negroes. This discovery was easy to corroborate because of the very different forms of these various teeth and jaws, even though many people doubted that it was true. (In 1939, it was intended to send an expedition to Africa to check the facts, but nothing came of it.) This genetical work attracted the attention of E. Fischer, who had himself, in 1908, worked on the 'bastards of Rehoboth'.[167] He wanted to work on genetical associations in Man and this led to my moving from Vienna to Berlin, in 1931, to work with Fischer in his institute. There, I was looking above all at the inheritance of facial and cranial shape in hundreds of families and twin-pairs, and also at the inheritance of fingerprint patterns."

"When Fischer gave a lecture in the Harnack House on "Race and Mind" on 30 January 1933,* the same day that Hitler seized power, and in it stressed the intellectual qualities of the Jews, all hell broke loose in the institute next day. You should read the *Völkischer Beobachter* of 31 January and 1 February. Probably no one has told you about this. Professor Rüdin of Munich came to our institute soon afterwards and said to us assistants, G. Brandt and myself: "Well, your chief is a goner now." He was wrong. Fischer was elected Rector of the University of Berlin. There were still many liberals in the university."

"G. Brandt wanted to know after Hitler's seizure of power what H. F. K. Günther would say about this change of course. A few days later, he came back with Günther's answer. "If I could, I would buy up all my books and have them pulped." During all that followed, Günther refused any official posts and asked for no favours for himself. This was a time of turmoil and denunciation. I was denounced myself, as being friendly to the Jews, because I had a book by the well-known Professor Weidenreich, who was a Jew and one of my father's friends, lying on my desk. I was denounced three times, but, each time, my friend, G. Brandt, managed to calm things down. He urged me to keep my mouth shut. Other similar denunciations came from Rüdin's institute in Munich; they said that I had Jewish ancestry."

"Fischer was asked to write an article about the German people, and he passed this task on to me. I used the old investigations of Virchow on skin, hair, and eye colour of schoolchildren from the whole of Europe as a basis for the determination of the distribution and frequency of Germanic hereditary elements. At that time, these frequencies had been deter-

* The lecture was given on 1 February 1933 and had a different title (see p. 84).

mined in Germany, Holland, Poland, Belgium, Austria, and in some parts of Italy. For example, on the basis of allelic determination and the dominance of dark pigment in the eyes and hair, a frequency of 18 per cent for hereditary elements for fairness had been found in Sicily, and, of course, much higher frequencies in West and North Europe. My intention was to put an end to what might be called the 'racial conflict' which went on in Germany after 1933. This conflict even reached the schools, where teachers classified children according to the ideas of H. F. K. Günther, and this led to serious problems for the children. I have always rejected such classifications, and stressed other traits as being important, so as to prevent the development of inferiority complexes, especially in children. However that may be, the publication of the article led to the editor of the journal being visited by an officer who said: "If you allow Abel to write another word in your journal again, you will be dismissed as editor." Since that time, I have only published specialized articles. I even refused a splendid offer from the Springer publishing house to write a textbook of anthropology."

"You also worked as an expert on cases which were sent to the institute from the Reich Kinship Bureau. Could you tell me something about that?" I ask. "Before 1933, we had to provide expert reports in normal paternity cases, which E. Fischer mainly did himself. Because of the new legislation, the number of cases increased enormously after 1933, so that Fischer involved me in this activity, and, later, I took over most of it. Neither Fischer nor I wanted to write these 'Jewish expert reports' and he offered several times to train people in the Reich Kinship Bureau to do it, but these offers were rejected. We had to go on. "How many?" you ask. About 800 expert reports. Fischer and I refused any payment. From the poorest of the poor, as he called them, we took no money, except for the costs of the paper and photographs involved, so as to cover ourselves with respect to the KWI. That was 20 marks, but often we charged nothing at all. The other institutes were often not so generous, and charged 700 marks or more. Thus, we were reproached for "unfair competition". We tried to help; we were able to do so because a chance incident had made things easier for us."

"I had a telephone call from a gentleman from the Kaiserhof,* who wanted to speak to me about an expert report. I was prepared to go to visit him, but he wanted to see me at the institute. At two o'clock, a big May-

* A luxury hotel in Berlin.

bach* drove up to the institute, and the gentleman spoke to me about an expert report which had turned out to be unfavourable. I fetched it and said: "Judge for yourself, his father, whom I am supposed to exclude, looks like his twin brother." He then said: "Well, well. We can still do something about that. You're a young man, and you'll want to make anthropological research trips abroad, isn't that right? I would be happy to help with the expenses." I showed him the door. The result was a telephone call from the Reich Kinship Bureau. "But, Abel, are you crazy? Do you know whom you threw out?" "No." "The president of the German paper industry, worth sixty million marks." As a result of that, a letter came from Bormann to Fischer, transmitted through the Reich Kinship Bureau, saying that we should be lenient in writing our expert reports (see p. 85)."

"Fischer discussed this with me, and we were in agreement that we would continue to write accurate expert reports according to scientific criteria, and that leniency was not a scientific concept. In addition, if we were to accept this demand, we would immediately become subject to blackmail. As a result of all this, I was considered to be incorruptible. I could turn that to good account, since I had become *the* expert in the field of human facial and cranial shape because of my genetic studies—just as the Norwegian, Dr Quelprud, in our institute was *the* expert on the inheritance of the shape of the ear. No one could check my decisions, and so it was not usual for other institutes to write expert reports on the same cases. We made ours, they made theirs. All the expert reports which came to us were about cases which couldn't be clarified by blood tests."

"How often was the legal father considered not to be the biological father?" I ask, in order to get an idea of the sort of expert reports, or, rather, revisions of destiny, which were written.

"That's not so easy to answer. When the earlier law was in effect, there were cases of sexual intercourse with two or more men, and there was really no possibility of throwing light on paternity for the mother and children through expert reports. In the majority of cases, legitimate children were involved, who were ostensibly conceived by another father, and then there were those expert reports where two or more possible fathers had to be considered. I had a case where the seventh possible father turned out to be the real one. I'll give you an example. An actress is in love with a medical student but, before she realizes that she is pregnant, she falls in love with a

* An expensive car comparable to a Rolls-Royce.

prosperous Jew, who is proud to have a child by her. She moves to another town, falls in love again, her fiancé is not supposed to know anything about the illegitimate daughter. The actress reveals the existence of this daughter to her fiancé's parents, who adopt the child before the wedding. Another example; a girl has sexual intercourse with two officers, long before 1933. The names of the men involved are known, but, of course, it's not known which is the father. One of them, a general, comes to see me; the other, who's abroad, is a Jew. The general says: "To get to the point, if he is my son I will shoot myself." "Not here, please." "I don't have any children. My wife wouldn't understand." "You should be happy, at the age of seventy, to acquire such a well-educated and capable son." "What does he look like?" I come back with the son, whom I have forewarned that the general is his father, and I say to the general: "Embrace your son." "

"One day, a Gauleiter arrives, escorted by an officer, and asks if I will provide an expert report on his wife. I agree to do it. Soon afterwards, the officer comes back and asks me to give an opinion on a photograph without any supporting documents. I refuse. He says: "I am ordering you to do this in the name of Himmler." "I refuse to give an opinion about single photographs, just as Fischer does. Against my better judgment and the dictates of my conscience, and constrained by an order, I am giving the following opinion: "This woman has no Jewish traits, and she probably originates from a region which is east of the line Vienna—Königsberg." The next day, the Gauleiter returns with his wife. I say to her: "I already know you. I have already written my expert report." He becomes pale and says: "I understand now for the first time why, before introducing her to the Führer, I had to send a photograph." "

"Then there was an eighteen-year-old girl whose father was a Jew and who was adopted as a baby. The documents needed for the girl's marriage were missing. What would you have done?"

"An expert report, which had been written in a positive sense,* came back into my memory after some years, when a second expert report was requested for the brother. The names of the parents were the same, but the photographs were of different people. Since all the photographs for all expert reports were kept, as was a photocopy of the first expert report, I only had the choice between denouncing myself and withdrawing the report."

---

* The decision was that the person concerned was not Jewish.

I repeat my question about the percentage of cases where the legal father was not considered to be the biological father. "How many expert reports were deliberately falsified?" He is silent. Then he says: "Fischer's words still ring in my ears today. "Abel, be careful." "

"I had an audience of about eight hundred twice a week at my first-year lecture course. Here, too, I tried to play down any conflict between classes or races using four photographs, collected for expert reports. My slides provided an opportunity for judging who was the correct father and who was falsely accused, and whether they were of Jewish or of other origin. Almost everyone who saw the photographs made incorrect assessments. It was a cause for great amusement when the wrong combinations were picked out. This exercise was planned to educate them to be careful in judging a man by his appearance."

"I worked on a whole series of other projects during those years, such as the influence of the environment on human beings, and I chose the Gypsies as a group to test. They were supposed to have first crossed the Bosphorus in 1400, and in 1480 they were already described as being in Scotland. I needed a trait which was genetically recognizable for my tests, and I chose fingerprint patterns. I received fingerprints from all over the world, from Filchner from Tibet, Wegener from Greenland, Gusinde from Tierra del Fuego, and of Pygmies and Bushmen from the Congo. Besides this, I paid students to do investigations for me in eastern Europe. My first wife's aunt, who was married to the founder of Shell, Job Kessler, helped with the money necessary for these trips and investigations. Thus, I travelled to Rumania in 1935 and to Scotland in 1938. I was invited, with the help of A. Haushofer, to the house of the British Ambassador. The Archbishop of Canterbury was also present, and I was able to explain the nature of my investigations."

"My father-in-law, a Dutchman, asked me to come to Vienna in 1938–39. Unbridled corruption was rampant, and everyone was becoming rich out of it. A friend told me that the best thing to do was to talk to Kaltenbrunner about it. Kaltenbrunner, whom I had known since student days, was upset over these blunders, and told me about cases where Gauleiters were involved. He couldn't do anything about it; perhaps I could in Berlin. Through contacts, I found Bormann's liaison man in the Labour Front. He told me: "I can't take all this in verbally. Give it to me in writing." I wrote it all down, seven pages of it, with my signature at the end. A month later, he was dead. A heart attack. You can imagine how I felt."

"From 1940, I was in the Luftwaffe and, after a foot injury, I was then transferred to the Army High Command organization for testing of staff. We had to inspect prisoner-of-war camps during the first winter of the Russian campaign. I went with two first lieutenants of the army psychological corps, and we found conditions which, in some places, were horrifying. There was a huge number of prisoners, and the early onset of winter had led to deficiencies in their care and, in some respects, awful conditions. The prisoners lay in the open without cover and without sufficient food, or, in some cases, without any food at all, even though potatoes and root vegetables lay frozen in the fields because of a lack of manpower to lift them. Only Hindenburg's son was trying to provide normal conditions. The commander of another camp, who had refused to run his camp without an adequate supply of food, was disciplined and punished. I said to the person responsible, in the presence of the two first lieutenants, that it was simply out of the question to behave in this way. He just said: "I will pretend not to have heard that. We are acting on orders from higher up." I saw such handsome men among them. I shall never forget a Russian officer in a camp near Königsberg where I was making an anthropological survey. I took a liking to him at first sight, but, understandably enough, his eyes showed only hatred."

"At about this time, I had to give a lecture in Munich. When I got off the night express there, I spoke to an SS-officer, who was walking in front of me and whom I took to be SS-Brigadier Mentzel from the Reich Ministry of Science. He said: "Don't you know me? I am Kaltenbrunner." We went together to a hotel, where he was able to get some rooms. I told him about the Russian prisoners of war, and that they were not sub-humans but, on the contrary, practically our brothers from our Indo-Germanic past. I told him what handsome men they were and that we must help them. He said: "I can't do anything. Only Himmler and Rosenberg are authorized to deal with that. Come and see me in Berlin. Unfortunately, I've been transferred there." I was to show him photographs there. He then said: "I am already in the gloomy shadow of my new job, but I had to accept it.""

"I tried to make contact with Rosenberg through Dr W. Gross. The excuse I used concerned a question of nature conservation at his property on the Mondsee which was next to mine. This ruse succeeded, and, among other things, I was able to show him the collection of photographs of Russian prisoners of war which I had prepared. His reaction was menacing and very cold. "I have my eyes on your beautiful property." He would not even tolerate a Ukrainian slave labourer on his estate. "As long as he is there, I won't go near the estate." "

"Then there came a telephone call from the director of Rosenberg's Ministry of the Occupied Eastern Territories, who was a count. "We should like you to give a lecture about the ethnic connections between Germany and the Russian people, or something of the sort." I said: "You don't want to hear what I want to say, and I won't say what you want to hear." I was then given an assurance that I would talk to a very restricted circle of a dozen or so. The lecture took place at the Political Academy in front of an invited audience of a hundred and sixty people. Lenz was there, and many others whom I knew, including my friend Haushofer. I told them, with the help of my photographs, about these fine handsome men, whom we could not treat as sub-humans. I also told them that biological pressures had for millennia been driving nations from the east to the west, and that a Thousand-Year-Reich would be impossible without living together with the Russians."

"But Wetzel was referring to this lecture when he quoted you, in his comments on the General Plan for the East, as having said that we must either exterminate the great majority of the Russians or Germanize them," I say.

"Well, yes, after the lecture, as we sat in a restaurant, Wetzel said to me: "The boss [Rosenberg] is not going to be pleased with what you said about the Thousand-Year-Reich. You won't stay a professor very long." I began to have misgivings thinking that I might have said too much, and I left the room to telephone Professor Lenz. I asked him: "Did I say too much?" Lenz said: "But you are right, what are you worried about? What you said was not bad at all." "

"For a time, I felt that I was on very thin ice, as they say, and then a telephone call came: "This is the RuSHA of the SS, the Brigadier wants to speak to you." "I heard that you gave a very interesting lecture. Can you give it again for our department? I haven't heard anything so sensible for a long time." I was relieved. Then, a telephone call came from Rosenberg's office that I should repeat my lecture in Prague and illustrate it with photographs. After the lecture, there was a heated discussion for an hour. A former student of mine, Hertl, working in Rosenberg's office, congratulated me during the journey home. He told me: "They wanted to finish you off in Prague." The plot miscarried."

"When I was released from the armed forces, I felt that I had to do something to cover myself, since, of course, the war was still going on. So I joined the SS. Sievers from the Research Foundation of the SS succeeded in having anthropological measurements of Russian prisoners of war sent to the KWI. Then the proposal came that prisoners in a concentration camp should work up the raw data. I put a stop to it, and said that there would be time for that after the war."

I ask once again about certificates of Jewish or Aryan ancestry given during the years after 1941. Instead of giving an answer about how many such certificates were provided, he said: "One day, Mayer from the Reich Kinship Bureau asked me to come to see him. He said that he had three hundred expert reports where the individuals concerned were wrongly classified (as Aryans, though he didn't use the word). He said that I should take responsibility for the these three hundred reports. I said that I already had too much work. Mayer said: "You must do it. You never make a mistake in your reports." Just think of it, to invalidate three hundred reports in 1942, when these people had been living free of problems for years. The very thought was absurd! So I said that I was prepared to take responsibility for two hundred as a first step. I received them and let them collect dust on my shelves."

"You ask about expert reports. There was one about a young soldier who wanted to become an officer. There was a suggestion that his father had been a pharmacist of the Jewish faith. At first sight, this seemed to be true and investigations of his parents, brothers, and sisters only confirmed the supposition. The mother, whom I saw alone, admitted the truth in a state of great alarm. It was difficult to help in this case because of the photographs. After a long time, I produced a positive report which was sent to the Reich Kinship Bureau. A short time later, he came back. "Professor, you were so kind to me that I want to speak frankly. A blood test, which had had to be done, came out negative, and excluded the man whom you had identified as my father." "You ill-fated young man, why didn't you tell me that it was going to be done?" In other instances, I had only provided reports when the blood tests were not informative. My report was rejected."

"As luck would have it, around this time, I often bought oil paints from a shop in Friedrichstrasse, near Prinz-Albrechtstrasse. At the court-yard gate of a house, I saw Kaltenbrunner getting into his car. I went past, but he picked me up: "Why don't you come and see me?" I replied: "Don't go to visit your prince, if you are not invited first." "Nonsense, come and see me next week." It was eighteen months after our meeting in Munich."

"At about the same time, Mayer, the Chief of the Reich Kinship Bureau, came to see me; he was dressed up as an SS-Colonel. He was rather arrogant: "Well, Abel, you've made a big mistake." "How?" "With the expert report about O.M." "Is that so? Well, to err is human." "As a punishment, you are going to prepare the two hundred reports I gave you eighteen months ago right now." I went out to my secretary, and I told her to come to see me in five minutes, and tell me not to forget to telephone Kaltenbrunner. "Which Kaltenbrunner?" Mayer asked. "Ernst, of course." "Don't make me laugh. You and Kaltenbrunner? Can I listen in?" "Please do." I got through, and made an appointment for Tuesday. Mr Mayer took his leave, and I heard nothing more about the two hundred expert reports. They all went back to the Reich Kinship Bureau shortly before the end of the war untouched."

"To protect my institute, I dictated to my secretary an application for a research grant for the study of sex-determination in cattle. As I was on the third sentence, there was a telephone call from Sievers of the Reich Ministry of Science. "I heard from Professor Sauerbruch about your successes in determining the sex of babies before conception." At that time I had been able to satisfy the wishes of parents for a son in 130 cases, by treating them before conception. Sievers said: "Our stud mares in Haflingern are having mostly male foals. Could you investigate this problem in cattle?" So, the estates of Dieke in Best, and that of Princess Bismarck in Varzin, both in East Pomerania, and Fischhorn Castle near Zell am See were chosen for investigation. Auschwitz was also proposed, but I was able to avoid that because Bang's disease,* an infection of the sex organs, was prevalent in the cattle of the area. Several members of my staff worked in Fischhorn until the end of the war, but in Varzin and Best we had done only some preparatory work when the war ended."

"In the summer of 1944, I asked Sievers for a train ticket to go to Fischhorn Castle. He said: "That's all right, but you must also go to a meeting in Papenschwandt, near Salzburg. You understand something about what's going on there." Sievers then told me that Pohl, Chief of the con-

---

* *Brucella abortus* is the commonest cause of brucellosis (undulant fever) and also causes infectious abortion in cattle, the animal reservoir of brucellosis. It is also known as Bang's bacillus, after Bernhard Laurits Frederik Bang (1848–1933), a Danish physician.

centration camps, had appeared at a meeting of SS-doctors, and had declared: "All that you are doing here is rubbish, do some jolly science* like Fahrenkamp in Papenschwandt. Heil Hitler!" Thereupon, a delegation of SS-doctors went to see the work in Papenschwandt and raised hell. Everything which was going on there was a fraud. Himmler then demanded that Sievers set up a commission to investigate the matter. Sievers now wanted my opinion as well."

"Fahrenkamp was a full- or half-Jew. He was a cardiologist who had once treated Himmler's mother. From that time on, he had been a friend of Himmler and Pohl, or so he claimed. The corridors in Papenschwandt were full of photographs of Fahrenkamp shaking hands with Himmler and Pohl. He had a research institute where he worked, assisted by SS-people who had heart diseases. His lecture lasted three hours. The SS-people had to stand all that time and show his demonstration posters. I've never seen anything like it. He claimed to have developed three drugs: Funktionin I for plants, Funktoinin II for animals, and Funktionin III for humans. Sievers had already given samples to various physiologists and botanists so that they could investigate the way these Funktionins worked. For example, his drugs were supposed to produce better grass, cows, and milk, cheese like Swiss Emmentaler, and higher yields of corn. Life expectancy in animals, fish for example, was supposed to be increased. He showed bigger and smaller fish in two aquaria; naturally, the larger fish were raised by his method. The possible applications of his Funktionins were endless, and they were said to be extremely useful for human beings too. I said angrily to my neighbour, Varesky: "It's all a fraud!" but he said: "Be careful! You'll be sent to a concentration camp." In the afternoon, the botanists and physiologists, who had already tested the Funktionins, gave their lectures. A botanist said that his experiments on the effect of Funktionin on tulip petals had not succeeded. A physiologist had tested himself and his associates. He had been ill, and his wife, assistants, and employees had vomited, and so on. Investigations in rats had shown that lactoflavin [riboflavin] was lost, first from muscles, and then from the heart and kidneys, until they died. "Perhaps," he said, "other essential materials are produced in the body to compensate for the lactoflavin, and the animals are really dying for quite other reasons." Cautiously spoken! The material was

---

* This curious expression was probably a reference to the book of that title by Friedrich Nietzsche, *Die Fröhliche Wissenschaft.*

eighty per cent methyl alcohol! All hell broke loose. Fahrenkamp said: "That's not true. I don't believe it. You must be mistaken. I will give you the material I started from. There is something fishy going on." And he went on and on in this vein. "Give me your addresses. I will send you the original material." We gave him our addresses, all sixteen of us, including Professors Tratz, Schäfer, Varesky, two physiologists, a botanist, and so on. Before I left, Fahrenkamp said to me: "I am no swindler. At the worst, I am a scientist who has been led astray." Again he went on and on in this vein. I calmed him down. No original material ever came, but, when I needed a train ticket again, Sievers said to me: "We only avoided a catastrophe by the skin of our teeth. R. Brandt telephoned me and asked me what on earth we had been up to. He told me that sixteen scientists, plus myself, were on a list for Auschwitz, which was ready for Himmler's signature, as being sabo-teurs of science." The list signed by Pohl was on Himmler's desk. Sievers asked for the document and added details about the truth of the matter. So it was that this cup, too, passed from me and from the others."

"I worked on many other problems before and during the war, such as preservation of fruit, for which I had a patent; on a drug against diabetes; on an antiseptic which saved the arms and legs of many soldiers, which otherwise would have had to be amputated. I spent some time in a leprosy ward in the hospital for tropical diseases in Bordeaux, with Dr Weddingen, studying changes in the skin and in fingerprint patterns. I didn't get lep-rosy, even though I took no precautions and didn't protect my hands. Leakey* sent me the first skull which he had found of early Man, and I described it in the first monograph on Australopithecus. He got his skull back after the war. I worked on the origins of Bushman remains in North Africa, the origin of the Negroes in Sudan, and so on and so forth."

"As the war was coming to an end, I brought my secretaries and co-workers, each with one suitcase, to my home to protect them from air raids. With my own suitcase, that made seven in all. When we reached the Mondsee, two of Rosenberg's underlings in uniform (we called them gold-en pheasants because of the yellow-brown colour of their uniforms) asked if they could come with us to Rosenberg's estate, which was nearby. The first cart, which was drawn by a team of horses, was full, and I had to wait for another one. They went on ahead, and we caught them up. This led to the assumption that I had removed Rosenberg's things. Rumours spread to

---

* L. S. B. Leakey, the anthropologist and archaeologist, worked in East Africa.

that effect and I was denounced. The whole house was searched, down to the last scrap of paper, but nothing was found. When the war ended, I was interned for two years in a camp. It was rather bad at the beginning; there was nothing to eat. There were many internees who were grossly under-nourished. We had three thousand of them with an average weight of fifty-four kilogrammes, and seven hundred even worse off. Then they gave us huge rations, but no greens or root vegetables. Everyone had hunger oede-ma. Even when they gave us four and a half thousand calories a day, the oedema took four months to go away and there were weight gains of only one or two kilogrammes."

"I was commissioned by my fellow prisoners from the Waffen-SS to make a bust of the American camp commander, as a present for him for Christmas 1945. But he preferred a portrait in oils. The commander asked me: "Why did you collaborate with the Nazis?" and answered his own question, without waiting for my answer. "As a farmer's son, I would have done the same. When we produced a lot of corn, the Jewish merchants paid us nothing, or very little, and, when we produced little, we could hardly pay for our seed corn." I was picked up every day by him or by other officers to paint, and, in the evening, I had to walk five kilometers back to the camp in the dark. That was a peculiar feeling! After my transfer, as a suspicious character, to another camp, I was shut up in a hole in the cellar at minus fourteen degrees centigrade. I was then brought to Salzburg to another camp. There I was interrogated for many hours about my acquaintance with Sievers, and finally released with a "Sorry, we made a mistake." "

"Subsequently I had two invitations from universities in Argentina and Chile, but I didn't have the chance to emigrate. So I decided to stay here. Camillo Castiglioni heard of my successes with sex-determination, and wanted to have me in Canada to continue this work. My mother was very ill at the time, and so I refused his offer. I lost my entire library, six-teen thousand volumes, which had been left in East Berlin, and I didn't get it back, even though a large part consisted of my Dutch father-in-law's zoological books. I didn't go back to university life; I remained a painter. I painted eight hundred portraits and earned my living this way. Later, I began to work on my methods of sex-determination again, and on prob-lems in biophysics. I discovered biophysical laws and new breeding meth-ods, especially in poultry. I took out international patents to protect these discoveries, even in America."

We had been talking for three hours, but nothing had been said about the extermination of the Jews. And nothing about the 'Rhineland bastards' (see p. 33). I ask about the latter. "That's a very sad story. Poor people. In my mind's eye, I can see one of them now. She had been playing a child's role in the Wiesbaden City Theatre. Such a dear little girl." I ask about their fate. "In 1943, by chance, I saw the same girl again. I don't know what happened to them all after that." "Perhaps they were included with the Gypsies in the final solution."* "What do you mean—with the Gypsies?" he asks. "There are still so many of them around." I tell him that the whole Gypsy camp in Auschwitz was exterminated under the direction of his colleague, Mengele.

"Did Fischer and von Verschuer know about the extermination of the Jews? Did you know?" I ask. "I didn't want to work in a camp and I didn't want to know what was going on there. It's probable that von Verschuer didn't know anything. He was a reserved man. Fischer? That I don't know." "Was Fischer an anti-Semite?" "No, never," says Abel. "But Rosenberg invited him to be the chairman of a workshop at the Anti-Jewish Congress in Cracow in 1944," I say. "Sometimes, one gets an invitation which one doesn't necessarily want." "But Fischer accepted," I say. "I don't believe it," he says. "I saw a copy of his letter," I say. "I don't understand that. Fischer would have been the last person to help with such a thing," he says.

"What significance did anthropology and human genetics have for Nazi policies?" I ask. "None at all," he replies emphatically. Fischer often said: "Politics destroys science for us." "

The conversation has come to a premature conclusion. Abel's wife rushes us, since they have to get up early the next day, and we still have to go to Salzburg. Abel drives. Very quickly. We are already in the car when he says: "In short, you say that the inheritance of mental traits cannot be proved. I say that I don't want to do such a thing, because, if we were able to do it, we would have to evaluate people and make judgements. I don't want to evaluate and judge any more. You use your argument as a protective shield, but what will you do if the inheritance of mental traits is demonstrated? I am not able to write expert reports any more, and I don't

---

* There has not been any survey of the subsequent fate of these coloured children. I have been able to locate two of them, now adult women, who did not suffer any major institutional persecution. On the other hand, I know of one coloured boy who was sent to a concentration camp for asocial adolescents.

want to. Too many are false. What should I say to a Jew who reproaches me that I have falsely made him into a half-Jew?" He tries to engage me in conversation again during the journey. His wife, worried about driving safely, interrupts him. I get out at the railway station in Salzburg.

Dr Engelhard Bühler

The Rhine valley is covered in mist. The sun shines on the Vogelsang pass. A blue sky and a red sun plunging into the mist. The narrow road from Jechtingen to the Sponeck. Along the Rhine, peasants are working in the fields. During the Thirty Years War, the countryside probably looked just the same. On a little hill, there is a ruined house with empty window frames. Flowers grow among the ruins. Dogs bark. After a long while, Dr Bühler's housekeeper comes along, and drags one of the dogs away by the hair of his head. "He bites," she says. The house, called 'The Citadel' is an old one with thick walls, low ceilings, and large rooms. There are paintings by the elder Bühler. They depict every possible aspect of the Rhine valley, as seen from the Sponeck. The most beautiful are the small ones in the style of Altdorfer. But there are also large portraits. Dr Bühler takes me on a tour of the house after our conversation to show me the other paintings. Beautiful old furniture. Simple carpets. A lived-in, comfortable disorder. The large paintings are remarkable. Siegfried sits on a bench, between Krimhild, who lays her fair head on his shoulder, and the dark-haired Brunhild*, who looks out into the void with an angry stare. Siegfried, too, looks out into empty space. All three are completely naked. A ménage à trois in difficulties. Brunhild reminds me of the portrait of a woman in the entrance hall. "Mrs Faist," says Dr Bühler, "she was Jewish, a musician, and a friend of my parents. She wrote beautiful poems and songs." Then, a painting of a woman on the Sponeck welcoming a soldier returning home. He puts his head on her lap; his steel helmet is lying beside them. And "A new life arises from the ruins," from the Mussolini competition in Cremona. A woman sits on the scorched earth, and plucks the first flowers for her child. In the background the scorched Sponeck, and over it, a grail. And another painting of an angry-looking woman with dark hair sitting on the Sponeck. "Cassandra, painted in 1938," says Dr Bühler.

At first we remain in the sitting room, drinking tea and eating cakes. "I matriculated in 1927 and then I studied in Marburg. There, I joined the SA and, soon afterwards, the Nazi Party. I had a party number under 1 100 000. In November 1933, I came to work with Fischer. Fischer was the 'Chief' not the 'Professor' or 'Director'. Morale in the institute was

---

* Siegfried, Krimhild, and Brunhild are characters from the Nibelungenlied, a medieval German heroic poem.

high. All the assistants addressed each other in an intimate manner.* There was no anti-Semitism in the institute. For example, there was no connection between us and the Institute for Research on the Jewish Question." "But Fischer and von Verschuer wrote articles on behalf of Rosenberg's institute, and visited it," I say. He has never heard this before. "Show me the anti-Semitism in these publications," he says, "I don't believe it."

"The only bad aspect was those courses for SS-doctors. Fischer was landed in this trouble by Walter Gross. The courses brought an unpleasant atmosphere into the institute. I taught Mendelian genetics. Fischer taught more advanced topics. Lenz had to organize the courses. Lenz was a socialist, and he didn't like organizing the courses at all. Later on, he used to read *Der Spiegel* and the socialist press. These SS-people thought that they knew everything. "We want to breed," they said, "Breed what?" I asked. "To select for race and achievement," said one of them. That was it; race and achievement. Some of them appeared later before the Nuremberg Tribunal, as concentration camp doctors." "Who?" "I've forgotten the names. The worst was a fat man, I don't remember any more what his name was."

"What work did you do in the institute?" I studied the inheritance of facial wrinkles and wrote expert reports in paternity cases. I was the institute's specialist on blood groups. I was the first to publish the methods developed at that time for basing expert reports in paternity cases on hereditary–biological facts. Then I went to Rome to the German Cultural Institute. There were three of us, a journalist, a musician, and myself, as an anthropologist. The director, who was decorated with the Order of the Blood,† invited the race–soul man, Clauss (see p. 55). I told him this was impossible, that Clauss was an outsider, and that he still had his Jewish lady friend. On the other hand, he behaved honourably when he was told to leave her; he refused and he lost his position. The director told me that I should be arrested for saying such things. He really didn't understand anything at all, that man. Of course, I wasn't arrested. Then the war came. At first, I was a military doctor and later, between other posts, adjutant for a time to the Chief Physician of the Luftwaffe, Professor Schröder. I had no time then for scientific work or for research in the institute. I just visited

* They used the second person singular, Du, rather than the more formal plural, Sie.
† The Order of the Blood was given only to those who could prove that they had taken part in Hitler's first and unsuccessful Putsch, when his supporters marched on the Feldherrnhalle in Munich on 9 November 1923. *Mein Kampf* was dedicated to the sixteen who were shot dead by Bavarian police.

from time to time." "Did you know Mengele?" He doesn't understand. He explains that he had never before heard that Mengele belonged to the institute, under von Verschuer. "I only know him from the illustrated magazines; he is still alive somewhere in South America. I never met him, either before or during the war."

"Did you arrange the move of the institute?" "Yes. In March 1945, I asked General Schröder for leave in order to undertake moving the institute at the request of von Verschuer. Then, I went to see Speer and told him that what was at stake was the KWI of Anthropology and its unique library. Speer gave me a lorry with a trailer, and, using this, I brought the irreplaceable contents of our institute, in particular the library, to the West. Later, I was captured by the Russians in Berlin. I ran away from them and made for the institute, where I put on a white coat. That was all right until the Americans arrived. Then, we were not allowed to eat any more in the Harnack House. I was beaten up. An American officer asked me what we had been doing and whether we had been involved with the Jewish question. I said to them: "We are a scientific institution." They laughed, and then they beat me up." "The institute had acquired a bad reputation because of Mengele," I say. "Even though Mengele was never in the Berlin institute. In any case, I travelled home from Berlin across the whole of Germany. I always travelled by day, even when crossing the zone border.* We waited until the Russian patrols were eating their midday meal, just as the foresters had described to us. Then, we ran across the border and, once over, we drank a bottle of wine we had in a rucksack. It was easier with the Americans. I had an identity card from my time in Rome, on it I was Angelo Bühler of Roma, and I showed it to them. We got something to eat, and then they gave me a lift in a lorry from Fulda to Frankfurt."

"It was difficult to start again after the war. I had to read a lot to become a general practitioner. But I like being the village doctor. I can talk to the people here in their own Alemannic dialect, and I know them all from the time of my youth." He smiles: "I talk to them in Alemannic even about the Russians." "Did you see any difficulties about expert reports concerning Jewish as opposed to non-Jewish paternity?" I ask, when he tells me that providing expert reports was his task. "No, they were not racial

---

* The border between the zones of Russian and Allied occupation, now the border between East and West Germany.

expert reports, they were only written in connection with maintenance payments. There wasn't any anti-Semitism in the institute. Professor Nachtsheim, Head of the Department of Animal Genetics, was Jewish. The psychologist, Professor Gottschaldt, was a Communist, but he stayed in the institute and was protected by Professor Fischer. Abel, Geyer, and Lehmann were in the SS.* But that was something entirely different. For example, when I was going to a congress in Copenhagen, I travelled in the same train compartments as Walter Gross. I expected a real harangue when I asked him about the Jews. But he said almost nothing. I remember even now how astonished I was at the time. Fischer joined the Party late on and was never a convinced National Socialist. He had a party number over 4 000 000. A high number." He laughs. "Mine was under 1 100 000.†
Father Muckermann, for example, privately encouraged me in my political views. He was close to the Nazis. He was a distinguished, well-educated, and able eugenicist. But, as a Jesuit, he couldn't talk freely in public."

"Günther?" "A quiet scholar. A great man. When anyone visited him in his agricultural college, he sat reading in his tiny room. He didn't give any public lectures. If he had been pushy, he would have had to give lectures all the time. He didn't want that. Of course, he also wrote a racial history of the Jews."

We go to his practice in Jechtingen. In the house, there hangs a portrait of Fischer by the elder Bühler. The hand on the rostrum is covered with rings; not a frank open look but, on the contrary rather sly and crafty. A photograph of General Schröder hangs over Bühler's writing desk. Many decorations. When I return home, I read that Schröder was sentenced to life imprisonment in the Doctors' Trial in Nuremberg because of his role as an organizer of human experimentation in Dachau.

Dr Bühler later added a note to the record of our conversation: "These

---

* The rush to join the Nazi Party after Hitler's accession to power on 30 January 1933, was so intense that a temporary moratorium on applications was introduced in April of that year. A number below 1 100 000 signified that its proud possessor joined the Party before that date.

† In general, I have tried not to correct the mistakes made in these conversations, but I should like to correct a few here. Dr Lehmann joined the Party in 1933, but he was never a member of the SS. Dr Geyer did join the SS but he had to leave, presumably because he or his wife had some Jewish ancestry. Professor Nachtsheim was not Jewish and Professor Gottschaldt was not a Communist. They both taught for a while at the University of East Berlin, which may account for Dr Bühler's views.

experiments were designed to establish whether a pilot shot down into the sea survives longer if he drinks sea water than if he does not. Similar experiments were conducted by both sides, by our former enemies as well as by ourselves, but over there, of course, no one was punished for it after the war."

Dr Adolf Würth

He lives in a small flat in a new building. He receives me in his small study. New furniture, many books and a small bookcase. He is seventy-seven years old, small, thin, yellowish-white hair. He is wearing an open-necked shirt and a summer suit. A typical Baden man, he is jovial and often laughs. "Do you smoke?" "No." "Then I won't smoke either."

"How did you come to work with Ritter?" "I learnt by accident that a psychiatrist in Tübingen, called Ritter, was looking for an anthropologist for research on Gypsies. Fischer warned me against it. He said that among these people you could never be certain who had fathered a child." "Did he want to reserve the Gypsies for his favourite student, Abel?" I ask. "At that time, Abel had already studied Gypsies in Scotland." He doesn't answer my question, but continues: "At the time, I had obtained my doctorate with Fischer, and I lived for some time in his villa, as a sort of night watchman. After a discussion with Ritter and with the president of the Reich Department of Health, I went to Tübingen in August 1936. In November 1936, we had to move to Berlin. The Reich Department of Health didn't have any branch offices, they said."

"I had already begun to work on the Gypsies of Württemberg, and I stayed in Stuttgart because I had found some very useful documents about these Gypsies in the records of the Criminal Police. Ritter placed great value on genealogical connections, and, with time, we constructed a family tree covering ten generations. We realized that family data had been kept in Württemberg for a long time, even for persons not settled there permanently, in the civic registry offices and earlier in church registers. Hermann Aichele's book[225] proved to be very useful for this work. Ritter first obtained a doctorate in psychology, then another in psychiatry. As chief physician, he was head of the children's ward of the psychiatric clinic in Tübingen (Professor H. F. Hoffmann was ahead of the department). Ritter was a remarkable man. He often came in to work in the morning only at ten o'clock, but then he stayed long into the night. Sometimes, he even needed two secretaries. On his ward, he had found children who suffered from a new form of feeble-mindedness, as he showed in his Habilitation dissertation. "A disguised form of feeble-mindedness," he called it. These children failed all the standard psychological tests, but in the outside world, for instance when picking berries, they were better than all the others. It was when he discovered that there were Gypsies among the ancestors of these children that he began to interest himself in Gypsies. At first, we were supposed to investigate the Gypsies in Württemberg and Baden. But when we were in Berlin, Gütt pressed for the investigations to be extended to all the Gypsies in the Reich. Rose, a spokesman for the Gypsies, writes today that the Gypsies were musicians, artists, and craftsmen. It's not true; the Sinti, whom I met, were mostly just poor devils."

"Ritter collaborated closely with Nebe (the chief of the Criminal Police). In the early days, I was present at their discussions. I had the impression that Nebe needed Ritter, and vice versa. Ritter, not being a member of the Party, sought Nebe's protection. When Nebe arrested Elser* as the man behind the assassination attempt in the Bürgerbräu [Citizen's Brewery] in Munich, we had to find out quickly whether he was a Gypsy or not. Naturally, we knew nothing of the assassination attempt or his capture. We were ordered to come with our results to the office of the Reich Criminal Police. When Mrs Justin and I arrived, they were all standing around in their dress uniforms. "What's going on?" we asked. "You really don't know?" they all said. Then Nebe arrived. They all clapped, and one of them presented him with flowers. Nebe immediately took us aside into Heydrich's empty office, and asked us for our results. We said that Elser wasn't a Gypsy. Nebe was disappointed, but there wasn't anything that could be done about it."

"Ritter and I weren't members of the Party. Those who were could allow themselves some liberties, but we couldn't. So, we always had to insert resounding phrases in our writings, to reflect National Socialist ideas. Ritter used to like to write a lot, so that some of these special phrases shouldn't be taken too seriously. For instance, the one about "the necessary solution of the Gypsy question" really should be interpreted against this background." Würth laughs.

"Today, people reproach Mrs Ehrhardt and me, saying that we meant the murder of the Gypsies by this phrase. We carried out our investigations

---

* Georg Elser, a journeyman carpenter, was arrested for attempting to assassinate Hitler with home-made explosives on 9 November 1939, the anniversary of the Feldherrnhalle Putsch of 1923, when Hitler traditionally came to Munich to address the 'old fighters' of the Party. It may be no coincidence that the Kristallnacht pogrom had been unleashed a year previously on the same date (see p. 39). He was not brought to trial, but was kept as a privileged prisoner, possibly for later use in a show trial. He was executed in Dachau in April 1945, shortly before it was liberated by the Americans. His captor, Nebe, was executed by the Gestapo a few weeks earlier.

in order to make a contribution to anthropological knowledge concerning a minority living in Germany, the Gypsies." I object: "But, later on, Ritter explicitly urged sterilization and internment in camps for the majority of the Gypsies." "But only within the framework of a law," Würth objects in his turn. "Everything prescribed by law is legal. Ritter himself wrote some drafts for a so-called 'Gypsy-law'."

"I was present at a discussion in the autumn of 1939 when plans were being made to deport Gypsies to camps. We insisted on postponing the deportations to the spring of 1940. I was then asked to come to Stuttgart in May 1940. Five hundred Gypsies were in Hohenasperg fortress.* "Where are they," I asked when I arrived. "In the cells," came the answer. "Why not in the courtyard? Let them out; they won't jump over the walls," I said." He laughs. "They were then loaded onto a train for an unknown destination. At first, they were told to get on in alphabetical order. I asked why they were doing it that way. I said that those who wanted to travel with each other should get into the next carriage, and so on. And that's the way it was done. The official from the criminal police who accompanied the train told me later, when I looked him up in Stuttgart after the war, that the train stopped in the middle of the countryside in the Generalgouvernement and that all the Gypsies had to get out. So it was nothing to do with a concentration camp. While in the Hohenasperg fortress, they had had to sign a document to say that they would never return to Germany. If they refused to sign, they were threatened with a concentration camp. We had already said, at that time, that no amount of threats would have any effect. And it came about as we had predicted. Soon afterwards some of Gypsies reappeared in the Reich. They knew how to slip back."

"At the beginning of 1941, an order was issued that all Gypsies were to be discharged from the army. The order was issued on the initiative of the representative of the Führer. The Higher Command of the Army and of the Wehrmacht did not think it up themselves. Gypsies and Hohenzollern princes are not allowed to serve, as people said at the time. During a holiday, I found out with great difficulty who was organizing this expulsion of Gypsies at Army High Command, and I went to see him. "How are you going about it?" I asked the Colonel responsible. "We issued an order that all company commanders should ask their men if they are Gypsies, and

---

* This fortress, ten miles north of Stuttgart, overlooking the town of Asperg, was for many years the Württemberg state prison.

that they should report anyone they suspect of being a Gypsy," he told me. "You'll never get them out that way," I told him." He laughs. "Then, I explained to him that it was we who had all the documentation about the Gypsies, and that any enquiry about whether a soldier was a Gypsy should be directed to the Reich Department of Health through the Reich Department of Criminal Police."

"I was called up for military service after the invasion of France, and I had the good fortune to spend the whole time as a driver and clerk with the armistice commission in Bourges. At the beginning of 1942, Ritter tried to have me classified as being in a reserved occupation. He made the mistake of having his request recommended by an SS-officer of the Reich Criminal Police Department. That made the army angry. They said that the SS should do their research on Gypsies themselves, and I stayed put in France until the end of the war."

"Was Fischer an anti-Semite?" I ask. "No," he says. Then: "Yes." After an interval of silence: "No." Then again: "Yes. He didn't want to kill them. He didn't like them, just like many Bavarians don't like Prussians. He had slowly developed from being a German Nationalist to being a Nazi. On the day of the Röhm Putsch (see p. xviii), he came back in the evening from an excursion with university personnel (he was still rector at the time), and he said to me: "But they can't do this kind of thing." When I was taking my oral examination for my doctorate in 1936, he asked me about the Jews. I talked about the biological basis of their power, their skills and their high intelligence. He drummed his fingers. He always did that when he was nervous. Then he asked about the Nuremberg laws. I said that was overdoing it somewhat. "When a plane is used, you will find shavings," he said. They all said something of the sort at the time, and also: "If only the Führer knew." Very many people thought that way at the time. What shouldn't exist, didn't exist. Fischer was a man richly endowed with imagination, but at times he showed a lack of resolve; he didn't have a solid character. Being a Baden man, he was perhaps also too conciliatory. We never spoke to each other about politics, either then or later."

It occurs to me to ask about Mrs Lüdicke. "Did you know her?" "Yes, I am still on friendly terms with her today. She was a convinced supporter of Hitler for a long time. Rommel (the Mayor of Stuttgart) has given an account of how he came to be an enthusiastic member of the Hitler Youth. Perhaps you would have been one too. We can't imagine today how things were at that time. Once, when I came home, I found that I had forgotten my key. I rang the bell, but my wife didn't open the door. And I could hear the toilet being flushed again and again." "I was tearing up Tucholsky's *Germany, Germany above everything*"* says his wife, who is sitting beside us with the coffee and cakes. "I can still remember today what the book looked like. We were terrified of a house search," he says, "because a colleague of mine, to whom my wife and I were very close, and still are today, was under investigation in prison at the time. Although she was a Party member, she had helped a Jewish doctor to flee."

"Then there was a certain Neese preparing his doctorate in the KWI of Anthropology. He was a longtime member of the Party and of the SA, and a very good friend of mine. He was one of those arrested at the time of the Röhm Putsch. They got as far as the cell next door to his when they were shooting them. He came back to the institute with all his hair shaved off. Later, he was a government adviser in the Ministry of the Interior, supervising films. He was a real ladies' man. He threw himself out of a window of the Gestapo building in the Prinz-Albrechtstrasse while being interrogated. Two veiled widows (actually they were his mistresses) were present at his burial." "Was Abel there too?" I ask. "No! The news of the so-called accident only appeared in the papers later." "Did you visit Berlin again after being called up for military service?" "Yes, for the last time in 1942, when the removal of the Gypsy archives to Mecklenburg was being discussed. I suggested the mental hospital in Winnenden for the anthropological material. Now I don't remember the reason for that suggestion at all. People reproach Mrs Ehrhardt today for having destroyed twenty thousand expert reports. Ridiculous! There weren't even that many in existence at the time. And besides they were already stored in the Reich Criminal Police Department. To my knowledge, the material consisted of: 1. Index cards of personal, genealogical, and other kinds of data. 2. Index cards or sheets of paper recording anthropological measurements of the persons who had been examined. 3. Index cards on which photographs were pasted. 4. Locator cards for family trees stored elsewhere." "In Koblenz, such documents for some sixteen thousand Gypsies are missing, and there are

* Kurt Tucholsky, a German writer, held left-wing views and was of Jewish origin. He was prominent during the time of the Weimar Republic. Born in 1890, he committed suicide as an exile in Sweden in 1935. His books, among them *Deutschland Deutschland über alles*, were burnt, together with those of 33 other writers, on a ceremonial bonfire in front of the University of Berlin on 10 May 1933, soon after the Nazis seized power.

no expert reports at all", I say. "Index cards do not represent signed expert reports," he says. "But the name of the investigator is noted on each index card with the anthropological measurements," I say. "But expert reports were another matter," he says. "They actually had to be signed. At the time, I told Ritter that we should prepare stamps with signatures. There were mountains of documents, and on top of that, the one-page expert reports which were intended for the Reich Criminal Police Department." "For those involved, it didn't make much difference whether they were signed expert reports or index cards," I object. "Describing them as 'part-Gypsy' meant a concentration camp at the time." "It was a recommendation, but it didn't necessarily imply internment," Würth contradicts. "Ritter had recommended sterilization and internment in a camp for more than ninety percent of the Gypsies, and at that time, for an 'asocial individual', 'camp' was synonymous with concentration camp," I say. "But a recommendation still isn't punishable," he says. "You could call it recommending genocide," I say. "None of us could have known that at the time."

"Ritter wasn't a Nazi," he says. "But he had a guilty secret in his past. When he was still in Zürich, he was supposed to have written, as a private psychiatrist, an expert report on Hitler, and to have sent it to Hindenburg's presidential office." "Who told you that?" I ask. "I can't tell you," he says. "After 1933, Ritter must always have been afraid that the report would come to light."

" "The Nazis made great difficulties for me because of you," Ritter told me, when I met him again in 1947. "You weren't a member of the party." "And I had difficulties on your account," I said. "Why was that?" he asked. And then I told him that a friend of mine, a party member, was instructed to report on the staff of the scientific institutes in Dahlem. "And what about Ritter?" I was asked. "Nothing wrong," I answered. People needed patronage at that time. As high up as possible. I don't know how it is today, but it's probably similar." I ask about the staff of Ritter's institute. "Mrs Ehrhardt?" "Mrs Ehrhardt got her doctorate in Munich. She had studied zoology and anthropology. Then she set up a laboratory for anthropology in Günther's department in Berlin. Günther was really a philologist and an historian; during his studies, he had done no more than one practical course in anthropology with Fischer in Freiburg. After Günther she then came to work with Ritter. In 1942, she went to work with Gieseler in Tübingen. He had to leave in 1945. She stayed with his successor, Just, and obtained her Habilitation there. After Just's premature death, Gieseler became director again." "Morawek?" "SS and SD. He was a real Viennese. As far as I know, he wrote his doctoral dissertation on the Gypsies of the Burgenland. "The enemy is listening," his co-workers used to say, when he came into their room. But he never actually denounced anyone. He was killed in the war." "And Stein?" "He was only with us for a few months." "Rodenberg?" "He didn't belong to Ritter's research division. As far as I know, he vanished without trace. He presumably had a reason." Continuing this line of questioning, I ask about Mengele. "Naturally, I knew him. As an assistant of Professor von Verschuer in Frankfurt. We anthropologists all knew each other, more or less." I ask about the eyes of Gypsies, which Mengele sent to the KWI from Auschwitz. "I don't know anything about that. Nachtsheim published something about it. I don't know where the eyes came from."

"During the war did you know about the mass extermination of the Gypsies?" "No." "About the mass extermination of the Jews?" "No. Only after the war!" "Mental patients?" "No. Wait a minute! Yes, I did hear that a bishop was protesting about that," (see p. 16). "In retrospect, what do you believe to be wrong with anthropology and these actions of anthropologists?" "Race-ideology was wrong, and it was wrong that anthropologists, and not only German ones, allowed themselves to be contaminated by it. This unfortunate mixture of so-called 'race research', and of National Socialist policies, led to Auschwitz." "After the war did you ever talk to your colleagues about what might have been wrong with anthropology and with what you and your fellow anthropologists did?" "I have spoken to some anthropologists who had been in the East as soldier. None of them said a single word from which one could conclude that they had been involved in Nazi crimes."

Professor Hans Grebe

A detached house on the edge of the Eder. Inside there are icons, rustic furniture, a head of Christ in stone (perhaps Gothic), two big rustic baroque altar-pieces depicting the Resurrection, books behind glass. A table is laid with coffee, plum cake, and two cups. Beside it, there are two chairs, parallel to each other. We sit down. We don't need to look each other in the eyes since the position of the chairs makes it impossible. He has a pale face and long white hair. He wears a pullover with a rolled collar. He looks fashionable and sporting despite his sixty-seven years.

"How did you come to work with von Verschuer?" "I obtained my doctorate in Frankfurt and received a prize from the University. At that time, Professor von Verschuer offered me an assistant's position. After I had spent a year in Berlin as an assistant in internal medicine, I heard my teacher, K., report my work at a meeting, without mentioning my name. So I decided to accept Professor von Verschuer's offer."

"In 1933, I was nineteen years old. As an active member of the Red Cross, I was absorbed into an SA medical unit with my Red Cross group. In 1932, there were forty-three political parties. To start from scratch is easier than to keep something going. (I am talking about the National Socialists building a new Germany as opposed to preserving the republic.) Just think of the difficult struggle today against extremists who want to alter everything again. When a Jewish friend of mine, who wasn't actively involved, was murdered during the Röhm Putsch in 1934, I volunteered for the army. Our leaders needed the Wehrmacht at that time. It represented security. My time as an assistant in Professor von Verschuer's institute began in the spring of 1938." "Who was in the institute at the time?" "Schade, Claussen," after a short pause, "Mengele." I ask about Mengele. "Mengele was our chief's favourite student. I didn't know him well. I was invited to his home once. We addressed each other formally."*

"Was there any anti-Semitism in the institute?" "No, there wasn't. I knew many Jews. I went to a gymnasium [secondary school with a classical curriculum]. In my matriculation class there were eleven Jews. I sat beside Richard Merton, whose family were among the founders of the university. I also helped many of them. For instance, I had a school friend who was accused in court proceedings of race-dishonour (see p. 35). I went

---

* Formal address is Sie rather than the more intimate second person singular, Du.

with him to the border near Aachen. There, a friend of mine from army days, who had become a customs official, showed him how to cross the frontier. My school-friend later came back with the Counter Intelligence Corps as an American major. He was a helpful witness for me before the Denazification Tribunal."

"Then again, for example, I went to the burial of a Jewish friend in Frankfurt. The caretaker of the Jewish cemetery said to me: "Good neighbour, please put on a hat!" He gave me one, and I put it on. When I was leaving the cemetery, I was stopped. "What are you doing here?" I explained. "Name?" I gave my name. Proceedings were instituted against me in the party court. I had a friend in the Party," Grebe smiles, "and so the whole thing was covered up. Later, an acquaintance of mine, a Jew, came to see me and asked me if I could help him. During the First World War, he had won the Iron Cross, First Class. Well, we considered various ways of going about his problem. His father had fought a duel after his birth. His opponent, who had since left for the United States, was an Aryan. I had a friend who worked in the Ministry of the Interior, as a genealogist," Grebe smiles, "and I talked the matter over with him. According to the conventional wisdom of those times, a Jew could not be brave and have an Iron Cross, First Class. So it was that he became a half-Jew, and his son a quarter-Jew. Professor Abel prepared the necessary expert reports at my request." "But wasn't Abel in the SS at the time?" I ask. "Yes, but he was Viennese. The Viennese have never been fanatics." "Did Professor von Verschuer ever do anything like that, or sign anything of the sort?" "I don't believe so. Professor von Verschuer was much too correct."

"At the beginning of the war, I was called up for military service. During the campaign in France, I was the first army doctor to win the Iron Cross, First Class. When I visited the institute in Frankfurt in my uniform, Mengele said to me: "You have the Iron Cross, First Class. I am going to volunteer right now for the Alpine Corps." He was a Bavarian, you know. He had already been in training in Füssen. But he was rejected because of a kidney ailment. That's why he joined the Waffen-SS. He became a camp doctor because he was not fit for front-line duty."

"Did Mengele tell you in Berlin that he had begun to study dwarfism in Auschwitz, and that he was picking out all the dwarfs on the railway ramp and having them brought to a special barracks for further investigation?" "No, I only met him there once, fleetingly. I was just going down the steps of the institute on my way to Rostock. I had lectures to give there. I only had a brief word with him about other matters." "Did you know that Mengele sent the skeletons of a father and son, who both suffered from the same bone deformity, from Auschwitz to the institute?" "That's news to me." "Did you also not know about the heterochromatic eyes of Gypsies (see p. 76), which Mrs Magnussen received from Mengele?" "No. I knew that she was working on eyes, but nothing more than that. She worked in another wing of the institute." "You don't know anything about Mengele's collaboration with the KWI?" "Nothing, I only learnt about this collaboration after the war."

"Professor von Verschuer was attracted to Frankfurt in 1946, because the Dean, his friend Professor de Rudder, had led him to hope that he would be offered a chair. But then an article (see p. 129) appeared against him." "Where?" "In *Das Reich*." "But, surely, the paper couldn't have been called that," I say. "Then I don't know. Anyway, a weekly or monthly published by Hans Habe.* This article put an end to any possibility of a chair for von Verschuer in Frankfurt. He had to wait a few years before he was offered one in Münster." I ask about Schade. "He was called up for service in the Waffen-SS, and was a prisoner for a long time after the war in Yugoslavia."

"Professor von Verschuer was a member of the Confessional Church and a devout man. When I was married in church, he came to the wedding. Afterwards he said: "I am pleased that you had a church wedding." He had soldierly inclinations. He was happy about my having won my Iron Cross, First Class, so early on." "Was von Verschuer anti-Semitic?" "No, certainly not." I persist with my question: "Isn't it strange that none of them was anti-Semitic?" "Von Verschuer's mother was a Balt. As you know, in those parts there were many marriages between members of the nobility and Jews," he says, smiling.

"Von Verschuer was an officer in the First World War. As such, he belonged to the Marburg student Freikorps and participated in the Kapp Putsch,† marching with them from Marburg through Thuringia (see p.

---

* The article referred to appeared in *Die Neue Zeitung*, which was published by Habe, a German-Jewish emigrant, who was one of the first to return to the American occupied zone. *Das Reich* was a Nazi paper, and it had ceased publication late in the war.

† In March 1920, Wolfgang Kapp seized power in Berlin for a few days, with the help of General Walther von Lüttwitz, the commander of the troops in the area. The Government ministers withdrew to Dresden and then to Stuttgart, but the Putsch came to an end after four days of a general strike by Berlin workers.

127). Boguslav von Selchow describes the episode in his memoirs, where his adjutant, von Verschuer, is mentioned and praised. Professor von Verschuer wasn't a Nazi. Quite the contrary. He once told me of a conversation with Gauleiter Sprenger, which was placed on record." "Why?" "I don't know. But whatever it was, conversations between friends aren't placed on record."

I ask about the political attitude of Eugen Fischer. "He belonged to the Herrenklub [Gentlemen's Club], like General Beck.* He was a sly fox. No one was able to get out of him what he really knew about 20 July 1944." "Was Fischer an anti-Semite?" "No, he certainly wasn't." I tell him about his Paris speech of 1942 (see pp. 50 and 87), and about his willingness to take part in the Anti-Jewish Congress in Cracow in 1944. "I don't know the speech," he says. "I must read it before passing judgement."

"What a time that was. I had an acquaintance who wrote a book about the Albigenses."† He brings the book from the case and he shows it to me, inscribed with a personal dedication by the author.‡ "My acquaintance then received a letter from Himmler, saying that he was the right man to be the founder of a German religion, and offering him a post in the RSHA. He accepted and became responsible for liaison with Rosenberg's office. In those days, careers sometimes got off the ground very quickly. I was offered a position with the Reich Physician for Sport. I refused. After the end of the French campaign, I obtained a temporary discharge from the army on a working leave. Then I was wounded three times in Russia as a doctor with an infantry battalion. While recovering in a Frankfurt hospital, I had obtained my Habilitation. Thus I gained the right to teach at the same time as my teacher, von Verschuer, was offered a chair in Berlin, after I was invalided out of the army. His successor, Kranz, was a mere party man. I didn't want to stay with him and so I went with von Verschuer to Berlin. I wanted to be a scientist in a reputable institute, and at thirty-one

---

* Colonel General Ludwig Beck was chief of staff of the German army until 1938, when he resigned in protest against Hitler's plans. He started to conspire to overthrow Hitler even before the war. He was one of the leaders of the assassination attempt of 20 July 1944. The Herrenklub, a right-wing club in Berlin, was closed after 20 July 1944.

† Heretics, especially Catharist, in the South of France of the twelfth and thirteenth centuries. Their beliefs were distantly derived from Manichaean dualism.

‡ The book was Rahn, O. *Kreuzzug gegen den Gral* [Crusade against the Holy Grail] Freiburg, 1933. See also Bernadact, C: *Le Mystère Otto Rahn* [The Otto Rahn Mystery] Paris, 1978.

I was invited to Rostock and became the youngest professor in Germany. This matter came under special scrutiny by the so-called Denazification Tribunal (see p. 132). I was completely exonerated. When I arrived in Rostock, I was asked: "Do you want to be the party delegate of the teaching staff of the department?" The previous party delegate had been killed in the war. His deputy had taken me into his house at the time of the night bombing raids. I said: "I am not very keen." At a meeting, a colleague asked me to give a report on Professor Gottschaldt. It seemed that he was under suspicion. It was said that he had been to Moscow, that there was a possibility that he was a Communist, and he was married to the daughter of the Japanese ambassador. I went to see Professor Gottschaldt, and I asked him to write the report himself. I just signed it."

"When did you hear about euthanasia?" "I had worked on dwarfs and similar topics. When I wanted to pursue follow-up investigations in 1942–43, I was repeatedly informed that my subjects had been transferred to state mental hospitals. I talked to Professor Fritz Lenz about it. Perhaps he knew the truth, and it was because of this that he suffered from a mild depression."

"Did you hear about the extermination of the Jews?" "A friend from army days wrote to me from Kiev that one day, while he was out for a drive, he had heard shots. An SS-soldier told him that he had better get out quickly, or else he would be shot too. He said that he had been ashamed to be a German."

I ask: "Is there such a thing as political guilt of the Institute of Anthropology as a whole?" "That is a very broad question, rather like asking about the relationship between gene and environment. I have always said that race is only the sum total of certain traits. But human genetics is not so simple. The Church is very interested in the subject. In 1953, I attended the First Congress of Human Genetics, which was held in Rome.* The Director of the Institute of Human Genetics in Rome, Professor Gedda, explained to me why the Church is so interested in twin research. Do twins have two souls or one? The Holy Father received us in audience. He came up to me and said: "I have good news for you. Adenauer† has been re-elected." Eugenics has its high and low points. The Holy Father spoke about

---

* He is referring to the Second International Congress of Human Genetics which was held in Rome in 1961.

† Konrad Adenauer (1876–1967) was Chancellor of West Germany (1949–63).

this. But we should continue to aspire to the heights. From 1952 to 1972, I gave lectures on human genetics in Marburg at the request of the Dean of the Faculty of Medicine. In Frankfurt, when they wanted to appoint someone to the chair, I was placed equal first with the successful candidate, as I learnt later from the dean. But since they had previously rejected my teacher, von Verschuer, they had to reject me too. At that time, a colleague in Marburg asked me why we needed all this Nazi genetics. I answered him: "You were in an SA uniform at such and such a meeting. If you say another word, I will tell everyone." That shut him up. It was like that. There was a universal amnesia." "Why did none of the scientists who were involved write about it after the war?" "Well, you know, after the war no one was quite sure which way the wind was blowing. Professor Lenz was glad that it was Professor Becker who replaced him in the chair which he had accepted in Göttingen after the war. You can't really understand the Germany of Hitler's time, if you haven't been there. You should read Haffner's *Comments on Hitler*.* I presented the book to my Rotarian friend, Teddy Kollek, the Mayor of Jerusalem, and also to Yssakar Ben Yakor, the Israeli ambassador in Vienna. Who knew in 1933 how things would turn out in 1945? It would have been simply unimaginable at that time."

* S. Haffner was a German journalist and writer best known for his book *Anmerkungen zu Hitler*. Munich, 1978.

Mrs Irmgard Haase, *Professor Otmar von Verschuer's medical technician*

Mrs Haase receives me in her small attic flat. I ask about her career. "I came to assist Professor von Verschuer in Frankfurt in October 1942, after passing my examination as a medical technician. I was told that I would be doing blood group serology, and I followed him on 15 October to the KWI in Berlin. Since von Verschuer was a theoretician rather than a practical man, he instructed me to set up a laboratory. We had about 6000 marks for a centrifuge, incubator, refrigerator, and so on. I received some further training in serology (blood factors M, N, Rh) with Dahr, who had been a student of Landsteiner. After that, I was with Abderhalden in Halle for three months from May 1943 to learn his protective enzyme reaction. It was a very difficult technique, used, for example, to detect a pregnancy, since one had to match colours by eye, without a photometer. My routine work involved paternity determinations, including those to distinguish between Jewish and Aryan fathers." "How many such Jewish-Aryan discriminations did you do?" "One or two a week, altogether about fifteen during the autumn of 1943. I thought that they were being done to help people. I was not accustomed to anti-Semitism. That was the way I was brought up at home. We had family friends who were half-Jewish. Half-Aryan too, of course; that compensates for the Jewish part." "Did you see the expert reports?" I ask. "No," she says, "not a single one."

"On top of that there was the research work, which included enzymes in the blood of Gypsy twins and of Russian prisoners of war. I remember there were samples of Uzbek and Kirghiz origin. [Uzbekistan and Kirghizia are Asiatic republics of the USSR. Their inhabitants are of Turkic origin.] From the middle of 1943 onwards, there were several consignments of 30 ml samples of citrated blood." "Where did these consignments come from?" I ask. "I don't know. The specimens were in boxes which had been opened. I never saw the sender's name." "Did you learn where the consignments came from?" I ask. "I thought that they were from a camp for prisoners." "Even the Gypsies?" I ask. "Yes," she says. "Auschwitz?" I ask. "I never heard the word at that time." I ask about Mengele. "I never heard of him, and I never saw him. My work was interrupted for a time because a part of the institute had to be moved because of intensified air-raids. Then I worked from the end of November 1944 until February 1945 in the KWI of Biochemistry, where Hillmann gave me technical advice. I didn't know what he did himself. I didn't get far there. I had just sensitized the first rabbits with dried serum. The analysis was only just beginning." "What did you want to get out of it?" I ask. "Specific enzymes in the blood were being investigated by means of Abderhalden's protective enzyme reaction." Mrs Haase cannot explain in any more detail.

"At the time, did you have any misgivings about the work which you were doing?" I ask. "No, we didn't have any misgivings. It was science after all. We even took control blood samples from each other. Taking blood is not dangerous. During the war, we never talked about these things. I only learnt about all those terrible things after the war." "Did you talk with von Verschuer after the war about these things, or did you ask him about Mengele or the blood samples?" "No, such an idea never entered my head."

Professor Georg Melchers

An opportunity occurred to speak briefly with the plant geneticist Professor Georg Melchers of Tübingen during a symposium to commemorate the first anniversary of Max Delbrück's death. Max had been the founder of the Institute of Genetics where I work, and so the symposium was held in Cologne. Professor Melchers, who had been a close friend of Max, had worked with Fritz von Wettstein, as a student, as a fellow, and as an assistant, in Göttingen, Munich, and Berlin-Dahlem, from 1927 to 1945. I asked him about von Wettstein. "Von Wettstein did the minimum necessary so as not to lose all his influence, and to keep that of the Nazis out of his institute as far as was possible. But he was never a member nor even a supporter of the Nazi Party. For example, Glum, the Secretary General of the KWG, had to leave partly because his wife had some Jewish ancestry, and he was replaced by Telschow. At the same time Max Planck, the President, resigned. At the time, von Wettstein said to me that the events leading to the change-over were extremely unpleasant, but that, in order to preserve the KWG, he would co-operate with the new Secretary General." "Did you have contacts with the KWI of Anthropology?" "Not really, contacts between the KWI of Biology and the KWI of Anthropology were minimal." I asked about the heads of departments and the scientific staff. "Someone told me a story about Abel. He went into a photography shop to find a photograph of a 'particularly Aryan-looking' girl. He thought that he had found the ideal candidate, a blonde with blue eyes, a Nordic-shaped head, and so on. He went to see the girl's mother, and asked her if she would allow him to publish the photograph. She was alarmed and refused: "No, my daughter is half-Jewish. She already has enough problems in her job as a dancer." "But come to your senses, dear lady, your daughter is most certainly not half-Jewish," said Abel, and she thought better of it. In this way, the girl was 'Aryanized'." I asked about von Verschuer and Mengele. "I didn't know them personally, but I did come into contact with one of their co-workers, whom I had previously met as a student in Göttingen, when she was already a committed National Socialist. I was asked to referee a paper by Mrs Magnussen about the inheritance of eye-colour in Gypsies when I was a member of the editorial board of the *Zeitschrift für Induktive Abstammungs und Vererbungslehre*. I was struck by the fact that the whole family, grandparents, parents, and children, had died at the same time. I could only assume that they had been killed in a concentration camp. I didn't send the paper to the publisher. The end of the war was near, so that I managed to avoid an argument about printing it."

The conversation again comes round to von Wettstein's department at the KWI of Biology: "In the institute, we never said "Heil Hitler!" as a greeting, but always "Good day." Only the gardeners were greeted by many of 'those in white coats' with "Heil Hitler!" Finally, the gardeners went to complain to the Nazi Party delegate, who was the mechanic in the institute: "This is not a real community! We gardeners and workers are not worse comrades than the academics and the technicians." We were no heroes of the resistance, but we muddled through. There was very little real resistance in Germany, since most of the time it led straight to a concentration camp. I don't know of any example of resistance in our institute. Fortunately, I have never received an invitation to Israel. Possibly, my refusal would be interpreted quite wrongly. The fact is that I would find it very difficult to face meeting the survivors, whose close relatives were among the millions systematically exterminated, without any active opposition on our part. But many colleagues in my age group think differently."

Professor Werner Joachim Eicke

He is waiting for me in front of his consulting rooms in the Frankfurter Strasse. A sturdy man, with sparse hair, who doesn't look his age. Glasses, a suit. He drives me to his home in his car. We are welcomed by a dog. "Don't touch the big beast," he warns me. After being told several times, the dog disappears into the adjoining room behind a curtain, where he growls now and then. Coffee is prepared, and Professor Eicke offers me a cup. I say: "You will have gathered the nature of my interest from my manuscript." With this, I give him the cue for a longish statement. "I have read it," he says. "It's a completely worthless and clumsy piece of work. I was on the point of writing to you to say that I didn't consider your visit worthwhile. You didn't take any trouble with your work. You spelt names wrongly." I object that the wrong spelling of von Baeyer had been corrected in the meantime. "No, I am talking about someone else." "About whom?" "I won't tell you. It's not my job to correct your manuscript." In the course of the conversation, he mentions the psychiatrist, Kranz, whom he thinks I have confused with Kranz, the anthropologist. I try to explain that this is his misunderstanding, and not mine.

"You write that there wasn't any opposition from the psychiatrists. That isn't true. My father was the chief physician at the psychiatric clinic in Buch. He made a protest in 1933. The director of the clinic, Birnbaum, was dismissed, and my father was supposed to succeed him, provided that he joined the Party. He refused. So he was demoted to senior physician, and another person became the director. When the Russians arrived in 1945, it was they who made him director of the clinic."

I object that I had specifically mentioned the lack of any *written* protests. "But the director of the Eichberg clinic avoided taking part in the euthanasia programme by joining the armed forces." "That's true," I say, and I add: "There are other cases of doctors who rejected euthanasia without suffering reprisals. But all the same, that's not the type of protest which I meant." "But everything was kept secret at that time," he says. "You can't imagine what it was like. My father didn't know anything about euthanasia. When his patients were transferred to another mental hospital, he thought that it was a good idea, since it was a pleasant place, and they would be less exposed to danger from air raids."

"But surely you knew about euthanasia?" I object. "No," he says. "I didn't know anything about it. I heard about it for the first time in 1944. I advised a technician to send one of his relatives, who was ill, to a particular mental hospital. He said: "But I can't do that. They will kill her there." That was the first time that I had heard about it. As a neuroanatomist, I had no contacts with psychiatrists, or hardly any contacts. It was all secret."

"It was the same with the Jews. We had many Jewish acquaintances. When they left Berlin, they came to say goodbye: "We are going to an uncertain future." Later I was able to reassure my father, when I saw German Jews in Przemyśl, while I was on official travel. In fact, at the time, they weren't doing too badly there. No, it's simply not true that everyone knew about euthanasia and about the final solution. But my wife did tell me once, when she came back home after buying some soap, that someone in the store had said that it would soon be made from the fat of Jews."

"It was all kept secret. No one knew anything." "But, all the same, Hallervorden must have known something about euthanasia!" "Yes, he probably did." "Did you ever speak to him about it at that time?" "Never," he says. "And, later, after the war?" I ask. "Only once, very briefly. He said that Heinze had told him that there were many brains available from Görden, and that if he didn't want to take them, they would have to be thrown away. So he took them." "That contradicts the record of his interrogation," I say (see p. 72). "That record is in English. Why do you quote it in English?" "It's in English in the original," I say. "I know how much can be lost or altered in its meaning in translation," he says.

"You worked as a pathologist and you performed post-mortems in Görden. Did you ever have any contact with Professor Heinze there?" I ask. "No," he says. "Heinze told me that in the dining room "Heil Hitler!" was being used as a greeting. From that time on, I didn't go there any more, but had my meals brought to the post-mortem room. There I ate alone." "Didn't you know Dr Asmussen and Dr Schmorl in Görden?" "No", he says. "So you didn't know anything about the 'observation ward' in Görden either, where those doctors worked, and which functioned in a similar way to Professor Schneider's research establishment in Wiesloch (see p. 72)?" "No, that is news to me." (Later Professor Eicke told me in a letter that according to information he had received from a colleague who had died in the meantime, the 'observation ward' was in the Brandenburg jail, and not in the Görden mental hospital.)

"The brains from the euthanasia programme didn't go through my hands. I only worked on the normal deaths in Görden. There were about a hundred and sixty a year. If there had been an increase, I would have noticed." "How big was the hospital?" I ask. "Twelve to fourteen hundred beds," he says. "That's a death rate of over ten per cent a year," I say. But he insists that he only worked on the normal deaths. "The corpses from the euthanasia programme must have been separated. I never worked on them." "Did you see Dr Rauch in Görden or in Buch?" "No," he says. "You weren't even born at that time. You simply can't understand what went on. I was considered to be unreliable. De Crinis had written me a very unfavourable reference. Of course, I didn't go around after the war bragging about it. I was interrogated once in Frankfurt. I told the judge that he knew more about my father and about me than I know myself. He apologized, and I was released. I was working day and night on the dissertation for my Habilitation. It was a very interesting piece of work about meningitis in foetuses and adults. Later, during the fifties, I gave lectures about it at international congresses. People were simply too busy to worry about these secret matters. And remember that I was considered unreliable anyway." "Why wasn't anything said about these things later?" "When I came back from Siberia in 1946, I had seen things which were very similar to those with which we are reproached." He smiles. "Quite rightly so, of course. Later on, when I started to talk about them, when I was a medical assistant in Würzburg, no one wanted to know. They were repressing this knowledge, as we psychiatrists would say."

He returns to the worthlessness of my work. "The case of the person damaged in the womb by carbon monoxide shows how badly you did your research" (see p. 72). "It wasn't a child, but a woman between forty and fifty. I saw her myself. She was a patient in our clinic." He puts his hands in front of his face and draws his legs up to his chest to imitate the patient's posture. "I am sure that she died a natural death." I think I remember, from the record of his interrogation, that Hallervorden mentioned that she was a victim of euthanasia, but I am not sure and, therefore, I do not contradict Professor Eicke.*

The conversation is drawing to its end. I ask about Professor Spatz. "He was a mild-mannered man. Hallervorden was harder. Both of them always stood by us." I mention the politically inflammatory and adulatory address delivered by Spatz when he became director of the institute. "I am sure that he thought it necessary to talk like that in order to be in a better position to protect his co-workers." "Did you have anything to do with

* My recollection is proved correct when I return home (see p. 72).

Professors Abel, Fischer, or Lenz, from the KWI of Anthropology?" "No, but as a student of medicine, I went to Lenz's lectures. Once, Lenz pointed out a certain student as being particularly 'Nordic' in appearance. The student said: "But, I am a Jew." Lenz was completely taken aback. There was a big rumpus."

The conversation is ended. He drives me into the town. "You didn't ask about Hallervorden," he suddenly says in an annoyed tone of voice. "Since you only talked to him about these matters fleetingly, there wasn't much I could ask you," I answer. After a short while, he asks: "In which institute are you?" "In the Institute of Genetics of the Faculty of Natural Sciences," I say. "And who is your director?" "I am. Four colleagues and I direct the institute collectively." "Will you send me a record of this conversation as you remember it?" "I will," I say. We have arrived. We part with a handshake.

Professor Hans-Joachim Rauch*

Our appointment is at the university psychiatric clinic in Heidelberg. A neoclassical building with columns in the inner courtyard. The door-keeper leads me down to the basement. A little cellar room. Book-cases round the walls. Rauch sits behind his desk at the far end of the room. White coat, white hair. A large, wrinkled, but not unfriendly, face.

I explain once again the purpose of my visit. He had read my book *Philosophers and living matter.*[1] I begin by asking: "How did you get into psychiatry?" He had first become interested in psychiatry as a student, but his original intention was to practise internal medicine. He spent the practical year of his medical studies in a camp in the Saar, which at that time was still administered by the League of Nations. Subsequently, he was unable to find a position as an assistant, since membership of the Nazi Party or of one of its organizations was required everywhere, and he was not a member. So he applied to enter the army as a career medical officer.

Having seen an advertisement in the medical press, he went to the psychiatric-neurological clinic of the University of Heidelberg as a volunteer assistant, while the decision on his application to the army was pending. The director of the clinic at that time was Professor Carl Schneider. He left the clinic after five months, having been accepted as a candidate medical officer by the army. Since he was not sent for specialist training in psychiatry and neurology, as had previously been agreed, but was asked instead to undergo training in another speciality, he requested his release, which was granted, albeit with great difficulty, in January 1938. He then obtained a position as an assistant in the psychiatric-neurological clinic of the University of Heidelberg under Carl Schneider. In August 1939, he was conscripted for military service as a reserve medical officer. In 1942, he was released from the army for a year in order that he should return to work in Heidelberg. From 1943 until shortly before the end of the war, he was assigned to the military reserve hospital in Heidelberg, but he worked almost entirely in the civilian sector. About a fortnight before the arrival of the Americans, he was released from the army, in order to care for the civil-

---

* This conversation was originally written in direct speech, like the others. It was changed into its present form when Professor Rauch revised the manuscript. After these revisions, the only original parts by the author which remain are his questions and remarks.

ian population. After Carl Schneider left, he was acting director of the clinic, until it was taken over by Kurt Schneider.

"Were requests for sterilization made in the Heidelberg clinic?" Requests for sterilization were made by the clinic in those cases prescribed by law. "But such requests were not made in all university clinics; many only forwarded the expert reports." He says that he does not believe that. Under the provisions of the law on hereditary health, the heads of psychiatric clinics and hospitals were obliged to make requests for the sterilization of patients falling into the classes defined by the law. Besides that, hereditary health tribunals demanded expert reports in doubtful cases.

"Did you know about the plans for the euthanasia programme?" He did not know. "When did you first learn that the programme was being carried out?" He heard about it for the first time, but only as a rumour, after the French campaign, when a lieutenant in his unit told him that his mother had been admitted to a mental hospital because of her schizophrenia, and that he had heard that patients in mental hospitals were being killed. He had told the lieutenant at the time that he could not believe such a thing, and this had in fact been his conviction. On his next leave, however, he made enquiries from Professor Carl Schneider, who, as head of the department of psychiatry, should have been one of the first to know. Professor Schneider denied that such a euthanasia programme was being carried out or was planned.

"Did you hear the truth later on?" When he heard talk about it, after his return from the front in 1942, it had already been ended. Only after the war did he learn that Professor Carl Schneider had been one of the experts who had marked names on selected lists, thereby giving their opinions on whether the patient should be killed or not, solely on the basis of the patient's records. He himself never saw such a list or such a record. In the patient records of the clinic or of the other psychiatric institutions, the question of euthanasia was never mentioned. He certainly never wrote expert reports about individual patients. Lastly, the whole euthanasia programme was treated as a state secret. The programme was concealed, using every possible means such as false entries in civil registers, as had been learnt after the war from the relevant literature.

"Did you know about the murder of Soviet mental patients?" The unit in which he was a medical officer was always at the front. They had never learnt anything about what was going on behind the lines. "Did you know about the murder of Jews?" As in the case of euthanasia, he only learnt the facts about the murder of Jews after the war. On the front in Russia, he was cut off from all information and he had no opportunity to listen to foreign radio stations. The German radio and press had been silent about the matter. He travelled through the Warsaw ghetto, which was overcrowded at the time, and he saw the distress and misery of the Jews living there. While travelling through Poland before the beginning of the Russian campaign, he saw a temporary concentration camp from the outside; it was disguised as a quarantine station. As he knew some Polish, he had asked a passer-by about it, and he had explained that it was a camp for Jews.

I ask about psychiatry in the Wehrmacht, especially the treatment of war neurotics. He says that there were psychiatric wards in the military hospitals, which served principally for purposes of diagnosis, since those with mental illnesses, especially soldiers suffering from endogenous psychoses, were discharged from the Wehrmacht and sent home as quickly as possible. There had been advances in scientific knowledge about so-called war neurotics since the First World War. For example, there were no soldiers quaking with fear anywhere near the front lines, as there had been during the First World War. It had been learnt that they were neither physically nor mentally ill, but, rather, that they had abnormal psychological reactions. They needed psychiatric treatment if these abnormal reactions could not be controlled by the medical officer in their unit. The unit medical officer was compelled to intervene, since these abnormal reactions were contagious, and dangerous for the troops' morale. In his own experience, for example, one unit medical officer had been able, by drastic treatment, to save a soldier from being court-martialled, after he had disobeyed orders and thrown away his rifle during an attack. Occasionally, despite the regulations, a soldier who was reacting abnormally had to be separated from the fighting troops, and sent to the dressing-station, because his behaviour was alarming his fellow soldiers. I ask about the research wards of Wiesloch and Görden, which had connections with each other and had profited from the euthanasia programme. Research wards, operating jointly in Wiesloch and Görden, never existed, as far as he knew. Indeed, this was impossible because of the distance between the two.*

"But patients underwent physiological and psychological investigation in Wiesloch and then were killed elsewhere, for example, in Eichberg." He didn't know anything about that. Investigations conducted after the war

* Wiesloch is near Heidelberg and Görden is near Brandenburg.

showed that no patients had been killed in Wiesloch. He himself never worked in Wiesloch.

"But did you not go, as it says in the letter which Professor Schneider wrote to Professor Nitsche on 2 September 1944,[138b] to Eichberg to look for the brains of the children who had previously been investigated?" That was not true; he had never collected any brains from Eichberg. The few brains which were sent to the histopathological laboratory of the clinic did not originate, according to the documents which accompanied them, from former patients of the clinic or of the mental hospital in Wiesloch. It had been the practice for decades to send brains from various institutions to the histopathological laboratory for investigation.

"At that time, were you in Berlin or Görden?" He had never been in Görden. As a visiting physician, he worked for six weeks in the KWI of Brain Research in Berlin-Buch. At that time, Professor Spatz was director and Professor Hallervorden a head of department; both of them were neuropathologists of worldwide renown. I interrupt and say: "Professor Hallervorden previously directed the post-mortem department in Görden. Later, one of his assistants took over this job. Professor Hallervorden received hundreds of brains from the extermination centre in the Brandenburg jail." He was convinced that Professor Hallervorden had never previously seen the patients whose brains he examined.

"Did Schneider talk to you about the purpose of the research ward?" No, Professor Schneider had never talked to him about euthanasia or about a research ward. There was no research ward in the Heidelberg clinic. "It seems that you are in a situation exactly the opposite of Professor von Verschuer's. He didn't know what his assistant [Mengele] was doing, and you didn't know what your professor's plans were", I say.

"What happened to Schneider?" He had disappeared, on his bicycle, shortly before the arrival of the Americans. He had told the head nurse that, as consultant psychiatrist of war-zone XII, he had to inspect hospitals behind the lines, and that was, in fact, one of his duties. As far as he knew, Schneider entered the psychiatric clinic in Erlangen as an in-patient, and, subsequently, he was interned in a camp in Moosburg in Upper Bavaria. From there, he smuggled out a letter in which he asked for what was then called a 'Persilschein' (see footnote p. 91). Shortly thereafter, he learnt that Professor Schneider, who had been called as a witness in the Mennecke trial in Frankfurt, had committed suicide in captivity.

"When did Schneider become a follower of National Socialism?" One of Carl Schneider's fellow assistants, from the time when he was at the university clinic in Leipzig, told Rauch that Professor Schneider had earlier had ties with the Social Democratic Party, and had had an intimate friendship with a Jewish colleague; only around 1933 did he join the Nazi Party. The same colleague told him that Professor Schneider's father, who had been a pastor in the Evangelical Church, had given up his ministry and probably died as a tramp. Professor Schneider was an idiosyncratic man who showed inner contradictions. Rauch opened Schneider's writing desk after his disappearance from Heidelberg to see if it contained any incriminating material. He found nothing of that sort, but in the top drawer there was a booklet, obviously much-used, which contained sayings of the Moravian Brethren, a Protestant sect. This was a strange thing to find, since Professor Schneider had often made anticlerical remarks. Professor Schneider was a very reserved man. Contrary to the usual custom in university clinics, he did not cultivate any social contacts with his co-workers. Rauch himself only visited Schneider's house once, when he delivered the dissertation which he had written for his Habilitation. Professor Schneider was a very hard worker. His mood fluctuated often and wildly. Rauch heard that, before he joined the clinic, a former senior physician had intrigued against Schneider in 1935–6, maintaining that he suffered from manic-depressive psychosis and should be sterilized himself.

"Was Schneider an anti-Semite?" During the early years of his time as a professor in Heidelberg, Schneider, as a party orator, was said to have spread anti-Semitic propaganda. In the clinic, there was nothing noticeable. For example, he treated 'non-Aryan' private patients. He did not reject Freud's psychoanalysis because Freud and many of his students were Jewish, but because he held psychoanalysis to be an unscientific ideology. He had no objections to citing Freud and other Jewish authors in scientific publications. He was very much in favour of insulin-therapy for schizophrenia and that had been introduced by Sakel, a Jewish neurologist from Vienna. In Rauch's opinion, Carl Schneider had no racist or nationalistic prejudices in his scientific work.

"What is your assessment of Carl Schneider's professional work as a psychiatrist?" Carl Schneider was recognized as a good clinician who felt a strong bond with his patients. He not only used occupational therapy as a means of combating emotional disturbances, but he also mastered what is now grandiloquently called 'milieu-therapy'. He attached much importance to the contribution of mental influences to the symptomatology and natural history of psychoses, and he concentrated on a therapeutic approach, contrary to the tradition of the Heidelberg school. He was also a very fine psychopathologist. According to Rauch's information, it was for this reason that Jaspers and von Weizsäcker, among others, had recommended that Schneider be invited to accept the Heidelberg chair. There were no posthumous legal proceedings against Professor Schneider. His widow received a pension, as far as Rauch knew. After the war, as a result of denunciations, the Americans had begun to investigate his involvement in the euthanasia programme and had even begun a preliminary judicial inquiry. All legal proceedings were stopped, however, since no incriminating material was found. The patient-records from Wiesloch would surely have provided such evidence, if there was anything to the story. The investigating authorities were astonished that some of Schneider's assistants, including Rauch himself, were not members of the Party.

"Zucker?" Zucker was not a Nazi. He revered Carl Schneider in a somewhat uncritical manner. Towards the end of the war, he was the doctor in a torpedo boat flotilla and had a nervous breakdown. When the war ended, he was an in-patient in the Heidelberg clinic. Rauch did not know how Zucker was classified by the Denazification Tribunal but, in any case, he worked for the disability board until his retirement. He had died about a year before.

"Did you speak among yourselves about Schneider after the war?" The facts about Carl Schneider's role in the euthanasia programme had become known only gradually. His attitude towards euthanasia came as a surprise, since it was in such sharp contrast to his behaviour towards his patients in the clinic. Naturally, all the assistants in the clinic had completely rejected euthanasia, just as Rauch himself did. Attitudes towards sterilization varied. Schneider himself rejected all compulsory sterilization, but he believed that sterilization should be offered to individuals who wanted it.

"Why are there so few descriptions of the history of the euthanasia programme?" The question is too complicated. Those who were involved in the programme, and who knew the background, have remained silent since no one likes to incriminate himself.

I recount the story, told by Bürger-Prinz in his memoirs,[211] of the high-ranking Nazi official who did incriminate himself, and was treated and cured by Bürger-Prinz. "Is that a case for a psychiatrist?" Naturally, only a psychiatrist can evaluate and treat such a case. From the diagnostic point of view, the psychiatrist is interested first and foremost in the form, and not in the content, of pathological ideas. Of course, the content of morbid ideas also interests the psychopathologist, as do other psychopathological phenomena, but it is the form of the abnormality which is decisive in making a diagnosis. The absurdity of the content of an idea is not proof in itself that the person who holds it is ill. If it were, the scientifically trained physician would, for example, have to regard many religious ideas, which are absurd according to our modern views of the world, as the products of a mind deranged by disease; take, for example, the Catholic Church's dogma concerning the Assumption of the Virgin Mary. "Was Schneider a psychiatric case?" Professor Schneider was mentally healthy, at least as judged from a psychiatric point of view. Naturally, there are other possible interpretations, drawing on depth psychology, but these are unscientific.

I ask about the truth of the story that Schneider's predecessor, Willmanns, lost his chair because he had said that Hitler had a hysterical personality. Rauch says that Willmanns had said in a lecture that Hitler became hysterically blind; he heard this story himself when he was a student. Willmanns had been told about this by Bumke, who treated Hitler at the time (see p. 106).

After a short discussion about the concept of psychiatric illness, during which our points of view prove irreconcilable, the conversation comes to an end.

Afterword

Five Days in Berlin

In late April, when flying off to Berlin to give the keynote talk before a German-organized Congress of Molecular Medicine, I was apprehensive that my forthcoming message on "*Genes and Politics*" was not what my hosts had bargained for in wanting a genetic celebrity on hand to mark Germany's long-delayed return to a prominent role in human genetics. For more than a decade, Great Britain and France, as well as the United States, have been leading players in the Human Genome Project, the worldwide effort to determine the sequence of the 3×10^9 bits of DNA information encompassed within the 24 different human chromosomes (the human genome). More recently, Japan, always beset by the need for a time-consuming, broad consensus before accepting a new challenge, also opted to become a major participant. So among the major technologically advanced nations, it has been only Germany, which up until now has played no significant role in this profoundly exciting effort to vastly speed up our knowledge of human genetic information.

In one sense, this German reluctance to join was not to be expected since it was obvious that medical research would be speeded up immeasurably by the finding of those genes that, when miscopied during DNA replication, lead to human diseases like cancer, diabetes, or Alzheimer's. In having no genome program, before this time, German scientists have been virtually excluded from current disease gene-finding successes and their valuable patentable consequences. Second, those pursuing the Human Genome Project invariably will be generating new DNA methodologies pivotal for future advances in biotechnology, that is, the use of cells for generating new commercial products (drugs, diagnostics, foods, etc.). Major nations that stay away from the human genome are bound to imperil their long-term commercial futures.

Germany's absence from the "genome table" thus never reflected financial considerations. Instead, politics were involved. Germany's past involvement with eugenics ("genetics used for human improvement") was a moral disaster in which all too many of their leading human genetics practitioners eugenically preached racial Nordic superiority and willingly participated in the 1933–1945 Nazi era elimination by scientific selection of Germany's mentally ill, Jews, and Gypsies. After World War II ended and these atrocities became known, their most direct perpetuators were tried under the Nuremberg Laws, and among those that did not commit suicide, a number were executed. However, those academics whose hands were not so directly bloodied and who claimed to never have been more than scientific advisers slowly crept back into leading academic positions in genetics, psychiatry, and anthropology. The German nation thus never directly faced up to the moral depravity done under the name of genetics. Far better would have been an effective moratorium on the teaching of these subjects for a decade or two following the war. Then a new generation of teachers trained abroad could return to Germany. Instead, the rot of Nazi genetics tainted the German university system until the late 1960s.

So neither genetics nor geneticists had the smell of integrity in Germany when the recombinant DNA era began in the 1970s and opened up the possibility of gene cloning and genetic manipulation. That this was not a new era we should blindly rush into was immediately realized by the DNA community, which quickly instituted an effective self-imposed moratorium until serious consideration was given to whether the novel genetically modified microorganisms (viruses, bacteria, and yeast) that we would create in our laboratories might pose a realistic threat to either human health or the world's ecology. A large international meeting was convened in Asilomar, near Monterey, California, to discuss these issues, which later became the province of specialist-dominated governmental committees formed in those countries whose scientists wanted to use recombinant DNA procedures for either understanding phenomena like cancer or the immunological response, or to create genetically engineered cellular factories for the making of important new pharmaceutical drugs or diagnostics. Virtually all such committees, independent of national origin and usually containing members drawn from the general public, opted to effectively end the moratorium for most research and biotechnology uses by the end of 1979.

Though at first there were discussions that the public would be more reassured by the creation of laws than government agency–promoted regulations, the inherent complexity of writing laws to handle the extraordinarily broad ways in which recombinant DNA might be employed made more easily changeable government regulation the preferred way of handling the fast-moving pace of innovation in recombinant DNA use. Partly because of ever-decreasing regulations, recombinant DNA–based research has thrived in the Western Hemisphere, in Japan, and in most parts of Europe. Not surprisingly, the major exception has been Germany, which all too long has been accustomed to viewing geneticists as individuals more responsive to their own needs or those of the state rather than the public good.

For almost two decades the totally unjustified German public perception that recombinant DNA manipulation per se is inherently evil has led to much unnecessary if not ludicrous regulation and legislation that has greatly set back their country's biological and medical research, as well as long stifling the use of DNA technologies by German industry, be it large or small. Instead of analyzing individual RNA recombinant products for their potential risks to humans or to the broader issue of world ecology, German opponents of DNA have misleadingly raised the moral threat of Nazi-type geneticists working to overturn the established natural order of life. In letting hysteria triumph over the use of reason, recombinant DNA products like insulin cannot be industrially produced in most parts of Germany. As a result, there has been an exodus of much German pharmaceutical research to other countries. Likewise, the unwarranted belief that any plant modified by a recombinant DNA procedure is inherently dangerous and never should be grown outside the protective custody of a greenhouse resulted in the vandalized destruction of each of 14 attempts to grow such plants in open German fields last summer. And not only the labs but the homes of prominent German scientists interested in human genetics have been threatened by terrorist bombs.

More concerned that they be perceived by their citizens as seeming to do good than actually doing good, the German government, never coming to grips with why the anti-genetics feeling remained so high among its people, long sat on its hands unrealistically hoping that the anti-DNA feeling would die down. If the German economy had remained in high gear, I suspect that both biotechnology and human genetics research would remain stifled, even today. But with the massive economic readjustment necessary to bring the former East German economy back to life, 2 years ago, a worried German government finally had the sense to initiate a modest Human Genome Project as well as to finally jump-start German biotechnology through federal and state subsidies.

Knowing of this most welcome turnabout, a year ago I accepted an invitation to come to Berlin for a meeting the following year. No longer would my hosts have to be inherently gloomy at effectively being kept out of the ever-growing excitement of today's human genetics and biotechnology. My main reason for going, however, was that the occasion was sponsored by the Max Delbrück Center for Molecular Medicine (MDC), a large research institution created after German unification in Berlin–Buch on the grounds of a former East German institute for biological research. Even earlier, it was the site of important 1930s research on the gene by the highly talented Russian geneticist Nicolai Timofeeff Ressovsky, collaborating with the young German theoretical physicist Max Delbrück, whose interests were switching from physics to biology. Strongly influenced several years earlier in Copenhagen by Niels Bohr, Max worked in Berlin–Dahlem at The Kaiser-Wilhelm Institut für Chemie with the famed Lisa Meitner. Later, as a refugee in Stockholm, she, along with her nephew Otto Frisch, correctly interpreted the uranium fission process discovered in her former institute by Otto Hahn and Fritz Strassmann.

In 1935, Delbrück and Timofeeff wrote a seminal paper that attempted to measure the size of the gene through the rate at which it inactivated by increasing doses of X rays. Their approach, given the name "Target Theory," became widely known later through Erwin Schroedinger's 1944 *What Is Life?* This small but vastly influential book appeared after a series of lectures that Schroedinger delivered in Dublin, where he had gone as a refugee from Nazi Austria. Its discussion of the Delbrück model of the gene first caught my attention in the late 1940s when I was a biology student at the University of Chicago. As a result, I stopped thinking of birds as my future career and instead saw the nature of the gene as biology's most important objective.

By then, Max Delbrück, whose high Protestant academic background proved immiscible with a Nazi indoctrination weekend was in the United States, moving to the genetics world in 1937 at the California Institute of Technology. Soon after his arrival in Pasadena, Max hit upon bacterial viruses (phages) as perfect experimental systems for the gene studies and soon set into motion incisive research which, over the next decade, led to his 1969 Nobel Prize.

My getting to know Max during the summer of 1948 at the Cold Spring Harbor (N.Y.) Laboratory was a revelation, with his tall youthful esprit soon becoming the model for what I wanted out of my own life. How one gene becomes two identical genes was the problem to solve. When Francis Crick and I found the answer through our March 1953 discovery of the double helical structure of DNA, Max instantly rose to the occasion proclaiming to all that the double helix would be the starting point for all future biological research. From him I had learned that Dahlem, before Hitler's time, had been one of the world's great scientific centers, and I now looked forward to seeing what luster, if any, from the past still enveloped the Dahlem scene.

During a day's stopover in Oxford before going on to Berlin, I began to worry more whether I would soon be complicating my life unnecessarily. Instead of praising my hosts for finally starting a human genome program, I would be telling them that the world wants them to finally shape up about their Nazi genetic past. I could do so in part because I was not making them responsible for all the genetics misdeeds of the past. A prominent eugenics movement also existed previously in the United States between 1910 and 1940. In fact, it was centered at the Cold Spring Harbor Laboratory, where I had first gotten to know Delbrück and of which, since 1968, I have been its Director and now its President. Like the German effort, the American eugenics agenda was primarily political, rather than scientific, and irresponsibly preached prejudice as scientific fact.

To restrict the level of Italian immigration into the United States, Harry Laughlin, the director of the Laboratory's Eugenics Record Office, gave testimony in 1923 before the American Congress that the people from Southern Europe were genetically prone to criminality. Furthermore, the equally unjustified belief of many then practicing human geneticists that race mixing leads to degenerate offspring helped pass laws in many American states that forbade interracial marriages. So I could start my talk with American misdeeds before going on to the clearly much viler German situation, where, for example, the "incurable" psychiatric patients with supposed inherited defects were called "socially inferior, empty shells, or ballast existences." So identified between January 1940 and September 1941, some 70,000 already sterilized psychiatric patients were murdered in gas chambers to free up their hospital beds for the war wounded.

Until World War II began, notwithstanding the anti-Semitic Nuremberg decrees of 1935, the American and German eugenics movements remained enthusiastic partners, with Harry Laughlin receiving from the German Consul in New York an honorary degree from Heidelberg University for his promotion of racial hygiene. At a "eugenics rally" in Pasadena, California, Laughlin praised the great benefit from the July 14, 1933, Nazi law for the prevention of progeny with hereditary defects. It allowed for compulsory sterilization for 16 different supposed genetic defects, including congenital mental defects, schizophrenia, manic-depressive disease, hereditary blindness and deafness, hereditary epilepsy, and severe alcoholism. Over the next 6 years, almost 400,000 persons so diagnosed were sterilized.

Though I never speak from written manuscripts, in this case not wanting to be misquoted, I saw the need to have one prepared to hand out after my talk. Worried that I might have some facts wrong, just before getting on the plane I arranged for a copy to be faxed to my friend of the late 1960s at Harvard, Benno Müller-Hill, now a Professor of Genetics at Cologne and whose 1988 English translation *Murderous Science* of his 1984 *Todliche Wissenshaft* had first alerted me to what had not happened to the Nazi co-opted geneticists after the war. To my relief, soon after my arrival in Berlin, Benno phoned me at the InterContinental Hotel that my facts about the past were right on the mark.

With a free day ahead of us, my wife, Liz, and I spent the morning in former East Berlin at the Pergamon Museum, famed for its almost intact Grecian temples and the extraordinary Assyrian brick gates from Babylon that several generations of German archaeologists sent back to Berlin beginning around 1870. In the afternoon, once back in the former West Berlin, we walked around the Prussian kings' Berlin palace at Charlottenburg, noting in particular the relatively petite, two-floored "summer home" designed for Karl Frederick IV by Karl Frederick Schinkel, the great German classical architect of the early nineteenth century whom our late architect friend Charles Moore much admired. Schinkel's English equivalent, Sir John Soane, was also a favorite of Moore's, and the Soane-like features of *Ballybung*, our new home at Cold Spring Harbor, would not have been out of place in Schinkel's summer house.

For the early evening, our host Detlev Ganten, the Director of the MDC, arranged for a predinner visit to the former atelier of Jeanne Mammen (1890–1976), the Berlin-born painter whom Max formed a close friendship with just before he left for the United States. Until the Nazis took over, she was a successful magazine illustrator, drawing and painting men and women of 1920s Berlin with a George Grosz–type sting. Such drawings became impossible to do with Hitler in power, and during the war her painting had Picasso-like features. After the war, Max brought back several of these 1940s pieces to his Caltech home, where they dominated the big room in which Max played the piano and entertained the always continuous stream of young guests to which he and his wife, Manny, were partial.

Mammen's atelier was on the top floor of a large early twentieth century building on the Kurfurstendamm, now maintained as a mini-museum by several friends who helped look after her in her last years. Being 23 years older than me, Max had once had a father-like role to me. So with Ganten following me out of breath, I bounded up the staircase imagining that I was still the 20-year-old youth in awe of everything that was Delbrück. It was my hope that I could somehow buy a 1920s drawing from the Jeanne Mammen Gessellschaft but soon found that those pieces had largely found their way to museums like the Busch Reisinger at Harvard. Instead, I happily settled on a bronze statue of a head from the war years that I took to be a haunted soldier of the Third Reich. With other guests wondering whether it might have been modeled upon memories of Max, I silently noted its resemblance to an oil of a wartime soldier that hung in the next room.

The occasion had begun with a short speech in German and Ganten sitting between us on the couch whispering in English into our ears. Before coming to Berlin, I only thought of how unique Max had been to me but never the other direction. So I felt awkwardly happy when Max's feelings about me were highlighted as well as his just post–double-helix notion that I was the Einstein of biology. Max used to emphasize that both Albert Einstein and Werner Heisenberg were only 25 when they did their best science, leading me later to take satisfaction in the fact that I was 1 month short of being 25 when Francis Crick and I found the double helix. Such feelings, however, always were accompanied by the realization that our finding of the double helix did not represent a particularly difficult intellectual effort. But now before new acquaintances not in the know I only smiled and accepted the champagne that was brought out to mark our still warm memories of Max.

Initially I was attracted to giving the keynote speech by knowledge that it was to be preceded by a talk from the German Science Minister. So my arrival in Berlin was clouded by learning that a more junior representative, Elke Wulfing, was to give the Bonn government presentation. Her speech, nonetheless, proved most informative both for what she said as well as what she did not. Emphatically the driving force behind Germany's belated entry into the genome game was economic—to directly help its pharmaceutical companies as well as to push forward Germany's fledgling biotechnology efforts. Nonetheless, she gave no encouragement that the $24 million now allocated for genome efforts would soon grow. And when she said that research that did not lead to patents had no place in her research portfolio, virtually everyone was stunned, turning their heads to catch the reactions of their compatriots. I fear that her desire for immediate commercial research payoffs represents the thinking of most equivalent governmental ministers elsewhere.

All in all I got the unmistakable impression that Germany was now only getting into the genome game to help itself, as opposed to the world as a whole. Immediately explainable was why Germany was not going along with the unselfish data-release policies agreed on more than a year ago by scientists from the United States and the United Kingdom whereby all of their genome data were put on the World Wide Web within a day of generation. In contrast, the German government now wishes to give its industry a 90-day first look at German-generated genome data before letting the rest of the world see them.* In so going alone and not being part of the now very efficient USA–UK collaborative programs, Germany's genome effort may not turn out to be the locomotive its government wants to pull its biotechnology industry into world prominence. My feeling of angry despair was compounded when her talk ended without any significant mention of the ethical uses of genetic information.

With my adrenalin levels then clearly raised, I improvised the starting words of my own talk by saying that Ms. Wulfing should report back to Bonn that the outside world saw little to cheer about in the way Germany was entering the genome world. This was not the occasion for her to portray genes as potential servants of the commercial interests of the German state. Instead, she should be emphasizing, particularly before a Congress of Molecular Medicine, the desire of the people of the world to find ways to

---

*Germany has now decided to go along with the British and USA immediate release policy. JDW (30 September 1997)

combat the pernicious effects of gene-related diseases. My necessary scorn directed toward Bonn brought forth enthusiastic applause by the audience, almost all connected to medically related research in Germany.

Later, it was much more difficult to judge their reactions to my many slides illustrating what eugenics really stood for prior to World War II. Certainly the squalid American story to which most of my talk was devoted was new to their eyes. And I suspect few of them had been consciously exposed to the grisly details of how the German eugenicists gave wholehearted support to the Nazi doctrine of race purity and their program to exclude anything Jewish from future German life. At the end of my hour I emphasized how bad it had been for the postwar German government to bring back Professors Fritz Lenz and Otmar von Verschuer into German academic life. Both had continued working on behalf of the Nazis even after they knew the genocidal final solution to the Jewish problem had commenced. Here, I had to say that the 1939 Nobel Prize winner Adolf Butenandt should be most remembered for his participation in the 1949 whitewash of Professor von Verschuer, then well known for wartime research using materials sent to him from Auschwitz by his former student Josef Mengele. Mildly reprimanded for "a few isolated events of the past," von Verschuer afterwards became the Professor of Genetics at Munster while Butenandt went on to lead the Max-Planck-Gesellschaft.

I had to pose the question whether anyone really should be surprised that so many Germans still mistrust their geneticists, if not their entire scientific community. Had not the time come for the German genetics community to finally admit that they are deeply ashamed of their forbearers' past? In my mind, only by doing so will they stand the chance of finally escaping from the ghost of Hitler that still haunts them as well as geneticists all over the world. We do not want Hitler's name brought up over and over as we try to somehow mitigate the genetic inequalities that diminished so many innocent peoples' lives.

Though there was much applause from the audience of over 1500 scientists, I had to wonder whether my true message got across. To most who came up to me, I gave copies of my written manuscript, particularly to reporters who wanted 1-minute type quotes, which by then I was too exhausted to give. By attacking the integrity of Butenandt, I knew I would go deep into the German psyche, but it was his actions and not Hitler's that are Germany's problem now. To my relief, Detlev Ganten turned warmly to me, telling me he was glad that I brought up the issue that Germany has never really purged itself of the sins of its Nazi era geneticists. Soon I was being congratulated by Peter Fischer, the biographer of Max Delbrück and now Professor of the History of Science at Konstanz University.

Later, at dinner at the Funkturn Restaurant, atop the radio tower next to the Congress Hall on the outskirts of Berlin, I sat next to Elke Wulfing and told her about how our American genome effort was committing 5% of its funds to discussion of the ethical, legal, and social consequences of genome research. Telling me that her field of past expertise was textiles, she emphasized that her ministry had delayed starting its genome effort until they sorted out the ethical issue. In our Congress packet was a March 1997 pamphlet from her Ministry of Science and Technology, entitled "Biotechnology, Genetic Engineering, and Economic Innovation." In it was the statement that there was need for interdisciplinary research into ethical, legal, and social questions. Nowhere in the text did I find the word eugenics mentioned, nor was there any discussion of why Germany faces greater difficulty than any other nation in pursuing the study of human DNA. As the dinner ended, I got the unmistakable impression that Ms. Wulfing thought genome ethical issues were now at last behind the backs of her ministry.

The next afternoon, Liz and I were given a car and driver to take us out to Dahlem, where Max had grown up, to see the prewar buildings of the Kaiser Wilhelm Institutes (KWI). To help us, Detlev Ganten arranged for us to be guided by a professor interested in medicine. Upon picking him up in a nearby suburb, I explained that I was particularly interested in seeing the building that once housed the KWI for Anthropology, Human Genetics, and Eugenics. It had been created especially for Professor Eugen Fischer, the leader of the German eugenic movement, who for more than 20 years was in close correspondence with Charles B. Davenport, the founder of Cold Spring Harbor's 1910 Eugenics Record Office. Then Fischer's worldwide reputation, gained in part through his studies on race mixing in German Southwest Africa (Namibia), gained him funds from the Rockefeller Foundation to cover his building's 1926 construction. Later, as the 1933–1934 Director of Berlin University after Hitler came to power, Fischer signed the dismissal notes of its Jewish professors.

Officially retiring in 1942, Fischer was replaced as Institute Director by Otmar von Verschuer, who had moved from Berlin to Frankfurt as Professor of Genetics 5 years before. In 1937, in a letter to Fischer, von Verschuer mentioned his report to Alfred Rosenberg (later the Reich Minister of the

Occupied Eastern Territories) containing his proposals for the registration of Jews and half-Jews. Later that year, von Verschuer protested to the Reich Minister of Justice Gurtner that his expert opinion (written with the help of Josef Mengele) incriminating the defendant in a race dishonor trial (marriage of Jews with Aryans was then forbidden) had not been accepted and that as a result the defendant had been set free.

After looking up at the turreted, four-story building where Hahn and Strassman had split the uranium atom in 1939, we walked toward the KWI for Anthropology building with our guide explaining that its last professor had been Professor von Verschuer, who after the war had moved on to the University of Munster from where he had traveled to an international meeting in Venezuela to talk about his twin research. Sensing that the guide had not been at my lecture, I quietly let him discover that von Verschuer's brand of genetics was not my type. So he knew what I might be thinking when we came upon a bronze plaque next to the front door of the two-story, some 400-foot-long KWI building. Its 21 lines described the past history of the building and how its science had been perverted for political purposes. After the war, this building became part of the Frei University of West Berlin. With its lower floor bracketed by New York subway–type graffiti, which now cover so many Berlin buildings, social scientists now make it their home. In leaving it, I thought how much better for it to have been bulldozed to the ground immediately after the war.

In later passing first the KWI building once housing the preeminent biochemist Otto Warburg and later the building built for Einstein before he saw good reason not to return to Berlin, I brought up the awfulness of racism, thinking of how grand Dahlem had been when it welcomed Jews among its institutes. Our guide, however, not understanding my words, quickly voiced agreement saying that with today's bad unemployment, racism was again a real feature of existence in Berlin.

With our guide now gone, Liz and I drove farther out to Lake Wannsee and across the bridge where spies were once exchanged between East and West Berlin, to the once grand Potsdam in former East Germany, which still looked as if World War II had just ended. There, we first walked about Cecilianhof, the last Kaiser's eldest son's Lutyens-style great lakeside 1916 mansion, where Stalin, Churchill, and Roosevelt met just after Europe was liberated. Then on to Sans Souci, the Prussian House of Hohenzollern's several mile square grand estate of palaces and gardens. In admiring its yellow-gilded Chinoise teahouse, its sprawling Italianate bath house, and its Charlottenhof elegant blue-windowed, stone Schinkel mini-palace of the 1830s, I appreciated better a key fact told to us soon after our arrival in Berlin. Until this visit I had assumed that Berlin's becoming the capital of the 1871 unified Germany was a successful reflection of Prussian militarism. Instead, we were told that Berlin's preeminence had come about in large part because the eighteenth century Prussian kings welcomed immigrants and new ideas, eagerly accepting the Huguenots forced out of eighteenth century France. Likewise, Berlin, more than any other German city, gave its Jews full rights, allowing them to become highly prominent members of its academic and commercial worlds by 1900. As a result, many Jews fought valiantly on the Kaiser's side in World War I. It was Prussian enlightenment and not military might that allowed Berlin to become perhaps the world's most important cultural center for the first third of this century.

A free last day in Berlin gave us the opportunity for the 45-minute drive north to Berlin–Buch to see how the newly created MDC was faring. In driving us out, Detlev Ganten wanted us to walk about an adjacent set of some 20 hospital buildings that soon would be totally vacated. One possibility for their subsequent use would be as a conference center for continued medical education. The entire complex was almost a small town, with all of the buildings, from gatehouse to the grand doctors' homes to the several-hundred-room hospital buildings, constructed of handsome red brick and topped by roundish Flemish gables. For a moment I felt that I might be in the midst of a large group of early twentieth century American college dormitories. How the East Germans used these buildings did not seem to interest our hosts, with my getting the impression that tuberculosis patients once might have roamed its gardened grounds.

Then we moved past a gated lodge into the MDC, where Detlev Ganten's office was on the second floor of the massive four-story, long research building. Its total reconstruction only partially compensated for the shoddy East German construction of only 15 years ago. Also being converted for use by Max Delbrück scientists was the large brick-covered "1920s modern" building that once housed Oscar Vogt's prestigious KWI for Brain Research. In the mid-1920s, Vogt had been asked by Stalin to come to Moscow to examine Lenin's brain. Though Lenin's thinking parts proved anatomically similar to all others, the visit let Vogt meet the talented young geneticist Timofeeff Ressovsky, whom he persuaded to join his Berlin–Buch Institute. Living in the large gatehouse that Ganten hopes soon will be transformed into the Institute's clubhouse, Timofeeff, at the war's end, remained in Buch after virtually all of its other scientists had fled to western parts of Germany. As such, he was soon captured by the Russian army and transported back to Russia. There, he was imprisoned for several years until moved to a military research lab in the Ural Mountains where he remained until his death in 1981.

By 1937 Oskar Vogt no longer could work under the Nazis and moved to a private lab in the Black Forest. At that time, Professor Julius Hallervorden from the Brandenburg Psychiatric Institute arrived in Buch. There he took particular interest in the brains of the feeble-minded that he obtained after they were "euthanized" by the Nazis. Much additional material came to him from the mental hospital at Brandenburg Görden that was closely connected to an extermination center in nearby Brandenburg. Hallervorden was actively involved with this center, not only providing it with a technician from his institute but letting one of its physicians come to his lab to do research and learn advanced anatomical techniques. Yet after American interrogation, he somehow avoided postwar imprisonment, becoming head of the Max-Planck Institute of Brain Research in Giessen in 1948.

When our tour of the MDC was over and I had signed its new large guest book, we went to dinner at Detlev's new home built on land just over the boundary from the MDC in the state of Brandenburg. With his house cheerfully new and having a garden to step out into from the living room, it was a welcome relief to his physician wife, who lived for 2 years in the once grand Oscar Vogt house after they arrived from Heidelberg. Admitting that her first reaction to life in the former East Germany was of deep despair, the large new complex of modern flats across the field into Brandenburg provided visible proof that East Germany was mending, albeit slowly. Dinner was dominated by conversation with two of the rare East German scientists kept on when the MDC was formed. They still read the newspaper of East as opposed to West Berlin, and they liked the way child care had been handled in East Berlin more than the system now taking over.

At dessert time, I raised the question of whether any state funds could be used to give the MDC a more distinguished visual appearance but learned that the bureaucrats do not allow such frivolities. A few years ago, German industry might have risen to the occasion. Now with their profits low they are miserly even with monies for supporting research that may have industrial payoffs. Asking whether private philanthropy will soon take off in a big way, I was told that virtually all Germans, rich to poor, assume that the state takes care of all important tasks. With Prussian kings no longer to be counted on and Berlin's Jews reduced to at most a few thousand, the federal and state governments remain the only bodies on which people can rely.

When we got back to our hotel, Liz immediately opened the English language version of the thick book that we had bought at the massive Potsdamer Platz construction site to read about the Berlin region's architectural riches. In the chapter dealing with Berlin–Buch, she found a writeup of the early twentieth century Flemish gabled hospital buildings. As we suspected but did not say earlier, the Kaiser's 1906 government took great care of and chose distinguished architects for their lunatic asylums.

Ten days later Germany ever haunts me.

J.D. Watson
Cold Spring Harbor Laboratory
Cold Spring Harbor, New York
15 May 1997

The Specter of Kakogenics

One may see eugenics with different eyes. One may see it as the sum of all the eugenic utopias proposed by great men of science, for example, Francis Galton, Alexis Carrel, H.J. Muller et al.—I do not see it as that. Or one may see eugenics as the social reality created and organized by politicians with the advice and help of human geneticists—that is how I perceive eugenics. But before I touch on the question of a new eugenics I must comment on early eugenics.

This eugenic reality has varied greatly in different countries. In Britain, for example, there was a lot of talk about eugenics but no action. In contrast, in Sweden 63,000 people, mostly women, were legally sterilized between 1934 and 1975, as decreed by eugenic legislation. The main reason given was antisocial behavior. Most Gypsies (*tattare*) living in Sweden were among the victims. It is doubtful whether even a minority of the victims consented to the procedure, as the law demanded. Here, we have an example of a democratic country run by a social democratic government from which one would not have suspected such an action. This history has in fact been presented only rather recently in two books in Swedish which, to the best of my knowledge, have not been translated into English.

The case in Germany from 1933 to 1945 was much worse, where it involved close and efficient cooperation between human geneticists and the Nazi government. One may call it kakogenics. Here, both sides had great advantages, but both sides also had to pay. The human geneticists got the involuntary sterilization law they had asked for and subsequently were envied by the international eugenics establishment. As a result, about 350,000 persons were sterilized between 1934 and 1939. The human geneticists received ample support for their research, their positions within the universities were strengthened, and their students got jobs in the eugenics administration. In return, the geneticists had to accept and support the violent anti-Semitism of the Nazis. They did so. On the other hand, the Nazi politicians received the support of scientists in solving unambiguously racial questions. They could claim that their racial projects were supported by science. In return, they had to accept the independence of the scientists who, for example, did not agree with the mythical claim that blood may be poisoned by interracial sexual intercourse. So there were disagreements, but both sides collaborated to the bitter end.

Let me now look briefly at Nazi euthanasia in the context of eugenics. Between January 1940 and September 1941, about 70,000 permanent psychiatric patients were murdered in gas chambers so that their hospital beds could be made available for the wounded of the war. It was the idea of the eugenicists among the German psychiatrists to call the schizophrenics and other incurable psychiatric patients with inherited defects *socially inferior*, *empty shells*, or *ballast existences*. These terms made it easy for the young psychiatrists involved in the euthanasia action to make the selection. While the euthanasia mass murder was going on, one of the leading eugenicists, Fritz Lenz, wrote in his introduction to a dissertation on euthanasia that euthanasia was *not* a eugenic measure, at least not in Germany where all psychiatric patients had been sterilized! This is a case where reality should count and not impeccable scientific logic. Thus, I see this mass murder as an outgrowth of eugenics, or kakogenics, as practiced in Germany.

It has become the habit of many geneticists to claim that these German geneticists were not doing genetics at all but *pseudoscience*. This would free the geneticists from this past. I believe the term *pseudoscience* is grossly misleading. If you read the old German papers and books you will see that in general they do not differ from the international standard. For example, almost all human geneticists then believed that race mixing led to bad results and should be resisted or restricted. However, there is no doubt that human genetics reached its lowest point in Nazi Germany, because the geneticists sold their knowledge to robbers and murderers.

There was a most interesting philosophical debate on this sort of problem shortly after the French Revolution. Benjamin Constant, then 30 years old, wrote in his essay *Les Reactions Politiques* (1797), that situations exist where the truth should *not* be spoken. He had experienced such situations during *la terreur*. Hence, he believed that one should not follow the teaching of a certain German philosopher who proposed that the truth should always be told, even to the murderer who asks for the address of one's friend, whom he wants to murder. The German philosopher Immanuel Kant, then 73 years old, read Constant's essay and answered immediately (*Berliner Blätter* 1: 301–314, 1797). He claimed that he was quoted correctly, and that indeed you should tell the murderer the truth and only the truth, because if you should lie only once, the truth may disintegrate for you and for others forever. So Kant's teaching not only allowed, but actually demanded, that the German human geneticists tell the scientific truth to the Nazis, irrespective of what the Nazis would do with this truth. I will document the infamous destructiveness of this proposition with two examples.

1. There were thousands of persons in Germany who had a Jewish father and a non-Jewish mother. To religious Jews, these individuals were non-Jewish, but in the system of the Nazis they were treated almost as badly as full Jews. As the mistreatment increased and as their situation became more and more hopeless (in 1941, the possibility of emigration ended completely), many of these half-Jews attempted a last means of escape. They claimed that their legal father was not their biological father. The human geneticists were officially asked to do a paternity analysis of these people. In 1941, the major blood groups could be determined, and physical analysis was well advanced. Now what would a geneticist do with such an analysis in 1941? If his result indicated that the legal father was indeed the biological father, the person asking for help would almost certainly be deported to the East to an uncertain future and, presumably, a violent death. I have asked every German human geneticist I could find who had been involved in such work. All of them claimed that they always related the scientific truth. They reported what the science revealed, even if the result of their analysis indicated that the legal father was the biological father, that is, that the person was half-Jewish. It was not their business to worry about the fate of the person. In contrast to the Germans, the Austrian and the French experts were corrupt; they could be bribed to falsify the data. I prefer that! One Austrian human geneticist actually told me he had lied so often on this subject that after the war he simply could not go on making a living with paternity cases, so he gave up science.

2. In those years, about 30,000 Gypsies lived in Germany and Austria. Their ancestors, who were Caucasians or Aryans, had come from India to Europe around 1400. From a racial point of view, these ancestors were acceptable to the Nazis. But there was good evidence that in the 550 years that these peoples lived in Europe, they had intermarried with the lowest

criminal underclass of Europe. So it was believed that the genes for anti-social and criminal behavior had been accumulated in their group [Note that such genes are still taken for granted today (see *Ciba Foundation Symposium* **194**; *Genetics of Criminal and Antisocial Behavior* 1996).] For this reason, the German human geneticists proposed that more than 90% of the Gypsies be sterilized. This became the general policy. About half a dozen families were selected to be allowed to live unharmed, as examples of true Gypsies, and about 20,000 were transported to Auschwitz. There, most died from hunger and infections, with the survivors finally perishing in the gas chambers. The other 10,000 Gypsies were deported to other camps or shot, or they escaped in various ways. The analysis of "pure Gypsy," or *Mischling*, was done according to standard criteria by human geneticists in a special institute that was part of the German National Health Institute. The problem was not in the analysis (they did a thorough job) but what was done with the analysis. *Mischling* became a death sentence, and the human geneticists who performed the analysis knew this. So, again, it was not the scientific truth, which one might question in detail, but selling the truth to the murderers, which became most objectionable. I might add that none of these experts ever had real legal problems after 1945.

I will now leave the past and comment on the eugenics of today. I mention in passing that the Chinese government has passed a law (Order of the President of the People's Republic of China No. 33, October 27, 1994) that reads like a modernized, short version of the German sterilization law of 1934. Embryos with genetic defects must be aborted, and people with genetic defects are not allowed to marry or to have children. We should learn from this that the eugenic reality will be very different in economically poor as opposed to wealthy countries. I will concentrate first on the future of the wealthy countries.

Genetics has advanced in the last hundred years. The difference between old and new eugenics is the knowledge of the human genotype. In the last 25 years an enormous amount of such knowledge has been amassed. But our knowledge about human genotypes is still very minimal. I predict that it will increase drastically in the next 30 years. I also forsee that the mutant genes leading to schizophrenia and manic depression will be isolated (of course, their phenotypes will be redefined!) and that genes and mutations determining very high, medium, or low intelligence (again redefined) will be found. I am not going to discuss the possibility that their carriers may be stigmatized in Europe or in the United States, this has been done by others.

I anticipate that the frequency of such mutations in these genes will be found to vary among ethnic groups. Interracial genetic differences for intelligence, for example, were claimed by the human geneticists of the 1930s without any evidence. It was a hypothesis that was accepted as truth and was amalgamated with value systems present in Europe and in the United States. After the defeat of Nazi Germany, widespread opinion held that no evidence for such differences exists (true) and that such differences do not exist (possibly true, possibly false) and cannot exist (most likely false). The claim that such differences might exist is regarded today as a sign of racism. Now, we sit in this trap built by well-meaning people after World War II. There is something fundamentally wrong with the claim that such differences cannot exist. Science determines truth but not values. From a scientific point of view it should be possible to make the statement that ethnic groups are genetically different in such genes, if there is hard proof that they are different. For me, racism begins when it is claimed that genetically different groups may be stigmatized and should not have equal rights; however, this is not the general opinion.

The history of Nazi Germany is the history of massive discrimination and murder committed in the name of eugenics, or race hygiene, as the Germans liked to call eugenics. Now, let us assume that murderers are waiting for scientists to stigmatize some peoples as genetically *inferior* so that these individuals can be eliminated. Is not low intelligence and schizophrenia a sign of *inferiority*? If this were the case, ethnic groups that have a higher frequency of such mutant genes should not be identified. What is true for individuals should also be true for groups. After all, individuals are not publicly identified when they are found to carry particular mutations. Whether such "anonymization" of ethnic groups is possible remains to be seen. If after "anonymization" some ambitious scientist or clever journalist breaks the code and announces the truth, a moratorium of this type of research should be announced. But how will people with such easily testable genotypes be treated in economically poor but ambitious countries such as China? What might be prohibited in Europe and in the United States might be accepted there and in other similar countries.

James Watson has been quoted as saying,: "We used to think our fate was in our stars. Now we know, in large measure, our fate is in our genes" (*Time Magazine*, March 20, 1989). This is a curious statement. Who were those who believed previously that their fate was in the stars? Many medieval Christians did, but certainly not religious Jews (I do not know about Muslims). The Rabbis read the last chapter of the *Treatment in Eight Chapters of Maimonides*, from which they learned that human freedom to vote for good or bad actions is *not* abolished or determined by the stars. Should *we* now believe that the genotype determines our moral decisions in large measure? I say emphatically "*no*." But we should be aware that the intellectual and emotional limitations within which we analyze the world and plan our actions may differ drastically among people with different genotypes. So it depends on what we understand when we use the words "our fate." I interpret these words as our limitations. (Please note that words and language determine our actions.)

I have stated that science produces truth but not values and that everyone can exercise his/her free will within the differing limitations of his/her genetic setup. This is also true for schizophrenic, manic-depressive, intelligent, or not so intelligent persons. But what about a man who carries on his X chromosome a mutant *MAO A* gene, which is claimed to lead to violent crime (Brunner *et al. Science* 262: 578–580, 1993)? Here, science has transgressed its borders. Crime should not be made part of a phenotype. Fortunately, in spite of an intense search, *MAO A* mutations have so far only been found in one Dutch family. The moment another "crime gene" is found, where null mutations differ in percentage in various ethnic groups, all hell will break loose. This may happen tomorrow.

To sum up, it is the duty of human geneticists to predict the possible social consequences of genetic research and to act accordingly. I fear that new eugenics will again become kakogenics with massive misuse of genetic knowledge. Indeed, I would be most happy if I am proven wrong by history.

Benno Müller-Hill
Institut für Genetik der Universität zu Köln
D-50931 Köln, Germany
May 1997

Bibliography

When the original, German edition of Murderous Science appeared in 1984, it was one of the first books which exposed the collaboration of German anthropologists, psychiatrists and human geneticists with the Nazis in their attempt to cleanse the German people from "undesirables" such as the handicapped and the insane, the Jews and the Gypsies. Since then, several books have appeared which deal with the matter from various points of views. I list here some of them.

The eugenic movement; prehistory of mass murder

Kevles, D.J. *In the name of eugenics: Genetics and the uses of human heredity.* New York, 1985.
A detailed history of the eugenic movement in the English-speaking world. The author presents his story as if a European and, more particularly, a German movement had never existed.

Kühl, S. *The Nazi connection. Eugenics, American racism and German national socialism,* Oxford, 1994.
A first attempt to demonstrate the tight links between American eugenicists and German race hygienists before and after 1933.

Adams, M. ed. *The wellborne science. Eugenics in Germany, France, Brazil and Russia,* New York, 1990.
The first attempt to present the international history of eugenics. Yet many countries, like Sweden, Switzerland or Japan are absent.

Paul, D.B. *Controlling human heredity. 1865 to the present,* Atlantic Highlands, New Jersey, 1995.

The German universities under National Socialism

Weinreich, M. *Hitler's professors. The part of scholarship in Germany's crimes against the Jewish people.* New York, 1946.

Still the best account of the criminal nature of anti-Semitism in German universities. It is characteristic of the neglect of this topic in Germany that the book has never been translated into German. The published version is an English translation of a text originally written in Yiddish [Hitlers profesorn. Der cheylek fun der daytsher visnshaft in daytshlands farbrekhns keygn yidishn folk, *Yivo-Bleter* (Journal of the Yiddish Scientific Institute), Vol. XXVII, Parts 1 and 2, 1945] by the research director of the Yiddish Scientific Institute in New York.

Race hygiene in Germany

Saller, K. *Die Rassenlehre des Nationalsozialismus in Wissenschaft und Propaganda* [The racial theories of National Socialism in science and propaganda]. Darmstadt, 1961.
The author had collaborated with Professor Fischer and was, as a young man, an enthusiastic supporter of eugenic ideas. He was dismissed from the University of Göttingen on 14 January 1935. His excellent book remained for a long time the only one which dealt with this topic. Its publication led to its author becoming a pariah among his German colleagues [In German].

Proctor, R. *Racial hygiene. Medicine under the Nazis.* Cambridge, Massachusetts, 1988.
A comprehensive account of the German medical involvement in the sterilisation of the handicapped, euthanasia and the attempt to "solve the Jewish problem".

Weindling, P. *Health, race and German politics between national unification and Nazism, 1870–1945.*
A detailed account of German health policies particularly before 1933.

Burleigh, M. and Wippermann, W. *The racial state: Germany 1933–1945,* Cambridge, England, 1991.
Theory and practice of the racial ideology in Germany.

Weingart, P., Kroll, J., and Bayertz, K. Rasse, *Blut und Gene. Geschichte der Eugenik und Rassenhygiene in Deutschland.* Frankfurt a.M. 1988.
The most detailed history of eugenics and race hygiene in Germany. (In German).

Seidler, H., and Rett, A. *Das Reichssippenamt entscheidet. Rassenbiologie im Nationalsozialismus* [The Reich Kinship Bureau decides. Race-biology under National Socialism]. Vienna and Munich, 1982.
An account of the co-operation of Austrian anthropologists with the Reich Kinship Bureau. The book is in part a self-justification; some of the anthropologists who were involved are not mentioned by name [In German].

Pommerin, R. *Sterilisierung der Rheinlandbastarde. Das Schicksal einer farbigen Minderheit* [Sterilization of the Rhineland bastards. The fate of a coloured German minority]. Düsseldorf, 1979.
An account of the illegal sterilization of German coloured children. Their subsequent fate is unknown [In German].

Persecution and extermination of the Jews

Reitlinger, G. *The Final Solution. The attempt to exterminate the Jews of Europe 1939–1945.* London, 1953.
The first comprehensive and detailed description of the Holocaust.
Hilberg, R. *The Destruction of the European Jews.* New York, 1961.
A more recent description of the Holocaust.
Gilbert, M. *The Holocaust: The Jewish tragedy.* London, 1986.
The story of the Holocaust told through the experiences of the individuals involved.
Friedlander, H. *The origins of Nazi genocide. From euthanasia to the final solution.* Chapel Hill, North Carolina, 1995.
A path breaking description of how the Nazi program of secretly exterminating the handicapped and disabled evolved into systematic destruction of Jews and Gypsies.
Schoenberner, G. *The Yellow Star.* London, 1969.
Photographs of all stages of the persecution of the Jews.
Kennzeichen, J. *Bilder, Dokumente, Berichte zur Geschichte der Verbrechen des Hitlerfaschismus an den deutschen Juden 1933–1945.* [Identity badge J for Jew. Pictures, documents, and reports of the history of the crime of Hitlerite Fascism against the German Jews, 1933–1945], ed., H. Eschwege. East Berlin, 1981.
A comprehensive account of the entire period [In German].

Persecution and extermination of the Gypsies ('asocial individuals')

Kenrick, D., and Puxon, G. *The destiny of Europe's Gypsies.* London, 1972.
The only book available in English on the persecution of the Gypsies.
Kalikow, T. Die ethologische Theorie von Konrad Lorenz: Erklärung und Ideologie, 1938–1943 [The ethological theories of Konrad Lorenz: Commentary and ideology, 1938–1943]. In *Naturwissenschaft, Technik und NS-Ideologie* [Science, technology and National Socialist ideology], eds., H. Mehrtens and S. Richter. Frankfurt, 1980.
A cautious critique by an American scholar of Konrad Lorenz's early papers. Lorenz, who won a Nobel prize after the war, had advocated the eradication of 'asocial individuals' [In German].

Persecution and extermination of mental patients

Klee, E. *'Euthanasie' im NS-Staat. Die 'Vernichtung lebensunwerten Lebens'* ['Euthanasia' in the National Socialist state. The 'destruction of lives unworthy to be lived']. Frankfurt, 1983.
An excellent and comprehensive book written by a journalist who has made extensive use of documents gathered by the courts which tried, very leniently, the psychiatrists involved [In German].

Wertham, F. *A sign for Cain. An exploration of human violence.* New York, 1969. The author, an American psychiatrist, describes the mass murder of German mental patients in one chapter.

The series, *Beiträge zur Nationalsozialistischen Gesundheits- und Sozialpolitik* [Contributions to the study of National Socialist health and social policy] includes: Aly, G., Ebbinghaus, A., Hamann, M., Pfäfflin, F., and Preissler, G. *Aussonderung und Tod. Die Klinische Hinrichtung der Unbrauchbaren* [Elimination and death. The clinical execution of the useless], Berlin 1985, and Aly, G., Masuhr, K. F., Lehmann, M., Roth, K. H., and Schultz, U. *Reform und Gewissen. 'Euthanasie' im Dienst des Fortschritts* [Reform and conscience. 'Euthanasia' in the service of progress], Berlin, 1985.

The first two volumes in this series provide a promising start to a detailed analysis of the period 1933–1945. Note that this excellent series is being produced outside the usual channels of university-based historical research [In German].

Auschwitz

Nyiszli, M. *Auschwitz: A doctor's eyewitness account.* New York, 1960. Confessions of a Jewish slave pathologist, who was forced to collaborate with Dr Mengele.

Perl, G. *I was a doctor in Auschwitz.* New York, 1948. The story of a Jewish physician who met Dr Mengele but who chose to help other prisoners rather than become his assistant.

Hill, M.M., and Williams, L.N. *Auschwitz in England.* New York, 1965. Dr Dering, a former assistant to Professor Clauberg in Auschwitz, attempted and failed to obtain legal compensation for defamation of character.

Levi, P. *If this is a man.* London, 1959. An Italian chemist describes his work as a slave-labourer in the IG-Farben factory near Auschwitz. Originally published in Italian as *Se questo è un uomo.* Turin, 1958.

Vrba, R., and Bestic, A. *Escape from Auschwitz. I cannot forgive.* New York, 1964. This book documents the first successful escape from Auschwitz in April 1944 by two young Slovak Jews, Vrba and Wetzler. After reaching Slovakia, they wrote an incisive report about Auschwitz in order to warn the Hungarian Jews of their imminent fate (see *Zeitgeschichte* 8, 413–442).

Müller, F. *Sonderbehandlung* ['Special treatment']. Munich, 1979. The account of one of the very few survivors of the Sonderkommando, the special squad who assisted in the gassing of the victims and the burning of the corpses [In German].

The Auschwitz album. A book based upon an album discovered by a concentration camp survivor, Lily Meier. Text by Peter Hellman. New York, 1981. The prisoners as seen by an SS-photographer.

From the past into the future

Chorover, S.L. *From genesis to genocide, the meaning of human nature and the power of behavior control.* Cambridge, Massachusetts, 1979.
Attempts to use behaviour control in the USA are documented and analysed.

Rose, S., Lewontin, R.C., and Kamin, L.J. *Not in our genes. Biology, ideology and human nature.* London, 1984.
A book, intended for a general audience, which deals critically with the use of psychology in human genetics.

Kevles, D.J. and Hood, L. eds. *The code of codes: Scientific and social issues in the Human Genome Project.* Cambridge, Massachusetts, 1992.
An outline of the present state of human genetics and the Human Genome Project. The future may bring unexpected surprises.

The attempt to understand

Adorno, T.W., and Horkheimer, M. *Dialectic of Enlightenment.* Translated from the German [*Dialektik der Aufklärung.* Amsterdam, 1947] by J. Cumming. New York, 1972.
Even before the war ended, these two exiled philosophers attempted to show that the Enlightenment had carried within itself the seeds of its own destruction.

Lifton, R.J. *The Nazi doctors. Medical killing and the psychology of genocide,* New York, 1986.
The first attempt to understand what went on in the mind of the murderers.

Lerner, R.M. *Final solutions. Biology, prejudice and genocide.* Pennsylvania Park, Pennsylvania, 1992.
Biological determinism, one of the pillars of Nazi ideology, is analysed here in detail.

Notes and References

In the notes which follow these abbreviations are used for the major archives which were used as sources. An English translation of their titles appears in the Acknowledgements on p. ix.

B. Arch. Kobl.—Bundesarchiv, Koblenz
Pol. Arch. A. A. Bonn—Politische Archiv des Auswärtigen Amtes, Bonn
Z. A. Potsdam—Zentralarchiv der Deutschen Demokratischen Republik, Potsdam
Z. A. Merseburg—Zentralarchiv der Deutschen Demokratischen Republik, Merseburg
Nat. Arch. Wash.—National Archives in Washington and Suitland (Maryland) USA
Arch. Yivo, New York—Archives of the Yiddish Scientific Institute, New York
Doc. Center Berlin—Document Center, Berlin.
Arch. Centre Doc. Juive Contemp.—Archives du Centre de Documentation Juive Contemporaine, Paris
Arch. MPG Berlin—Archiv der Max-Planck-Gesellschaft, Berlin
Univ.Arch. Münster—Universitätsarchiv, Münster
Inst. Zeitg. Mü.—Institut für Zeitgeschichte, München

The following abbreviations are also used.

RIM—Reichsinnenministerium [Reich Ministry of the Interior]
RMdI—Reichsministerium des Inneren [also Reich Ministry of the Interior]
REM—Reichsministerium für Wissenschaft, Erziehung und Volksbildung [Reich Ministry of Science, Education, and National Culture]

1. Müller-Hill, B. *Die Philosophen und das Lebendige* [Philosophers and living matter]. Frankfurt, 1981.
2. Fischer, E. In: *Bekenntnis der Professoren an den deutschen Universitäten und Hochschulen zu Adolf Hitler und dem nationalsozialistischen Staat* [Vow of allegiance to Adolf Hitler and the National Socialist state by the professors of German universities and colleges] pp. 9–10. Dresden, 1933. [This book contains not only a German text but also its translation into English, French, Italian, and Spanish.]

3. Von Uexküll, J. *Staatsbiologie. Anatomie—Physiologie—Pathologie des Staates* [Biology of the state: Anatomy, physiology, and pathology of the state] 2nd edn. Hamburg, 1933.
4. Arch. MPG Berlin, Material zum Gesetz zur Wiederherstellung des Berufs-beamtentums [Material on the law for the restoration of the professional civil service] *a* p. 21. Pfundtner to Planck, 24.4.33. *b* p. 22. Telegram from Planck to Glum, 25.4.33. *c* p. 28. Glum to the directors, with questionnaires attached, 27.4.33. *d* p. 35. Record of a meeting of the directors of the KW Institutes in Berlin on 5 May 1933 at 4 pm in Berlin Castle. *e* p. 36. A note for the record concerning the KWI of Medical Research: "Showing great foresight, he [Professor Kuhn] had dismissed one of his Jewish assistants a long time previously, and was going to dismiss the second one, a son of the writer Wassermann, within the next few days." *f* p. 107. Glum to Buttmann, RIM, 4.10.33. [As far as I (BMH) can tell only one assistant was dismissed from a biological KWI for political reasons, and he was an assistant in the KWI of Brain Research, who was a Communist. The American geneticist, Muller, who thought of himself as a Communist at that time and who had come to Berlin because of an interest in eugenics, was working as a visiting scientist in the same institute. He drove the dismissed assistant to the Danish border, if court evidence to that effect is to be believed]. *g* p. 196, Kuhn to Glum, 27.4.36.
5. Arch. MPG Berlin, A1–541, pp. 11–14. Haber to Glum, 2.5.33 with a copy of letter of Haber to Rust, 30.4.33, enclosed. [Haber sent copies of his letter to Rust to several directors.]
6. Arch. MPG Berlin, 126. Report of the 22nd General Assembly of the KWG in the Harnack House in Berlin-Dahlem on Tuesday, 23 May 1933.
7. Planck, M. Mein Besuch bei Adolf Hitler [My visit to Adolf Hitler] *Physikalische Blätter* 3, 143, 1947.
8. Inst. Zeitg. Mü. I/vDB(d) G2–4. V. Brack, evidence under oath from O. Warburg, 3.2.47.
9. *Gesetz zur Verhütung erbkranken Nachwuchses vom 14. Juli 1933* [Law for the prevention of progeny with hereditary defects. 14 July 1933]. Published with explanatory commentary by Arthur Gütt, MD, Ernst Rüdin, MD, and Falk Ruttke (Doctor of Law). Munich, 1934.
10. *Veröffentlichungen aus dem Gebiete der Medizinalverwaltung* [Publications in the field of medical administration] Vol. XXXVIII, part 5, Eugenics in the service of public welfare. Report of the proceedings of a committee convened by the Prussian State Health Council on 2 July 1932, p. 98, Berlin, 1932.
11. Goldschmidt, R. B. *Im Wandel das Bleibende. Mein Lebensweg* [What endures in a changing world. My life's road] p. 264. Hamburg and Berlin, 1963.
12. Arch. MPG Berlin, *Material zum Gesetz zur Wiederherstellung des Berufsbeamtentums* [Material on the law for the restoration of the professional civil service] pp. 8–9. Goldschmidt to Planck, 24.7.33: "Dear President; In

answer to your letter of 21 July, I am informing you that I have carried out your order to give notice to three employees of my institute from 1 September . . ."

13. Kallmann, F. Die Fruchtbarkeit der Schizophrenen. In: *Bevölkerungsfragen. Bericht des Internationalen Kongresses für Bevölkerungsfragen*, Berlin, 26.8–1.9.1935 [The fertility of schizophrenics. In: Population Problems. Report of the International Congress on Population Problems Berlin, 26.8.–1.9.1935], eds. H. Harmsen and F. Lohse. Munich, 1936. Dr Kallmann gained little from his enthusiasm. As a Jew he lost his livelihood. He continued to work untiringly on this theme in the USA. He was a defence witness for Professor Rüdin in judicial proceedings before the Denazification Tribunal.

14. Z.A. Potsdam, REM 965–108. Professor Ewald was called the "only champion of those with hereditary defects".

15. Z.A. Potsdam, RMdI 1501–26250, p. 88. Minutes of a meeting on 13.11.33.

16. Z.A. Merseburg, Rep 76 Vc section 2, Tit 23 Litt A 128a I. Minutes of a meeting of the Expert Advisory Council for Population and Race Policy on 26.6.34.

17. Z.A. Potsdam, RMdI 1501–26251, p. 101. Gütt to the NDW, 1.6.34; RMdI 1501–26252, p. 485. Record of the deliberations of the NDW on 20.6.34.

18. Z.A. Potsdam, RMdI 26229, pp. 412ff. Minutes of a meeting of the Expert Advisory Council for Population and Race Policy on 25.6.34.

19. B. Arch. Kobl., NS2–90, p. 13. Hofmann to the Reich Physician of the SS and Police, 24.9.42. "The Reichsführer-SS decided on 19.9.42, at the time when I presented my report, that vaginal examinations are no longer to be included as part of the medical examination of brides of SS-men."

20. Pol. Arch. A.A. Bonn, Inland I, Partei 84/4, pp. 471160ff.

21. Pommerin, R. *Sterilisierung der Rheinlandbastarde. Das Schicksal einer farbigen deutschen Minderheit* [Sterilization of the Rhineland bastards. The fate of a coloured German minority]. Düsseldorf, 1979. [The publisher used the pejorative expression 'Rhineland bastard' on the book cover without quotation marks or explanations.]

22. Abel, W. Über Europäer-Marokkaner und Europäer Annamiten Kreuzungen [On matings of Moroccans and Indochinese with Europeans]. *Z.Morph. Anthr.* **36** part 2, 1937.

23. Z.A. Potsdam, 3001 Reich Minister of Justice. 10157–10160 Film 23063. Academy of German Law. *a* Constituent meeting of the committee for public care and welfare law, 29.4.38. *b* Another meeting of the committee, 19–20.8.38.

24. Grunau, Ein Jahr Gesetz zur Verhütung erbkranken Nachwuchses [One year of the law for the prevention of progeny with hereditary defects]. *Juristische Wochenschrift* **64** part 1, p. 3, 1935.

25. Z.A. Potsdam, RIM 10160, Film 23063.

26. Z.A. Potsdam, RIM 10161–10162, Film 23064. Lammers to Reich Minister of the Interior, 25.5.326: "The Führer does not think we will gain anything in our battle against the false reports which have been appearing in the foreign press, by publishing the number of sterilizations carried out in Germany."
27. Z.A. Potsdam, RIM 10161–10162, Film 23064. Rüdin to Reich Minister of the Interior, 10.6.36.
28. B. Arch. Kobl., R18–5585, pp. 431–527.
29. B. Arch. Kobl., a R18–5585, pp. 529ff. Lammers to Pfundtner, 13.8.37. b R18–5586, pp. 331–2. Lammers to Pfundtner, 30.4.38.
30. B. Arch. Kobl., R18–5586, p. 1. The Minister of the Interior of the Reich and of Prussia to Lammers, September 1937.
31. B. Arch. Kobl., R18–5586, pp. 327–8. Himmler to Gütt, 26.1.38.
32. Z.A. Potsdam, REM 4909–968, p. 28.
33. Z.A. Potsdam, REM 4909–968. a p. 4. Letter from the Ministry of Culture and Education of Baden to REM, 18.6.38. b p. 13. Pohlisch to REM, 8.12.38.
34. Z.A. Potsdam, Reich Ministry of Justice 3001–1389, pp 6–8. Minutes of a meeting of Ministers of Justice of the Länder on 6.5.33, point 7, mixed marriages.
35. B. Arch. Kobl., R22–852, pp. 75–328. Minutes of the 37th Meeting of the Criminal Law Commission, 5.6.34. Klee, p. 173; Metzger, p. 266; Dahm, p. 250.
36. *Allgemeine Zeitung*, 6.5.36. (There is a copy in the Z.A. Potsdam.)
37. Baur, E., Fischer, E., and Lenz, F. *Menschliche Erblichkeitslehre und Rassenhygiene* [The principles of human heredity and race-hygiene]. a 3rd edn., Vol. I, p. 562, Munich, 1927. b 4th edn., Vol. I, p. 753. Munich, 1936.
38. Z.A. Potsdam, REM 4901–965, pp. 19–20. Fischer to REM, 1.9.36.
39. Z.A. Potsdam, REM 4901–965, p. 29. Mollison to REM, 15.7.36.
40. B. Arch. Kobl., R22–486, pp. 112ff. Von Verschuer to Gürtner, 14.10.37.
41. Univ. Arch. Münster, papers of von Verschuer. a Von Verschuer to Fischer, 20.5.37. b Von Verschuer to Fischer, 5.11.37. c Fischer to von Verschuer, 10.12.38: "Your proposal for the study of the Gypsy question is very good."
42. a Von Verschuer, O. Die Juden und jüdischen Mischlinge im Deutschen Reich. *Der Erbarzt* 8, 162–3, 1940. b Von Verschuer, O. What can the historian, the genealogist and the statistician contribute to the investigation of biological aspects of the Jewish question? In *Forschungen zur Judenfrage* [Researches on the Jewish question] 2, p. 216, 1937. "I should like to begin by recounting an experience which came to mind while I was preparing this lecture. In the spring of 1924, that is to say thirteen years ago, I gave a lecture on race-hygiene at a training camp organized by a national student body. In the very lively concluding discussion, which was conducted both verbally and by means of written notes, one of the leaders of the student society, whose name now escapes me, asked our opinion on a certain matter. He deplored the fact that anthropological science had not yet provided any proof of the racial inferiority of the Jews. He believed that this evidence was absolutely necessary to provide a firm foundation for anti-Semitism. I

answered that anti-Semitism is, in the first place, a national-political struggle whose justification and necessity spring from the threat which Jewry poses for our people, and that it does not depend in any way on a racial assessment of the Jews. A nationalistic state must regard the preservation of its own people as its most important duty, and throw down the gauntlet to anyone who threatens the nation. Therefore, the German national struggle is directed primarily against Jewry, because the German nation is especially threatened by Jewish infiltration. When we put our nation first in this way, it should not be interpreted as underplaying the significance of race. In fact, its significance can be seen most clearly as we move towards a solution of the Jewish question."

43. Fischer, E. "Erbe als Schicksal [Heredity as destiny]", a lecture given to the 8th Technical Meeting of the Association of Mining Interests in Essen on 20 June 1939. (A reprint, without any indication of its origin, is included in the reprint collection of the KWI of Anthropology, now at the Institute of Human Genetics of the University of Münster.)

44. B. Arch. Kobl., R22–487, p. 191. Lenz to the district court in Cologne, 18.9.40. (The replies of his colleagues are to be found in the same place.)

45. Z.A. Potsdam, RMdI 1501–26369, p. 41.

46. Z.A. Potsdam, RMdI 1501–26252, p. 399. Minutes of a meeting on 5.7.34. (Gütt, E. Fischer, Linden, Ruttke, and others were present.)

47. Z.A. Potsdam, Reich Ministry of Justice 9937–9946, Film 22964. Rieffert to REM, 15.11.35.

48. Schneider, Carl. *Behandlung von Geisteskrankheiten* [Treatment of mental illness]. Berlin, 1939.

49. Nat. Arch. Wash., CIOS-Report item 24, file XXVIII–50. Reported by Leo Alexander.

50. *a* B. Arch. Kobl., R961–2. A copy of a letter of 11.8.39 from the Reich Ministry of the Interior to the Reich Chancellery is filed immediately before these 'expressed opinions'. The letter says: "Among the enclosures I am sending you, in accordance with your wishes, are the minutes of the 20th, 91st and 106th meetings of the Criminal Law Commission. These minutes have not been made public nor have they been transmitted to other ministries. I should like to ask you, therefore, not to share them with other departments . . ." This letter carries the stamp of the department which later organized the euthanasia programme. Do these 'expressed opinions' belong to the minutes of the meetings of the Criminal Law Commission mentioned in the letter? The American registration number of the letter is 125338. The 'expressed opinions' begin at 126660. The missing pages could very easily contain other material. In a telephone conversation with the author on 5.9.83, Dr A. Ullrich said that he participated in a meeting about the euthanasia-law which took place at the Reich Chancellery between 20 April and 25 May 1940. Some 70 persons were present, including most of the heads of university departments of psychiatry and almost all the directors of mental hospitals.

No opposition to the planned law was expressed at this meeting. *b* In general the Christian names of the 'experts' have not been noted with these 'expressed opinions'. This makes it impossible to identify them with complete certainty. I believe that the following persons were involved: Professor de Crinis (Berlin), Professor Fritz Lenz (Berlin), Professor Friedrich Mauz (Königsberg), Professor Berthold Kihn (Jena), Polisch = Professor Kurt Pohlisch (Bonn)—see also note 54, Professor Carl Schneider (Heidelberg), Dr F. Faltlhauser (director of the mental hospital in Irrsee bei Kaufbeuren), Dr Heinze (director of the mental hospital in Görden), Dr Jekelius (specialist in nervous and mental diseases, Vienna), Dr Kaldewey (director of the sanatorium in Eikkelborn), Dr Schumann (later director of the extermination centre in Grafeneck), Dr Renno (later director of the extermination centre in Hartheim), Dr Pfannmüller (director of the sanatorium in Haar near Munich), Dr Sprauer (chief of the Department of Health in the Ministry of the Interior of Baden).

51. Lenz, F. In: Stroothenke, W. *Erbpflege und Christentum. Fragen der Sterilisation, Aufnordung, Euthanasie, Ehe* [Christianity and the safeguarding of hereditary endowment: Questions of sterilization, eugenic improvement of the Nordic race, euthanasia, marriage]. Dissertation, Berlin, 1940.

52. B. Arch. Kobl., R22–4209, p. 1. A note by Hitler on his personal stationery dated 1.9.39.

53. Nat. Arch. Wash., NO-2275. Hildebrandt to Himmler, 9.1.40.

54. B. Arch. Kobl., R961–1., pp. 127891–3. The name Pohlisch is wrongly spelt as Polisch on one of the lists.

55. B. Arch. Kobl., R22–5021, p. 205. President of the Superior Provincial Court of Frankfurt to the Reichsminister of Justice, 16.5.41.

56. *Der Krieg gegen die Psychisch Kranken* [The war against mental patients] eds. K. Dörner, C. Haerlin, V. Rau, R. Schernus, and A. Schwendy. Rehburg-Loccum, 1980. Pages 112ff. quote the historic sermon preached by the Bishop of Münster: "Is the people of Israel the only people which God has chosen and protected and encompassed with his fatherly care and motherly love? And is the people of Israel the only people which did not want to accept this, the only people which rejected God's truth and cast aside God's law, hurling itself to ruin and destruction? Did not Jesus, the all-knowing God, gaze at the same time upon our own German people?" When Bishop (later Cardinal) Clemens August von Galen preached this sermon on 3 August 1941, in the Lamberti Church in Münster, the gassing of mental patients was already about to be stopped. Bishop Galen was a staunch anti-Communist and a supporter of the war against the USSR, and this may have saved him from reprisals.

57. Militärarchiv Freiburg, H20/480. Wuth to Bumke, quoted in: U. Geuter *Die Professionalisierung der deutschen Psychologie im Nationalsozialismus* [The professionalization of German psychology under National Socialism] p. 386. Frankfurt, 1984.

58. B. Arch. Kobl., R961–9. Collective ideas and suggestions concerning the future development of psychiatry by Professor Rüdin (Munich), Professor de Crinis (Berlin), Professor C. Schneider (Heidelberg), Professor Heinze (Görden), Professor Nitsche (Berlin). The memorandum is not dated but mentions as an annex a separate memorandum from Professor Heinze of 6.2.42.

59. B. Arch. Kobl., H20–463. Reich Board to Nitsche, 26.2.43.

60. Militärarchiv Freiburg, H20–482. Transcript of Professor Kurt Schneider's lecture: "The problem of psychopaths in the army in the field," delivered at a meeting on 18.4.42 held at the Academy of Military Medicine in Berlin by the working group of psychiatrists of the medical corps of the army of the Eastern Front.

61. Eissler, K. R. *Freud und Wagner-Jauregg vor der Kommission zur Erhebung militärischer Pflichtverletzungen* [Freud and Wagner-Jauregg before the commission of inquiry into injuries connected with military service]. Vienna, 1979.

62. Nat. Arch. Wash., CIO item 24, file XXVIII–49. *a* p. 40. *b* p. 61. [The text reproduces the original English of these sources.]

63. Nat. Arch. Wash., NO–1880. Himmler's memorandum of 28.11.40.

64. *Der Weltkampf* [The World Struggle] Part 1. Munich, 1941. This periodical subtitled *Monatschrift für die Judenfrage alle Länder* [Monthly for Jewish questions in all countries] was founded by Rosenberg in 1924.

65. Von Verschuer, O. *Der Erbarzt* [The Heredity-Physician] 9, pp. 91 and 264, 1941. "In this way it falls to this journal to play a significant role in our struggle against the Jews which is really a world-wide struggle."

66. Nat. Arch. Wash. NG978. *a* Lammers to Gross, 13.10.41. *b* Note to the record about a discussion with Lammers on 2.10.41, signed by Gross. Transcript, Berlin, 13.10.41.

67. Arch. Centre Doc. Juive Contemp., CXXVIII, Nuremberg Documents NO–203. Brack to Himmler, 28.3.41. "Report on experiments concerning sterilization by X-rays."

68. Arch. Yivo, New York, Einsatzgruppen documents, p. 2226.

69. Fischer, E. Le problème de la race et de la législation raciale en Allemagne [The problem of race and racial legislation in Germany]. In *Cahier de l'Institut Allemand*, pp. 84-109. Paris, 1942. ". . . les tendances morales et toute activité des Juifs bolchéviques décèlent une mentalité si monstrueuse que l'on ne peut plus parler que d'infériorité et des êtres d'une autre espèce que la nôtre."

70. Eichmann, A. Interrogations by Israeli Police, Vol. I, pp. 175–8, 1961.

71. Nat. Arch. Wash., NO–365. Draft of a letter from Wetzel to Himmler, 25.10.41.

72. B. Arch. Kobl., R6-37. Speech by Reichsminister Rosenberg on the occasion of a reception for the press on Tuesday, 18.11.41, at 3.30 pm in the Assembly Hall of the Reich Ministry of the Occupied Eastern Territories.

73. Von Verschuer, O. Erbforschung und Bevölkerungspolitik [Research on heredity and population policy] *Völkischer Beobachter* 1.8.42. Copy in Z.A. Potsdam. Compare also the following. O. von Verschuer: "Never before in the course of history has the political significance of the Jewish question emerged so clearly as it does today . . . Its definitive solution as a global problem will be determined during the course of this war." *Der Erbarzt* **10**, 1, 1942. H. W. Kranz: "In the disputes between Jewry and its host nations, it is a question for us of "you or me". We must carry on with this struggle to the bitter end according to the ancient Jewish commandment "an eye for an eye", even though this may be contrary to our own nature. Historical experience of Jewry compels us to take this attitude. Compassion and compromise would represent a betrayal of our own nation and of those who come after us . . . The solution of the Jewish question, and the liberation of our nation from the Jews, will only be permanent when the last Jew has left this German and European continent." In Kuhn P. and Kranz H. W. *Von Deutschen Ahnen für Deutsche Enkel* [German forefathers for German grandchildren] pp. 73–4. Munich, 1943. H. H. Schubert: "This notion which was put forward many years ago, and according to which the Jewish question constitutes the main theme of German racial history, has today lost its meaning since we are very close to a definitive solution of the Jewish question." *Volk und Rasse* **17**, 103, 1942. G. Teich: "The destiny and force of Jewry is, quite independently of its will, an assault on human society. Taking such a clear stance explains the impossibility of a solution to the Jewish question . . . A correct understanding of Jewry must dictate its complete annihilation." *Volk and Rasse* **17**, 92, 1942.
74. Nat. Arch. Wash., M887-Film 14-Frame 936. Mennecke to his wife, 14.1.42.
75. B. Arch. Kobl., R58–871–1.
76. Arch. Yivo, New York, Institut zur Erforschung der Judenfrage [Institute for the Investigation of the Jewish Question], 105a. Korherr to R. Brandt, 23.3.43: "The final solution of the Jewish question in Europe. A statistical report."
77. Nat. Arch. Wash., NG 2586. Minutes of the conference.
78. B. Arch. Kobl., R6-22, Rosenberg. A note for the record for the Führer, 23.3.42.
79. Inst. Zeitg. Mü., NO–2585. Report of the meeting of 4.2.42.
80. Inst. Zeitg. Mü., NG–2325. F. E. Wetzel: "Comments and reflections concerning the General Plan for the East of the Reichsführer-SS", 27.4.42. Dr Wetzel was a jurist who obtained his doctorate in Göttingen in 1928 with a dissertation entitled: "Exclusion of members from associations, with particular reference to legal aspects." Dr Wetzel was sentenced to a prison term in East Germany in 1950. In 1955, he made himself available for re-employment as a civil servant in West Germany. He received a pension until 1961. In 1961, an action was brought against him in Hanover but charges were withdrawn before trial. I do not know whether he was re-employed by the Government.

81. B. Arch. Kobl., R73–10005. Abel to Breuer (DFG), 13.12.44. Financial report on the research assignment "Race-biological investigations among the peoples of the East." [It is not widely known that the NDW was renamed the DFG by the Nazis in 1936 and that this new name was preserved after the war. It was the President of the DFG who was able to inform the Minister of Science, Education, and National Culture that no Jew or half-Jew was supported by the DFG on 2.2.37. Ibid., R73–63.]

82. Abel, W., conversation with BMH, 23.1.81.

83. Arch. Yivo, New York, Rosenberg files. Report by Dr. Hüttig, 15.10.42 and report by Dr. Holtz, 5.11.42.

84. Doc. Center Berlin, Clauss files.

85. *a* Inst. Zeitg. Mü., MA 292, 8575–8655. Beger to R. Brandt, 13.4.43 and correspondence of Clauss. *b* all the supporting documents are quoted in: Kater, M. H. *Das "Ahnenerbe" der SS 1935–1945* [The "Foundation for the Heritage of our Forefathers" of the SS 1935–1945] pp. 245–55. Stuttgart, 1972.

86. Arch. Centre Doc. Juive Contemp., CDXXXVIII–19 and B Arch. Kobl., Schumacher Collection 240 II 595–606. Hofmann to Himmler, 17.3.43: "Reichsführer! Regarding the question of the final solution of the problem of part-Jews . . ." Race-biological evaluation of quarter-Jews. Expert opinion of Professor B. K. Schultz, 18.1.43. Expert opinion on racial impact of far-removed alien [Jewish] ancestry by Professor B. K. Schultz, 12.11.43. Comment by Professor Astel, 12.2.44. This second opinion by Schultz also found its way to Himmler, adduced as evidence to support the requests of three SS-men, each with the same remote Jewish ancestor, to marry. Himmler granted these requests, albeit with reservations. At the same time, he was extremely displeased with Professor Schultz and wrote that he was not fit to be the Chief of the Race Bureau of the RuSHA (Himmler to Hildebrandt, 17.12.43, loc. cit.). That the Reichsführer-SS found it appropriate to devote his time to details of such problems when the military situation was so desperate illustrates the fact that, for Nazis, pursuit of the racial elements of their ideology had become as important an aim as the prosecution of the war, if not more so.

87. Arch. Centre Doc. Juive Contemp., CXXXXVIIIb, Nuremberg Documents. NO-1763. Note for the record about the discussion on 18.8.43 between representatives of the RSHA and the RuSHA of the SS, signed, Schultz.

88. B. Arch. Kobl., NS2–89, p. 85. Programme of the course for 'aptitude-testers' in Prague, 20.7.–8.8.42.

89. B. Arch. Kobl., NS2–89, p. 81. Hofmann to Schultz, 20.7.42.

90. B. Arch. Kobl., R75–9, p. 26. Report of the work of the Central Office for Migration (Zamość branch) from the beginning of the operation in Zamość of 27.11.–31.12.42.

91. Arch. Yivo, New York, Rosenberg files. Memorandum from Dr Gollert.

92. *a* Inst. Zeitg. Mü., MA 292. Dr Hagen to Hitler, 7.12.42. *b* Hagen, W., *Auftrag und Wirklichkeit. Sozialarzt im 20. Jahrhundert* [Duty and reality. Community doctor in the 20th century] Munich-Gräfeling, 1978.

93. Nat. Arch. Wash., NO–2418, Zörner to Frank, 24.2.43. NO–22021, Frank to Hitler, 25.5.43. On 4.6.43, Lammers forwarded this letter to Himmler.

94. Inst. Zeitg. Mü., Fa 506/12, order dated 9.3.43.

95. Perl, Gisella *I was a doctor in Auschwitz*, pp. 13–16. New York, 1948.

96. Höss, R. *Kommandant in Auschwitz* [Camp Commandant in Auschwitz] ed. M. Broszat, p. 162. Munich, 1963.

97. Gerstein report of 26.4.45. In: Rückerl, A. *NS-Vernichtungslager* [National Socialist extermination camps]. Munich, 1977. Historians have shown that Globocnik visited Hitler on 7.10.42. Professor Pfannenstiel has confirmed his role in Gerstein's account. "People wait in the gas chambers. But nothing happens. We hear their wailing. "Like in the synagogue" says SS-Major Professor Pfannenstiel, Professor of Health Sciences at the University of Marburg, as he puts his ear to the wooden door to hear better."

98. B. Arch. Kobl., R22–943. Draft of a law on the treatment of enemies of society, 10.5.40. For later drafts see R18–943, R18–3386, R22–949.

99. Lorenz, K. Durch Domestikation verursachte Störungen arteigenen Verhalten [Disturbances of species-specific behaviour caused by domestication] *Z. f. angew. Psych. u. Charakterkunde* **59**, 2, 1940. When interviewed on the German second television channel by Franz Kreuzer, Professor Lorenz gave the following account. "*Did you have to make compromises during the National Socialist period?*" "I hoped that National Socialism would have some good effects, since, for instance, it held the biological perfection of Man in such high esteem and had a poor opinion of attempts at domestication, and so on. At the time, I really didn't believe that these people meant murder when they spoke of 'eradication' or 'selection'. So naïve, so stupid, so credulous, call it what you will, was I at that time." "*When did the truth become apparent to you?*" "When I was already in the army. I saw deportation trains for the first time in Poznań, they were filled with Gypsies, not Jews. That made my hair stand on end. [The remark is revealing. As a behavioural scientist, Professor Lorenz was well aware that this phenomenon implies both fear and aggression. B.M.H.]" "*Do you believe that you have ever been politically active in your life, or have you ever wanted to be politically active?*" "During my whole life, from childhood onwards, I have always shunned political activity. I didn't even go on school excursions. . ." In Lorenz, K., and Kreuzer, F. *Leben ist lernen* [To live is to learn]. Munich, 1981. In 1940, Professor Lorenz, in a published paper, had called it "one of the greatest joys of my life" to have converted a student to "our concept of the world [Weltanschauung]", that is to say to National Socialism, during his course of lectures on evolution. Lorenz, K. Nochmals: Systematik und Entwicklungsgedanke im Unterricht [Ideas of systematics and evolution in education] *Der Biologe* **9**, 24, 1940.

100. Kranz, H. W. and Koller, S. *Die Gemeinschaftsunfähigen* [Social misfits]. Giessen, 1941.

101. Von Verschuer, O. Eine Kartei der Gemeinschaftsunfähigen [A register of social misfits] *Der Erbarzt* **8**, 235, 1940.

102. B. Arch. Kobl., R73–14005. *a* Ritter to the president of the NDW, 12.2.35. *b* Ritter to Breuer (DFG), 20.1.40. Report on work in progress. *c* DFG—Ritter files.

103. Ritter, R. Die Zigeunerfrage und das Zigeunerbastardproblem [The Gypsy question and the problem of bastard Gypsies] *Fortschritte der Erbpathologie* 3, 2, 1939.

104. Ritter, R. Bestandsaufnahme der Zigeuner und Zigeunermischlinge in Deutschland [An enumeration of Gypsies and part-Gypsies in Germany] *Der Öffentliche Gesundheitsdienst* 6, 477, 1941.

105. Arch. Centre Doc. Juive Contemp. CXXI–56. Nuremberg Documents, NG–845. Portschy to Lammers, 9.1.39. Includes a memorandum from the leader of the provincial government of the Burgenland, party member Dr Portschy, on the Gypsy question, Eisenstadt, August 1938.

106. Arch. Centre Doc. Juive Contemp. CXXI–42. Nuremberg Documents NG-684. Attorney General of Graz to the Reich Minister of Justice, 5.2.40.

107. B. Arch Kobl., *a* R18–6544. Pfundtner to the Head Office of the Security Police, 24.1.40. *b* RD 19–29. Yearbook of Department V (Reich Criminal Police) of the RSHA, 1939/40, p. 23.

108. Arch. Centre Doc. Juive Contemp. *a* Doc DXXI–1193. Notes of a discussion of 10.10.41 about the solution of the Jewish question. *b* CXXVa–23 Nuremberg Documents NG–3354. Notes on the results of my [of an employee of the Foreign Office] official trip to Belgrade, 25.10.41. *c* CI–31. Nuremberg Documents NOKW–1486; Lecture by Staatsrat Dr Turner on 29.8.42 to the staff of General Löhr. *d* Arch. Yivo, New York, Occ E3–61. Lohse to Landgraf, 24.12.41.

109. *a* Deposition of Dr Justin in judicial proceedings against Dr Maly and others. p. 700 24 Js 429/61 Sta Cologne. *b* Various depositions in judicial proceedings against Dr Maly and others.

110. Döring, J. J. *Die Zigeuner im NS-Staat* [The Gypsies in the National Socialist state] pp. 146ff and pp. 212ff. Hamburg, 1964.

111. Streck, B. Zigeuner in Auschwitz, Chronik des Lagers BIIw [Gypsies in Auschwitz, a chronicle of Camp BIIw]. In: *Kumpania und Kontrolle* [Clans and control] eds M. Münzel and B. Streck. Giessen, 1981.

112. Ehrhardt, S. Wirbelmuster in den Interdigitalräumen der Palma beim Menschen [Whorl patterns in the interdigital areas of the palm in Man] Z. *Morph. Anthrop.* 47, 316–30, 1956. This paper analysed palm prints of 307 Jews and 2183 Gypsies.

113. Fischer, E. Erbe als Schicksal [Heredity as Destiny] *Deutsche Allgemeine Zeitung*, 28.3.43. Six years earlier, Professor Fischer had given a lecture at the Prussian Academy of Sciences which was similar to this article but much more restrained. *Sitzungsberichte der Preussischen Akademie der Wissenschaften.* Öffentliche Sitzung am 1.Juli 1937 [Public Meeting on 1 July 1937].

114. Rüdin, E. Zehn Jahre nationalsozialistischer Staat [Ten years of the National Socialist state] *Arch. f. Rassen- u. Gesellschaftsbiol.* 36, 321, 1942/43.

115. Z.A. Potsdam, REM 967–57. Heyde to REM, 24.4.42.

116. Nat. Arch. Wash., M887–Film 17. NO–1556–PS. Dr T. Lang to Interallied Commission for the Investigation of War Crimes, 10.5.45.

117. Doc. Center Berlin, Rüdin files, Wolff to Wüst, 2.11.39. "The amount in question [30 000 RM] is provisionally granted by the Chief of the Security Police, SS-Lieutenant-General Heydrich with respect to those of Professor Rüdin's investigations in which the Reich Criminal Police is primarily interested. SS-Brigadier Nebe, Chief of the Reich Criminal Police will contact Professor Rüdin to agree on the details of the future evaluation of the results of this work."

118. Nat. Arch. Wash., M887–Film 13-Frames 24–5. Dr Pokorny to Himmler, October 1941.

119. Nat. Arch. Wash., NO–3963. Deposition of Dr Tauboeck.

120. Arch. Centre Doc. Juive Contemp. CLVII–16, Nuremberg Documents NI–4825. Sworn deposition of Viktor Lederer.

121. Nat. Arch. Wash., M887–Film 14–Frame 905. Himmler to the commandants of concentration camps, 10.12.41.

122. Nat. Arch. Wash., M887–Film 14–Frame 940. Pohl to camp commandants 27.4.43.

123. Hamann, M. Die Morde an Polnischen und sowjetischen Zwangsarbeitern in deutschen Anstalten [Murder of Polish and Russian slave labourers in German hospitals]. In *Beiträge zur Nationalsozialistischen Gesundheits- und Sozialpolitik, 1, Aussonderung und Tod. Die Klinische Hinrichtung der Unbrauchbaren* [Contributions to the study of National Socialist health and social policy, 1, Elimination and death. The clinical execution of unusable individuals], p. 121. Berlin, 1985.

124. B. Arch. Kobl., H20–465. Planning data for Baden, July 1942.

125. B. Arch. Kobl., R96I–2. Dr Rü/He to Professor Nitsche, 30.6.44. Rü–name unknown and He—Hefelmann, were working at Tiergartenstrasse 4, the headquarters of the euthanasia programme.

126. B. Arch. Kobl., R96I–6, p. 126516.

127. B. Arch. Kobl., R96–7. The owner of a private nursing home wrote to Dr Linden in the Ministry of the Interior on 21.9.41: "An entirely new phase in the economic management of our business has been introduced by the liquidation of the patients. The emptying of large buildings which this has caused spells economic ruin for us, and not through any fault of ours."

128. Source in: *Nationalsozialistische Massentötungen durch Giftgas* [National Socialist mass killings by poison gas] eds. E. Kogon, H. Langbein, A. Rückerl *et al.*, p. 62. Frankfurt, 1983.

129. Nat. Arch. Wash., M887–Film 14–Frame 482.

130. Wertham, F. *A sign for Cain.* An exploration of human violence. New York, 1969. *a* p. 155. *b* Ibid., p. 178. *c* Lafont, M. *L'Extermination Douce* [The gentle extermination]. Éditions de'AREPPI, Ligné, 1987.

131. Report of the KWI in Munich, the German National Research Institute of Psychiatry, 1.4.41–31.3.42. *Z. f. d. ges. Neur. und Psych.* **175**, 476, 1942.

132. B. Arch. Kobl., *a* R73–11449. Hallervorden to DFG, 8.12.42. *b* R96I–2 Haller-vorden to Nitsche, 9.3.44.

133. Klee, E. *Was sie taten—was sie wurden. Ärzte, Juristen und andere Beteiligte am Kranken oder Judenmord* [What they did—what they were. Doctors, lawyers and others involved in the murder of the sick and of the Jews] p. 116. Frankfurt, 1986. Also, Lifton, R. J. *The Nazi doctors. Medical killing and the psychology of genocide,* p. 106. New York, 1986.

134. Nat. Arch. Wash., M887–Film 17 [The text reproduces the original English of this source].

135. Hallervorden, J. Über eine Kohlenoxydvergiftung im Fetalleben und Entwicklungsstörungen der Rinde [A case of poisoning by carbon monoxide in foetal life and disturbances of the cerebral cortex] *Allg. Z. Psychiat.* **124,** 289, 1949. In a letter to the author, Professor Eicke has pointed out that the publication states that the post-mortem was carried out by Professor Anders, the director of the department of pathology of the mental hospital in Buch. This apparently contradicts what Professor Hallervorden told his American interrogating officer, that the brain had been obtained from some-one killed in the euthanasia programme. Were there two separate cases of this type or is one of these statements false?

136. B. Arch. Kobl., *a* R961–4. C. Schneider to Blankenburg, 11.8.44: "In any case I am asking the Reich Research Council to continue to grant us money and material support." Among the DFG documents, there is no entry in the index under C. Schneider. Possibly the payments went in a lump sum to the T4 office. It seems improbable to me that Professor C. Schneider was either mistaken or deceived about the financing of the project. *b* R 96I–4–127884. Supplementary report to the T4 office by Professor C. Schneider on 2.2.44: "After the installation of a ward in Wiesloch, it was possible to implement our work fully in December 1942. We set up two wards, one for women and one for men. Each ward contained about 20 patients, mainly feeble-minded individuals and idiots, but including a few epileptics . . ."

137. Nat. Arch. Wash., M887–Film 14–Frame 936. Mennecke to his wife, 15.6.42.

138. B. Arch. Kobl., R961-4. C. Schneider to Nitsche, 18.1.43. *b* C. Schneider to Nitsche, 2.9.44.

139. Doc. Center Berlin, Nitsche files. Nitsche to de Crinis, 30.10.43. See also Nietsche [*sic*] to de Crines [*sic*], 25.8.43. Professor Nitsche was suffering from cancer and underwent surgery between 18 and 25 August in Heidel-berg. He dictated and signed the letter of 25 August but did not correct it.

140. Rauch, G., conversation with BMH, 24.9.81.

141. An unknown person to Dr Kammler of the SS Head Office of Economy and Administration, 28.6.43, in *Kennzeichen, J* [Identity badge J for Jew], ed., H. Eschwege, p. 275. East Berlin, 1981.

142. Borkin, J. *The crime and punishment of I.G. Farben.* New York, 1978.

143. Doc. Center Berlin, *a* Mengele files. *b* Von Verschuer files, DFG index card.

144. Univ. Arch. Münster, von Verschuer's papers. Von Verschuer to Fischer 25.1.43: ". . . my assistant Mengele . . . has been transferred to work in an office in Berlin so that he can do some work at the institute on the side." It is no oversight that Professor von Verschuer called Dr Mengele "my assistant" here and elsewhere. Dr Mengele had kept his position as an assistant in Frankfurt when he was called up for military service. He did not actually lose this post until June 1945. Professor von Verschuer had no position for him with the KWG, but he still planned to take Dr Mengele with him to the Berlin institute. Thus, von Verschuer to Lehmann, 11.6.42, *ibid*: "In the meantime, many important events have occurred in my life: I received an invitation, which I accepted, to succeed Eugen Fischer as director of the Dahlem institute. Great trust was shown towards me, and all my requests were granted with respect to the importance and authority of the institute . . . I will take almost all my co-workers with me, first Schade and Grebe, and later Mengele and Fromme." Thereafter, Dr Mengele was included in the birthday list of the professors, assistants and visiting scientists of the entire Dahlem institute, and of the Department of Human Heredity in particular.

145. Wagner, G. *Rassenbiologische Beobachtungen an Zigeunern und Zigeunerzwillingen* [Race-biological observations on Gypsies and Gypsy twins]. Dissertation. Berlin, 1943.

146. Wagner, G. Partielle Irisverfärbung (Hornhautüberwachsung) ein neues Erbmerkmal. [Partial discoloration of the iris (corneal hypertrophy) a new hereditary trait] *Der Erbarzt* **12**, 62, 1944.

147. *a* Nyiszli, M. *Auschwitz. A doctor's eyewitness account*, pp. 64–5. New York, 1960. "I finished dissecting the three pairs of twins and duly recorded the anomalies found. In all three instances the cause of death was the same: an injection of chloroform into the heart. Of the four sets of twins, three had ocular globes of different colors. One eye was brown, the other blue. This is a phenomenon found fairly frequently in non-twins. But in the present case I noticed it has occurred in six of the eight twins. An extremely interesting collection of anomalies . . . During the afternoon Dr. Mengele paid me a visit . . . He gave me instructions to have the organs mailed and told me to include my report in the package. He also instructed me to fill out the "Cause of Death" column hitherto left blank. The choice of causes was left to my own judgement: the only stipulation was that each cause should be different . . . I shuddered to think of all I had learned during my short stay here, and of all I should yet have to witness without protesting, until my own appointed hour arrived. The minute I entered this place I had the feeling I was already one of the living-dead. But now, in possession of all these fantastic secrets, I was certain I would never get out alive. Was it conceivable that Dr. Mengele, or the Berlin-Dahlem Institute, would ever allow me to leave this place alive?" *b* p. 63. [This text reproduces the original English of this source on page 71.]

148. The testimony of Dr I. Vexler. In Bernadac, C. *L'holocauste oublié* [The forgotten Holocaust] pp. 145ff. Paris, 1979.

149. Melchers, G. Conversation with BMH, 10.3.82.

150. B. Arch. Kobl., R73–15342. Breuer to Sauerbruch, 31.10.44, includes von Verschuer to Breuer, interim reports of 20.3.44 and 4.10.44. Hillmann had a diploma in engineering and no doctorate at that time. He was originally a co-worker of Professor Hinsberg who had obtained a scholarship for him from the DFG. After the destruction of Hinsberg's laboratory, Hillmann continued to work with the aid of his scholarship. From 1943 onwards he was a guest in Professor Butenandt's laboratory in the KWI of Biochemistry. Professor Butenandt supported two applications for extensions to the scholarship supporting Hillmann; he was then working on methods for the diagnosis of cancer (see Butenandt to the DFG, 6.3.44 and 28.3.45 *ibid.*, R73–11692). In 1947, Professor Butenandt was on the committee for Hillmann's doctorate examination. Shortly thereafter Dr Hillmann joined Professor Butenandt's institute in Tübingen. Professor Butenandt told me in a conversation that Hillmann had not reported his collaboration with von Verschuer, or even given any hint of it, before, during or after his experiments with sera from Auschwitz.

151. Criminal case 4Js444/59, Public Prosecutor's office, Frankfurt (Auschwitz trial). Evidence of Dr Johann Cespiva: "During the time I was working in the Gypsy camp, I often encountered Dr Mengele and I was able to observe what he was doing . . . I was able to see with my own eyes how he infected twins with typhoid in the sickroom of the Gypsy camp so as to observe whether the twins reacted in the same way or differently. A short time after being infected, they were sent to the gas chambers . . ."

152. Univ. Arch. Münster, papers of von Verschuer. *a* Among these papers, of which they are very many dealing with other matters, there is no trace of this correspondence. His son, Helmut von Verschuer, told me on 12.6.82 that there are no other scientific papers left by his father. Since the contents of his institute were moved by lorry to the West in March 1945, the documents should have been preserved. *b* Von Verschuer to de Rudder, 4.10.44. *c* Von Verschuer to de Rudder, 6.1.45.

153. Archiv der Akademie der Wissenschaften der DDR [Archives of the Academy of Sciences of the German Democratic Republic] II-V-205.

154. Von Verschuer, O. *Westfälische Landeszeitung* 25/26.11.44. (There is a copy in Z.A. Potsdam.)

155. Ferencz, B. B. *Less than slaves.* Cambridge, Mass, 1979.

156. *Faschismus-Forschung* [Research on fascism], eds., D. Eichholtz and K. Gossweiler. 2nd edn. East Berlin, 1980.

157. Arch. Centre Doc. Juive Contemp., CLX–38, Nuremberg Documents, NIK–10746.

158. Arch. MPG Berlin, KWI of Anthropology files. Von Verschuer to local police in Beetz (where the institute had been evacuated from Berlin), 22.8.44.

159. Baur, E., Fischer, E., and Lenz, F. *Menschliche Erblichkeitslehre und Rassen–hygiene* [The principles of human heredity and race-hygiene] 3rd edn., Vol. II, pp. 317–18. Munich, 1931.

160. B. Arch. Kobl., R18–5518. Stenographic transcript of a discussion of pregnancy out of wedlock, 15.6.37.
161. Doc. Center Berlin, Lenz files. *a* Lenz to Pancke, 5.1.40, memorandum "Remarks on resettlement from the point of view of safeguarding the race." *b* Memorandum by Lenz, 5.3.41: "The road to further progress of population policy."
162. B. Arch. Kobl., R69–231. Report on a working meeting of the Central Office of Migration on 11–12 January 1941 in Dresden.
163. Doc. Center Berlin, Lenz files. Himmler to Heissmeyer, 31.3.41.
164. Tätigkeitsbericht der Kaiser Wilhelm-Gesellschaft zur Förderung der Naturwissenschaften für das Geschäftsjahr 1942/3 [Report of the KWG for the business year 1942/3] *Die Naturwissenschaften* **31**, 41, 1943.
165. Lenz, F. Über die rassische Beurteilung eines Menschen [On the racial assessment of an individual] *Informationsdienst, Rassenpolitisches Amt der NSDAP*, **137**, pp. 257–66, 20.5.43.
166. Lenz, F. Diesseits von Gut und Böse. Bemerkungen über das Verhältnis von Genetik und Glauben [In the realms of good and evil. Remarks on the relationship between genetics and faith] *Deutsche Universitätszeitung* [German University Gazette] Part VIII/23,9 1953 "Genetics is not in any way guilty for this [the persecution of the Jews]; on the contrary, the persecution of the Jews was fostered by political fanatics who knew little or nothing of genetics."
167. Fischer, E. *Die Rehobother Bastards und das Bastardisierungsproblem beim Menschen* [The bastards of Rehoboth and the problem of miscegenation in Man]. Jena, 1913. ". . . only idealists or fanatics can deny that Negroes, Hottentots and many other races are inferior. . ." pp. 330ff.
168. Arch. MPG Berlin, KWI of Anthropology files. Summary of Fischer's lecture on 1 February 1933: "Racial crosses and intellectual achievement".
169. Fischer, E. *Der Begriff des völkischen Staats biologisch betrachtet* [The concept of a national state considered from a biological point of view], 1933, and a somewhat more polemical version, *Der völkische Staat biologisch gesehen* [A biological view of the national state], 1933.
170. Z.A. Potsdam, RMdI 26243. *a* Astel and B. K. Schultz to Frick, 29.5.33. Dr Hans Spatz was the editor of the *Münchener Medizinische Wochenschrift*. This "Munich Medical Weekly" was published by J. F. Lehmanns Verlag. Julius F. Lehmann, the owner of this publishing firm, was one of the most ardent propagators of race-hygiene, anti-Semitism, and German nationalism. As such, he was much honoured by the Nazis and his firm flourished by publishing the most rabid tracts in these fields. *b* G. Brandt to Frick, 12.6.33. *c* Frick to Rust (draft), June 1933.
171. Z.A. Potsdam, RMdI 26245, p. 220. Memorandum from Fischer: "Evidence for my attitude to the race-question in relationship to the German people".
172. Doc. Center Berlin, Fischer/Lenz files. Himmler to the staff of the Führer's representative, 17.8.38.

173. Klee, E. *Was sie taten—was sie wurden. Ärzte, Juristen und andere Beiteiligte am Kranken oder Judenmord* [What they did—what they were. Doctors, lawyers and others involved in the murder of the sick and of the Jews] pp. 219–20. Frankfurt, 1986.
174. Fischer, E., and Kittel, G. *Das antike Weltjudentum* [World Jewry in Antiquity] *Forschungen zur Judenfrage* [Researches on the Jewish question] 7, p. 161. Hamburg, 1943. The book had been ready for publication in 1941 but was completely destroyed in an air raid.
175. Inst. Zeitg. Mü., MA 243, 3416–3420. Fischer to Rosenberg, 10.6.44.
176. Arch. Yivo, New York, Rosenberg files.
177. Arch. Yivo, New York, Rosenberg files. See also M. Weinreich *Hitler's Professors.* New York, 1946.
178. Univ. Arch. Münster, papers of von Verschuer. Fischer to von Verschuer, 20.1.45.
179. B. Arch. Kobl., NS 8–266, p. 108. Günther to Rosenberg, 21.9.44. Two months previously he had written to the Minister: "Since I am sure that my health would quickly break down if I were placed in a munitions factory or a military unit, I am considering in what kind of capacity I could usefully be employed." *Ibid.*, p. 106.
180. Loeffler, L. Conversation with BMH, 18.10.80.
181. Gauch, H. *Neue Grundlage der Rassenforschung* [New fundamental problems of race-research]. Leipzig, 1933.
182. Gauch's son later published some of his memories of his father. Gauch, S. *Vaterspuren* [The traces of my father]. Königstein, 1979.
183. Streicher, J. *Deutsche Volksgesundheit aus Blut und Boden* [German public health from blood and soil] 1.1.35. Quoted in *Kennzeichen J* [Identity badge J for Jew] ed. H. Eschwege. East Berlin, 1981.
184. B. Arch. Kobl., R22–486. Expert report by Loeffler, 27.3.35.
185. Report on Professor Otmar von Verschuer by A. Butenandt, M. Hartmann, W. Heubner, and B. Rajewsky, September 1949. (I thank Professor Butenandt for giving me a copy.)
186. Univ. Arch. Münster, papers of von Verschuer. *a* Fischer to Muckermann (draft). *b* Von Verschuer to Adrian, 8.10.46. *c* Von Verschuer to de Rudder, 28.3.46.
187. *Studien aus dem Institut für Natur- und Geisteswissenschaftliche Anthropologie.* [Studies from the Institute for Anthropology in the Sciences and in the Humanities] ed. H. Muckermann. Berlin-Dahlem, 30.8.52. Contains: Kirchner, W. Investigations of somatic and mental development in offspring of European-Negro matings in infancy with reference to social conditions.
188. Mühlmann, W. E. *Geschichte der Anthropologie* [History of Anthropology]. Bonn, 1948. cp. Mühlmann, W. E.: Die Hitler-Bewegung. Bemerkungen zur Krise der bürgerlichen Kultur [The Hitler-movement: Remarks on the crisis of bourgeois culture]. *Zeitschrift f. Völkerpsychologie und Soziologie (Sociologus)* 9, 129, 1933.

189. Saller, K. *Die Rassenlehre des Nationalsozialismus in Wissenschaft und Propaganda* [The race-theory of National Socialism in science and propaganda]. Darmstadt, 1961.

190. Platen-Hallermund, A. *Die Tötung Geisteskranker in Deutschland* [The killing of mental patients in Germany]. Frankfurt, 1947.

191. Klee, E. *'Euthanasie' im NS-Staat. Die 'Vernichtung lebensunwerten Lebens'* ['Euthanasia' in the National Socialist State. The 'destruction of lives unworthy to be lived']. Frankfurt, 1983.

192. Geyer, H. *Über die Dummheit* [On stupidity]. Göttingen, 1954.

193. Fischer, E. *Begegnungen mit Toten. Erinnerungen eines Anatomen* [Encounters with the dead. Memoirs of an anatomist]. Freiburg, 1959.

194. Lenz, W. Conversation with BMH, 14.10.80.

195. Rosenberg, A. *Der Mythus des 20. Jahrhunderts* [The myth of the twentieth century]. Munich, 1934.

196. Fischer, E. Zur Rassenfrage der Etrusker [On the question of the Etruscan race], *Sitzungsberichte der Preussischen Akademie der Wissenschaften, Phys.-math. Kl.* **XXV**, 250, 1938.

197. Fischer, E. *L'ereditarietà delle qualità morali* [The hereditary nature of moral qualities]. Leipzig, 1938.

198. *Hitlers Politisches Testament, Die Bormann-Diktate vom Februar und April 1945* [Hitler's political testament. As dictated to Bormann in February and April 1945] pp. 54ff. Hamburg, 1981.

199. Rosenthal, B. *Heimatgeschichte der badischen Juden* [The history of the native Jews of Baden]. Bühl, 1927.

200. Kant, I. *Der Streit der Fakultäten* [The strife of the Faculties]. Collected Works, Vol. XI, p. 321. Frankfurt, 1977.

201. Fichte, J. G. *Beitrag zur Berichtigung des Urtheils des Publikums über die französische Revolution* [A contribution to the correction of public opinion concerning the French Revolution]. Collected works, Vol. 1, p. 293. Stuttgart, 1964. "As for giving them [the Jews] civil rights, I for one see no remedy but that their heads should all be cut off in one night and replaced with others not containing a single Jewish idea."

202. Lichtenberg, G. L. *Schriften und Briefe I. Sudelbücher* [Writings and letters. I. Jottings] Part L358, p. 903. Munich, 1968. "The Jews have bargained and burrowed their way into the society of all nations. This betrays their likeness to vermin."

203. Aristotle, *Histoire des animaux* [History of animals] Greek-French bilingual text, p. 64. Paris, 1969. "The female is more soft-hearted and more inclined to tears than the male. She is more envious and more dissatisfied with her lot, more of a slanderous disposition, and more cantankerous. Besides this, she is more discontented, more shameless and more inclined to lie, more skillful in cheating and more vindictive. She needs less sleep, but she is also lazier. She is less inclined to take action, and she needs less nourishment."

204. *Alberti Magni Opera* [Works of Abertus Magnus] Vol. 11, p. 423. Paris, 1891.

205. Günther, H. *Ritter, Tod und Teufel. Der Heldische Gedanke* [The knight, death, and the devil. The heroic concept] p. 80. Munich, 1920.
206. Hitler, A. *Monologe im Führerhauptquartier, 1941–45* [Monologues in the Führer's headquarters, 1941–45] H. Heims and W. Jochmann, 1/2–12.41, pp. 148–9. Hamburg, 1980.
207. Hitler, A. *Mein Kampf. 1.Bd., Eine Abrechnung* [My struggle, Vol. 1, A reckoning] p. 64. 3rd edn. Munich, 1930.
208. Von Weizsäcker, V. *Ärztliche Fragen* [Medical questions] pp. 70ff. Jena, 1934.
209. Roth, K. H. Psychosomatische Medizin und Euthanasie: Der Fall Viktor von Weizsäcker (Psychosomatic Medicine and euthanasia: The case of Viktor von Weizsäcker). *1999 Zeitschrift für Sozialgeschichte des 20. und 21. Jahrhunderts* 1, 65, 1986.
210. Von Weizsäcker, V. *Euthanasie und Menschenversuche* [Euthanasia and human experimentation] pp. 14ff. Heidelberg, 1947.
211. Bürger-Prinz, H. *Ein Psychiater berichtet* [A psychiatrist speaks] p. 70. Hamburg, 1971.
212. Binding, K., and Hoche, A. *Die Freigabe der Vernichtung lebensunwerten Lebens, ihr Mass und ihre Form* [The sanctioning of the destruction of lives unworthy to be lived: Its limits and its form] 2nd edn., p. 32. Leipzig, 1922. "Again I find no reason, whether from the social, moral, or even religious points of view not to allow the killing (although not, of course, by just anyone) of these individuals who present a terrifying appearance which is the exact antithesis of that of real people and who inspire horror in almost everyone who meets them. In times when a higher morality prevailed (all heroism has been lost in our own time) we might have delivered these poor people from their mortal bodies officially. But who would steel himself to do it now when we have lost our nerve, and do not recognize the necessity and the justification for such actions?"
213. Wagner, G. *Reden und Aufrufe* [Speeches and manifestos] p. 178. Berlin, 1943.
214. Plato: *Sämtliche Werke* [Collected Works] Vol. III, 414c and 459c. After the German translation by H. Müller, edited by W. F. Otto, E. Grassi, and G. Plamböck, Hamburg, 1959.
215. Nat. Arch. Wash., 1919—PS. Himmler's Speech in Poznań, 4.10.43.
216. Goethe, J. W. *Gespräche* [Conversations] No. 461 (1200), ed. F. Biedermann. Leipzig, year of publication unknown.
217. Mitscherlich, A., and Mielke, F. *Das Diktat der Menschenverachtung* [The dictate of contempt for Man], pp. 19ff. Heidelberg, 1947.
218. Chargaff, E. *Bemerkungen* [Observations], p. 91 Stuttgart, 1981. This quotation requires some explanation. In sciences such as physics, chemistry or genetics, assertions are always qualified as "only being true to a limited extent". In sciences such as psychiatry or anthropology, diseases or races suddenly disappear as if they had never existed. Not only the explanations for phenomena, but the phenomena themselves seem to appear or melt away, according to whatever is the fashionable view at the time.

219. Klee, E. *'Euthanasie' im NS Staat. Die 'Vernichtung lebensunwerten Lebens'* ['Euthanasia' in the National Socialist state. The 'destruction of lives unworthy to be lived'] pp. 216ff. Frankfurt, 1983.

220. Recollections of nurse L.E. from the Weissenhof Hospital in Weinsberg. In Dörner, K., Haerlin, C., Rau, V., Schernus, R., and Schwendy, A. *Der Krieg gegen die psychisch Kranken* [The war against mental patients] p. 197. Rehberg-Loccum, 1980.

221. Levi, P. *Se questo è un uomo* [If this is a man] p. 196. Turin, 1973.

222. Aboth, Sprüche der Väter [Sayings of the Fathers] 1, 14. In *Der Babylonische Talmud* [The Babylonian Talmud] L. Goldschmidt, ed., Vol. 9, p. 666. Berlin, 1934.

223. Militärarchiv Freiburg, H20–465. Rüdin to Nitsche, 21.9.41.

224. Weinreich, M. *Hitler's professors. The part of scholarship in Germany's crimes against the Jewish people*, pp. 32–3. New York, 1946.

225. Aichele, H. *Die Zigeunerfrage mit besonderer Berücksichtung Württembergs* [The Gypsy question with special reference to Württemberg]. 1911.

226. Details in: Friedländer, H. Jüdische Anstaltspatienten in NS-Deutschland. In: *Aktion T4 1939–1945*, ed., G. Aly. Berlin, 1987. pp. 34–44.

227. An excellent account of the Baal cult of Rosenberg can be found in Lieb, F. Der Mythos des nationalsozialistischen Nihilismus [The myth of National Socialist nihilism]. In *Freie Wissenschaft* [Free science], ed., E. J. Gumbel. Strasbourg, 1938. Also see Poliakov, L. *Bréviaire de la haine* [Breviary of hatred] pp. 6ff. Paris, 1951. Lem, S. *Provokation* [Provocation]. Frankfurt, 1981.

Name Index

Besides the degrees of Dr. med. and Dr. phil. which are explained in the front material, other doctorates in this index are:

Dr.agr. (Agricultural Sciences); Dr.chem. (Chemistry); Dr.ing. (Engineering); Dr.jur. (Law); Dr.med.vet. (Veterinary Medicine); Dr.phil.nat. (Science); Dr.rer.pol., Dr.sc.pol. (Political Science) and Dr.theol. (Theology, Divinity). The titles Dozent, a.o. Professor, o. Professor are explained in the front material. After the war, the system described here changed gradually and the titles in the index are Dozent and Professor only. In a few cases 'lecturer' [Lehrbeauftragter] appears; this is a person with responsibility, usually temporary, for specific courses.

Abderhalden, E., Dr.med. Prof., 1877–1950, Swiss, Dozent Berlin 04, o. Prof. 08, Halle 11, biochemist. 169–170

Abel, W., Dr.phil. Prof., born 1905, Dozent Berlin 33, Department Head KWI of Anthropology Berlin and a.o. Prof. Berlin 40, o. Prof. 43, after 45 in private life. vi, 6, 12, 18, 32, 54, 85, 89, 118, 136–150, 154, 156, 160, 164, 171, 176, 215, 221

Albertus Magnus, 1193–1280, Dominican, teacher of Aristotelian philosophy and science, Cologne. 98, 230

Alexander, Leo, officer in American Counter Intelligence Corps. 217

Anders, Dr.med. Prof., Director Pathology Department of mental hospital Buch. 225

Aristotle, 384–322 BC, philosopher and scientist. 98, 230

Assmussen, Dr.med., collaborator at euthanasia research project Görden. 174

Astel, K., Dr.med., Prof., 1898–1945, suicide, SS-Colonel, President of Bureau of Race-theory [Landesamt für Rassewesen] of the Land of Thuringia 33, o. Prof. Jena 34, Rector Jena, 39. 57, 89, 122, 221, 228

Baur, E., Dr.phil., Dr.med. Prof., 1875–1933, a.o. Prof. Berlin 04, o. Prof. 11, Director KWI of Breeding Research Müncheberg 25. 8, 26, 121, 216, 227

Becker, P. E., Dr.med. Prof., born 1908, Dozent Freiburg 43, o. Prof. Göttingen 62. 5, 168

Berger, B., Dr.phil., SS-Captain, anthropologist, imprisoned West Germany. 56, 221

Benn, G., Dr.med., 1886–1965, poet. 104

Binding, K., Dr.jur. Prof., 1841–1920, o. Prof. Basle 66, Freiburg, Strasbourg, Leipzig. 8, 101, 231

Birnbaum, K., Dr.med., 1878–1950, a.o. Prof. 27, Director mental hospital Buch, dismissed 33, emigrated to USA 39. 173

Seraphim P.-H. Dr.rer.pol. Prof., born 1902, a.o. Prof. Königsberg 40, o. Prof. Greifswald 43, Lecturer Munich 48. 49

Sievers, W., 1905–1947, executed, SS-Colonel, Secretary General of Research Foundation of SS [Stiftung Ahnenerbe], sentenced in Nuremberg trials. 145–148

Spatz, Hans., Dr.med., 1892–?, Editor of *Münchener Medizinische Wochenschrift* published by Dr. J. F. Lehmann. 84, 228

Spatz, Hugo., Dr.med. Prof., 1888–1969, brother of Dr Hans Spatz, Dozent Munich 23, Director KWI of Brain Research 37–45, Director MPI of Brain Research 48–57. 84, 135, 175, 180

Speer, A., Diploma in Engineering, 1905–1983, Reichsminister of War Industry 42–45, sentenced to prison in Nuremberg trials. 153

Sprauer, L., Dr.med., Medical Councillor [Medizinalrat] responsible for euthanasia in Ministry of Interior of Land Baden until 45, prison 48–51. 218

Sprenger, J., 1884–?, Gauleiter of Land Hesse 33–45. 166

Stahlecker, W.Dr.jur., ?–1942, Commander of Einsatzgruppe A. 63

Stein, Dr.med., graduate student of Professor von Verschuer Frankfurt, collaborator of Dr Ritter Berlin. 162

Stengel-Rutkowski, L., Dr.med., born 1908, Dozent Jena 40. 122

Streicher, J., 1885–1946, executed, Gauleiter of Land Middle Franconia, editor *Der Stürmer,* dismissed 40–45, sentenced in Nuremberg trials. 88, 88n, 89, 99, 229

Stroer, Dr Prof., Dutch, Dozent Leiden, Department Head KWI of Anthropology 44–45, in Holland after 45. 78

Stroothenke, W., Dr.theol. 218

Stumpfl, F., Dr.med., born 1902, Dozent Munich 35, Assistent KWI of Psychiatry 30–39, a.o. Prof. Innsbruck 40. 84, 133

Suckow, J., Dr.med., born 1896, Assistent of Professor C. Schneider 42–43, Dozent Leipzig 50, Prof. Leipzig 57, Dresden 69. 73

Szamuely, T., Commissar for Police in Kun's revolutionary government in Hungary 19?. 36

Tauboeck, K. W. F., Dr., employed by IG-Farben. 68, 224

Teich, G., Dr Institute of Border and Foreign Questions [Institut für Grenz- und Auslandsfragen] Berlin until 45. 220

Telschow E., Dr.phil, born 1889, Secretary General of KWG 37, MPG 48. 171

Thannhauser, S., Dr.med. Prof., 1895–1962, o. Prof. Düsseldorf 27, Freiburg 31, emigrated to USA 34. 134–135

Thierack, O. G., Dr.jur., 1889–1946, suicide, Reichsminister of Justice 41–45. 53

Thums, K., Dr.med. Prof., 1904–?, Dozent Munich 39, a.o. Prof. Prague 40, private practice after 45. 133

Toller, E., 1893–1939, suicide, one of the leaders of Bavarian revolutionary republic 19, emigrated to USA 33. 36

Tratz, Prof.: presumably Trautz, M., Dr.phil. 1880–1960, o. Prof. Münster 36, chemist. 147

Trotsky, L. (pseudonym of Bronstein, L. D.), 1879–1940, assassinated in Mexico, Russian revolutionary and one of the founders of the USSR. 36

Weniger, J., Dr.phil. Prof., 1886–1959, o. Prof. Vienna 34, anthropologist. 136

Wentzler, E., Dr.med., member Reich Commission for Registration of Severe Disorders in Childhood 39–45, legal proceedings against him abandoned before trial 49, emigrated South America. vii

Wetzel, E., Dr.jur., born 1903, official [Regierungsrat] Ministry of the Occupied Eastern Territories, sentenced to prison term in East Germany 50, returned West Germany 55, requested and obtained reinstatement as civil servant, legal proceedings against him instituted but abandoned before trial 61. 17, 18, 50, 54, 143, 219

Wiedersheim, R., Dr.med. Prof. 1848–1923, o. Prof. Freiburg 1883. 117

Willmanns, K., Dr.med. Prof., 1873–1945, o. Prof. Heidelberg 26, dismissed 33, stayed in Germany. 183

Wimmer, K., Dr.med. Assistent of Professor Hirt Strasbourg 44. 56

Woltmann, L., Dr.med., 1871–1907, gentleman-scholar. 7

Würth, A., Dr., Assistent of Professor Fischer 33–36, collaborator of Dr Ritter 37–39, official in Bureau of Statistics of Land Baden-Württemberg, West Germany, after 45. vi, 156–162

Wüst, W., Dr.phil. Prof., born 1901, o. Prof. 35 Munich, President Research Foundation of SS [Stiftung Ahnenerbe], dismissed on full academic pension 45. 224

Wuth, O. Dr.med. Prof., 1885–?, Dozent Munich 21, a.o.Prof. 26, Berlin 39, chief physician of the army. 45, 218

Zerbin-Rüdin, E., Dr.med. Prof., born 1921, daughter of Professor Rüdin, Dozent Munich 72, Prof. 78. vi, 130–133

Zucker, Dr.med. Prof., 1893–?, euthanasia expert witness, public health service Heidelberg after 45. 14, 44, 182

Subject Index

A

Academicians, silence of, 108
Alcoholics
  as hereditary defective, 34
  sterilization of, 10, 30
Americans, interrogation of German
  scientists, 92, 153
Anthropologists
  as aptitude testers, 59
  ethical defects of, 109
  expert reports of, 37–38, 40, 160–161
  as exterminators, 19, 23–34, 81, 100–103
  goals of, 23–24, 32
  lessons for, 109–111
  loss of esteem, 45
  Nazi policies and, 149
  political guilt of, 167
  post-war behavior, 94, 111–112
  race research of, 12, 162
  research of, 20, 71–73
  as scientists, 81
  sexual relations, authorization by, 32,
    35–36
  studies of Russians, 54, 144
  views on Hitler, 95–96
Anti-Semitism. *See also* Jews
  absence, claims of, 6, 118, 119, 123, 126,
    132, 134, 152, 154, 159, 163, 165, 166,
    169, 181
  deplored, 9, 82
  German benefits of, 81–82
  justification, 81–82
  National Socialists' view, 84
  origins of, 97–99
  in post-World War I, 95, 97–99
  protests against, 25–26
  scientists' views on, 84–85, 174
  in universities, 24
  as vulgar, 36
Antisocial individuals
  adolescents as, 67
  concentration camp for, 161
  eradication of, 24, 67, 101
  laws, 13
  numbers of, 61
  research on, 12
  sterilization of, 13, 33
Armed forces, mental patients treatment,
  46–48, 179
Asiatics
  killing of, 56
  studies on, 56
Auschwitz
  additional reading on, 210
  as extermination center, 75
  gas chambers, 75
  gold collection at, 80
  gypsies to, 19, 64, 65, 66, 76, 149
  Jews to, 59, 61, 77
  operating capacity, 75
  public knowledge of, 128
  "research" at, 75–76, 77–78, 107
  responsibility for, 125
  selection for, 59–60
  sterilization at, 20
  twins studies at, 76–77, 78

C

Carbon monoxide gassing
  at Auschwitz, 75–76

I

Idiots, studies on, 75
Illegitimate children, status of, 82–83, 88
Inferior people
  basis of, 23
  in Germany, 7–8
  "rights" of, 23
Intellect
  of persons of mixed blood, 84
  racial crosses and, 10
Interviews of
  Dr. Buhler, E., 151–155
  Dr. Wurth, A., 156–162
  Mrs. Haase, I., 169–170
  Prof. Abel, W., 136–150
  Prof. Eicke, W.J., 173–176
  Prof. Fischer's graduate student,
    134–135
  Prof. Fischer's technician, 134–135
  Prof. Grebe, H., 163–168
  Prof. Lenz's son, 120–125
  Prof. Melchers, 171–172
  Prof. Rauch, H.J., 177–183
  Prof. von Verschuer's son, 126–129
Interviews, techniques used, 4–5
Interviews, verification of, 5–6

J

Jews. *See also* Anti-Semitism
  as aliens, 13, 39
  anthropological studies of, 38
  at Auschwitz, 59, 61, 77
  bibliography on, 209
  census of, 38–39
  classification of, 57
  contributions of, 36
  defense of European culture against, 21,
    86
  defined, 203
  deportation, 15, 39, 48, 57
  as different, 84
  dismissal from civil service, 10
  dismissal from universities, 10, 122–123,
    196
  expert reports on, 138–141, 144, 145,
    150, 152, 153, 160, 164
  extermination of, 15–17, 22, 52, 53, 56,
    103–105, 118, 120, 149

  in financial circles, 13
  gassing of, 17, 50–53
  Hitler's views on, 94
  "inferiority" of, 17, 23, 35
  intellect of, 36, 84, 137
  marriage to Germans forbidden, 11
  mass murder of, 16
  Nazi views on, 23
  numbers killed, 22, 52
  one-half, 19, 28, 57, 61, 203
  one-quarter, 19, 29, 49, 56, 57, 61
  pauperization of, 49
  Polish, 18, 45
  psychological studies on, 40–41
  registration of, 12, 38
  Russian, 48, 51
  shooting of, 49–50, 63
  starvation of, 53
  sterilization of, 49, 57, 61
  as unfit to work, 17
  "of value", saving of, 27–28
  virtues of, 36, 159
Justice
  for Germans, 60–61
  in occupied lands, 60

K

Kaiser Wilhelm Institute (KWI)
  of anthropology, 22, 36, 40, 75
  of brain research, 18, 198
  creation of, 8
  directors of, 24, 30, 75
  expert reports of, 21, 40
  short courses of, 40
  Vogt, O, and, 198–199
Kaiser Wilhelm Society for Advancement
  of Science (KWG)
  administrators' conduct, 25, 27
  biology section, 172
  brain research unit, 180
  dismissal of Jews, 10, 25–26, 28, 30
  eugenics section, 8, 83
  library, 153
  psychiatric section, 71
  reorganization of, 25–27
  staff, 171
  use of brains of murdered patients, 71

Autobiographical Note

Benno Müller-Hill was born on February 5, 1933, in Freiburg i.B., a small town in South Germany. This was during the time of the collapse of the Weimar Republic and the Nazi takeover. His father was a liberal lawyer, his mother a Swede. He grew up in a protected home. Shortly before the end of the war, he entered the *Jungvolk* at the age of ten where he collided with his superiors. He then went to a *Gymnasium* where he learned Latin, classical Greek, and French. He studied chemistry at the Universities of Freiburg and München. In 1962, he received his Ph.D. in the chemical laboratory of the University of Freiburg on a thesis dealing with β-galactosidase of *Escherichia coli*.

He left Germany with a Green Card in 1963 and went to Howard Rickenberg's laboratory at Indiana University. There he set out to isolate the Lac repressor, whose existence had been proposed in 1959 by François Jacob and Jacques Monod. In 1965, he went to the laboratory of Jim Watson and Wally Gilbert in the Bio Labs of Harvard University, still with the goal of isolating the Lac repressor. In 1966, he isolated a mutant of the *lacI* gene and produced a variant of the Lac repressor that binds inducer more tightly than wild type. This made it possible for Wally Gilbert to isolate the Lac repressor with a radioactive inducer.

In the United States, he met many Jewish scientists who had fled the Nazis in Germany or Europe. This experience enhanced his sensitivity and awareness of the Nazi period. How could it have happened? What went on in the German Universities? In 1968, he returned to Germany and became professor at the Institute of Genetics at Cologne University. He continued to work on the Lac repressor, which he described in his recent book *The Lac Operon: A history of a genetic paradigm* (1996).

In 1981, he published a book on the philosophers' view of living things (*Die Philosophen und das Lebendige*, 1981). While writing this book, he discovered that the history of human genetics in Germany during the Nazi years was a black hole. Virtually nothing had been written on it. Everybody had kept silent, the geneticists and institutions such as the Max-Planck-Gesellschaft and the Deutsche Forschungsgemeinschaft. So he spent a sabbatical reading the old papers, visiting the archives, and interviewing the people. The result of this enterprise is *Murderous Science* (*Tödliche Wissenschaft*, 1984).

The book was reviewed only once in the German press. Its first review appeared in *Nature*. However, the book sold 15,000 copies in Germany. It may be understood that under these conditions, no honorary German medals or memberships are to be reported. He is Honorary Fellow of the Hebrew University of Jerusalem and a member of the Academia Europaea. He received the French Humboldt–Prize and the Medal of the Collége de France—he is happy with that. So he lives a quiet life with his (second) wife Rita and his two children Sarah and Jakob.